Life
Without the
Boring Bits

Books by Colleen McCullough

Tim
The Thorn Birds
An Indecent Obsession
Cooking with Colleen McCullough and Jean Easthope
A Creed for the Third Millennium
The Ladies of Missalonghi

The Masters of Rome series
The First Man in Rome
The Grass Crown
Fortune's Favorites
Caesar's Women
Caesar: Let the Dice Fly
The October Horse
Antony & Cleopatra
The Song of Troy

Roden Cutler, V.C. (biography)
Morgan's Run
The Touch
Angel Puss
The Independence of Miss Mary Bennet
Life Without the Boring Bits

The Carmine Delmonico series
On, Off
Too Many Murders
Naked Cruelty
The Prodigal Son

COLLEEN McCULLOUGH

Life
Without the
Boring Bits

HarperCollins*Publishers*

HarperCollins*Publishers*

First published in Australia in 2011
by HarperCollins*Publishers* Australia Pty Limited
ABN 36 009 913 517
harpercollins.com.au

Copyright © Colleen McCullough 2011

The right of Colleen McCullough to be identified as the author of this
work has been asserted by her under the *Copyright Amendment
(Moral Rights) Act 2000.*

This work is copyright. Apart from any use as permitted under the
Copyright Act 1968, no part may be reproduced, copied, scanned, stored
in a retrieval system, recorded, or transmitted, in any form or by any
means, without the prior written permission of the publisher.

HarperCollins*Publishers*
Level 13, 201 Elizabeth Street, Sydney NSW 2000, Australia
31 View Road, Glenfield, Auckland 0627, New Zealand
A 53, Sector 57, Noida, UP, India
77–85 Fulham Palace Road, London, W6 8JB, United Kingdom
2 Bloor Street East, 20th floor, Toronto, Ontario M4W 1A8, Canada
10 East 53rd Street, New York NY 10022, USA

National Library of Australia Cataloguing-in-Publication data:

McCullough, Colleen, 1937–
Life without the boring bits.
ISBN: 978 0 7322 9448 9 (pbk.)
A823.3

Printed and bound in Australia by Griffin Press
60gsm Hi Bulk Book Cream used by HarperCollins*Publishers* is a natural, recyclable product
made from wood grown in sustainable forests. The manufacturing processes conform to the
environmental regulations in the country of origin, Finland.

5 4 3 2 1   11 12 13 14

Dearest Anthony,

This is for you because we go back such an enormously long way, to days when you stuck your publishing neck out for me and began a friendship as deep as platonic, as enduring as chequered.

Thank you too for giving me the only title this present work can possibly sustain, for if it isn't life without the boring bits, what is it?

With much love, always loyal, Col.

CONTENTS

FREAKING AT THE CONTROLS

Freud divided people into two kinds: those with "oral" fixations and those with "anal" fixations. Pray understand that I merely parrot the undoubtedly inaccurate generalizations that represent the good doctor's output in the public's mind. And onward and upward! Oral people are untidy and methodically slapdash, see the grand picture and overall purpose of a plan or a scheme, but dismiss minor details as irrelevant. Anal people are tidy and meticulously organized, see every last and most trivial detail of a plan or a scheme, but fail to grasp its overall purpose or design. Naturally there are fusions of both types, as well as one type adulterated by the veriest drop of the other, and all the various shades of grey.

I am a fusion of both types, though the anal can appear to dominate; this happens in persons who exist on a higher plane than mixtures of the two types. I speak, of course, of that most irritating of all types: the control freak. This is another term open to misinterpretation; people tend to think of control freaks as persons who want to rule the world, or their work place, or their home—putting the verb "to rule" first in importance. Such is not the case. "Control" need not mean "rule." Control implies a judgement. Can he drive this car competently? Yes, he can, so I can sit back and relax. Can he sedate this cat without being scratched to bits? No, he can't, so I'd better do it for him. Control is about controlling a given situation, not ruling anything—unless it's being done badly, or, worse, incompetently.

Apropos Freud, has it ever occurred to anyone that the good doctor built a whole theory on toilet training infants/toddlers back in the days when diapers were revolting things had to be cleaned, then washed, dried, and used over and over again? A mommy couldn't wait to sit the kid on a potty productively. Now, who cares if the kid wears a disposable diaper until it's four? If, that is, the wallet can afford it. Kids toilet train themselves. And though world prosperity has pinnacled and is now on the decline, I predict that many domestic sacrifices will be made before the disposable diaper is abandoned. Interesting.

Okay, I have established that I am a fusion of oral and anal, and a control freak to boot. I am also an incorrigible nit-picker.

In my Yale days, I watched a neurology resident writing a report on a plain yellow pad.

"Since you can't keep a natural margin," I said when I had either to speak or to explode, "why don't you draw one before you start? And your tabulations are so *untidy*! Do you want to enclose your numbers in parentheses or circles?"

He put his pen down and looked up at me with mild interest. "I bet you get migraines," he said.

That's the perfect way to squash a nit-picker flat.

The trouble is, nit-pickers can't help themselves. There is an element of pure agony involved when, for instance, I look at sloppily presented work. I itch to write it out again for its author in glorious neatness, balm for my nit-picking soul.

Watching movies can drive me quite mad. It's said of directors that if they get the cars in a film right, they don't need to worry about getting anything else right. I believe it's because film directors tend to be men, and in adolescence the only thing that matters more than girls are cars. Men love cars, that's why the director gets them right. His accuracy also pleases the male segment of his audience. Ric will be snoozing gently through a film, then suddenly jerk and sit up straight. "There's a 1953 De Soto! I had one of those when I was a kid." The car drives off-screen, and he goes back to sleep. At the end of the session he'll vote it a good film. In the meantime I've noticed that the guy with the gammy leg can never remember which leg is supposed to be gammy; the redhead is suddenly a blonde, and then goes back to red again without any reason; the plants in the ducal conservatory are wrong; and Hitler's army in Russia is bogged down in mud and pouring rain, yet the sky is blue.

Roman films are money for jam to a nit-picker with knowledge of the period. They couldn't even get the name of the hero right in *Gladiator*! He had a *cognomen* for a *praenomen*, a *praenomen* for a *nomen*, and a *nomen* for a *cognomen*—three out of three wrong. Even the BBC made mistakes in *I, Claudius*, though it was a good effort. They had the famous bronze statue of the Tuscan wolf in the Senate House, and that was correct, but the lupine old girl was suckling Renaissance twins, added later. Cicero remarks in passing to Atticus that lightning struck the suckling Romulus—the Tuscan wolf hadn't nursed two babes, just the one who founded Rome. My favorite fluff out of this wonderful series illustrates a tragedy, despite its humor. A hefty Brian Blessed (Augustus) pins a willowy John Castle (Postumus) against a wall that bows and buckles dangerously—it's made of cardboard! I guess they didn't have the money for another take, so it stayed in. There's the real rub! Those who would genuinely try for historical accuracy are on a shoe-string budget, whereas those with money to burn don't give a tuppenny bumper anent historical accuracy. Sod's Law in action.

Here's one I must have seen half a hundred times over the decades: the cup of tea poured from the coffee pot. Directors clearly played hookey from a very early age, as they don't seem to remember the rhyme about the teapot—short and stout. Coffee pots are tall and slender, designed to pour anything from pea water to unwatered pee. There is no grille of holes at the base of the spout to block the onward progress of some of the tea leaves. But, as I have always said, God gave us teeth to strain the tea leaves. I'm sure the residents of Boston knew that.

I remember reading Baroness Orczy's series of novels about the Scarlet Pimpernel when I was ten years old. Quite why, I do not know, but the nuclear story became one of the most re-made of all beloved tales. I think my count on DVD is six versions of *The Scarlet Pimpernel,* starting with Leslie Howard and Merle Oberon, and going through mostly TV recreations. Perhaps it appeals to the British, who can't say they hate the French any more, but love anything that sees a Brit shove one up a Frog. And the Scarlet Pimpernel, safely back in the early 1790s, is ideal one-up-the-Frogs material. Impeccably historic, ahem.

Yet in every version they make the same mistakes, chiefly to do with knitting. Knitting, you say? But to knit is to knit! Not so. The Brits and the Frogs knit differently. What is more, the Frog way of knitting is faster and easier than the Brit. In the Frog method, one needle and the yarn do most of the work, which grows at the rate of one metre per guillotined head. The Brit method uses both needles on the yarn equally, so limps along at the rate of an inch per guillotined head.

Perhaps because Leslie Howard came from Czechoslovakia, he knitted the correct way, the Frog way, but no British actor since has got it right. Why is this so important? Because the Scarlet Pimpernel disguises himself as a crone at least as noisome as Madame Defarge and sits in the front row of crones watching the aristo heads fall into the basket. Knitting, knitting, knitting.

I want to see a version in which the crones whizz along Frog-style knitting, and thoroughly bored with counting aristo heads.

One crone says to the Scarlet Pimpernel, "Ma foi! Zis twenty denier yarn, she is incroyable for les turning of ze 'eels aftaire les jambons zey are feeneeshed, non?"

The S.P. leers at her evilly, sucks on his pipe. "Sure is, you reeking old crone! Excuse me, I'll lose count—

knit one, purl one, knit one, slip one, pass the slipped stitch over."

The crone jumps, shocked clear out of her sabots. "Sacre bleu! Zat kneeting, she is not le kneeting of la Belle France! Ze yarn she is 'undred denier et les niddles zey go flic-flic, flic-flic, à l'Anglais! En avant, citoyens, en avant! 'Ere ees le Pimpernel Rouge! Keel 'eem! Keel, keel!"

A dozen men wearing the tricolored cockade in their hats dive on top of Richard E. Grant/Anthony Andrews and, boom-boom, 'ees 'ead, she ees dans le basket—a basket case, we say.

My favorite continuity disaster concerns a disaster. In Series 5 of *Spooks* some terrorists hold London to ransom by threatening to destroy the Thames Barrier.

I have a very soft spot for Prince Charles, for two reasons that spring immediately to mind. One is that he adores the *Goon Show*, which won't mean anything to anybody, but he and I both adore it. The second reason is that he detests what modern architecture has done to London, and he's spot-on right. When one goes to Brasilia or Pamplona, or any other of dozens of places, modern architecture is thrilling. But in London it's a complete fuck-up of a grand old city that should have remained respectably old, in its architecture at least. I admire Prince Charles for speaking out when royalty isn't supposed to. Well, bugger that. Someone needs to say it! Though the damage is done: the Ferris wheel is an eyesore, the Millennium Dome worse—but *who* gave the go-ahead to that awful little skyscraper made of colored glass shaped like an anal suppository? If I knew who was responsible, I'd have a go at shoving it right up where it belongs.

Off the soap box, Col! The Thames Barrier has a definite purpose, so it's hard to criticise, but *yellow* like businesses trying to catch the eye? It should have been river-colored to blend in, not silvery-white and acid-drop yellow.

Anyway, to make a soap box go somewhere, these terrorists are threatening the Thames Barrier, which was built, as I understand it, to minimize the impact of floodwaters rushing down the Thames while simultaneously a king tide is rushing up the Thames. This particular disaster has happened before, and it can happen again; if left to its liquid fate, London would be submerged under feet of water.

We learn that the king tide peaks at 5 p.m. and the barrier has to be activated on the dot of 5 p.m. But don't king tides do what other tides do, and rise gradually? Or is 5 p.m. the leading edge of the sine, so to speak? *Spooks* is not very specific. And why aren't the super spies doing their thing clad in gumboots, macintoshes and sou'westers while the rain pours down? Against newsflashes of Oxfordshire under ghastly floods? I know that in Hertford and Hereford hurricanes hardly ever happen, but the plot surely calls for one. We may safely ignore the Hampshire weather.

Instead, the camera shows the sun shining and the Thames as placid as the wee in granny's potty. Can this be why a tsunami is suddenly added to the plot? But can the North Sea at the Thames Estuary really generate anything like a tsunami? Tsunamis are oceanic phenomena that occur when a seismically triggered wave suddenly strikes a very wide continental shelf, which is why most earthquakes don't cause damaging tsunamis.

The episode finishes at the beginning of Series 6, but I'm not holding my breath or rushing out to buy Series 6. It's a perfect illustration of a scriptwriter dumped on by the trillion-ton floodwaters of his too-fertile imagination.

I am never sure whether this kind of television torment is cynically inflicted on its audience, or in true ignorance of how bad it actually is. Are scriptwriters overpaid, or underpaid? I know Jerry Bruckheimer has an Outer Mongolia for his stable of scriptwriters—*CSI Miami* it's called. But whereabouts would Kudos/BBC send an erring *Spooks* scriptwriter? Composing the teleprompter weather for BBC Scotland? All I know about the matter is one thing: there is *always* an Outer Mongolia.

Control freaks don't really want much out of life. A perfectly organized, perfectly run world will do for starters. Having organized and run a couple of weeny worlds in my day, I can testify to the fact that once people get used to method and order, they absolutely love it. "Everything has a home!" I would snarl, advancing menacingly upon a shivering professor, and waving a jar holding two chimpanzee testicles under his nose. "You know where things live—put them there, or it's soprano time!" At first they hated this merciless treatment, but after they'd learned to put things in their homes—oh, it was so *wonderful* to be able to lay their hands on them immediately. If order and method weren't among life's necessities, control freaks wouldn't exist. But, as some NASA and other red faces can bear witness, it helps to have nit-pickers and control freaks around. Then billions don't get wasted for the want of a screw, or the difference between metric and imperial. Imperial is better for mensuration—stick to it!

I will tell you a true story that happened to me in another incarnation—no, no, I don't believe in reincarnation! I use it in the sense of doing a different job wearing a different hat.

I was marking time in England for six months, and working as a temp/sec in a little city that shall be nameless. It was a precision engineering works, and the engineers loved to grab me to type their specifications because I didn't make mistakes and would even query their calculations from time to time, thus saving the engineer a red face later on. But the pace of work in that office, which had a large pool of typists, was desperately slow; I always seemed to have time on my hands. The period, I must add, was prior to the computer age—mid 1970s will do.

One of the oldest engineers in terms of staff longevity was a man I'll call Bob, who was responsible for the factory's parts. For some years he had been working on a catalogue of every last part the factory contained, down to the tiniest washer. His list was long finished, but he couldn't persuade a typist to type it for him. This wasn't an ordinary typing job. Its object was to create a typed description on a sheet of mylar, using a sheet of yellow carbon paper in the mix as well as a carbon ribbon in the IBM machine, which had a phenomenal roller to accommodate the mylar sheet. Typewriters were massive then anyway, but the roller on this special machine was 27 inches in length. Each mylar sheet had been pre-printed into rectangular boxes that allowed for a full description of each part, each name, its code number, parts number, source—in all, I think each part had six or seven boxes across the two-foot width of a sheet. Then each sheet held the details of thirty different parts.

When Bob asked me if I would be willing to type his parts sheets in my spare time, I said yes, of course; it looked like the perfect job for a nit-picker. Bob himself was neat, precise, and ideally suited for his job. My answer was greeted with joy; I settled down with my gigantic typewriter and a parts list that ran over ten thousand items. How I loved it! The other typists could not believe that anyone could do the work and stay sane. Whereas what had driven me insane was twiddling my fingers and giggling over gossip. I pounded away with the yellow carbon reversed so it haloed the dense black print with yellow, and it was amazing how quickly I ploughed through the items. Within a month I had finished it, and done other work as well. It's my power to concentrate; absolutely nothing impinges on the work.

Bob was so overcome that he took a cartload of mylar sheets up to the general manager's office and showed them off, praising me to the skies. And the manager, not a tactful man, summoned the typists together (apparently the engineers had also been singing my praises) and harangued them about their lack of a work ethic. Using as his example of the work ethic my typing of the parts catalogue. Mercifully I wasn't asked to attend, any more than I had known of Bob's trip upstairs, but the filthy looks and cold shoulder treatment said it all.

Here I should say that Bob was a very elderly man, probably past retirement, working for interest's sake. He was paraplegic, couldn't move from the waist down, and spent his waking life in a wheelchair. A really pleasant man, he never complained.

I suppose he behaved a little as if he had just had the most exciting birthday present ever, but seeing his list done at last meant a lot to him.

That was a Friday. When we came in to work on Monday, we found that someone had taken a razor-sharp blade to the huge stack of mylar sheets and slashed them to ribbons. All my work had gone for nothing, reduced to shreds littering the office floor. Which wasn't the worst. That poor old man broke down and cried as if his heart were broken, and I suppose in a way it was. A paraplegic in a wheelchair! How deep can the poison run in some people, to do that, but especially to do it to someone who can't stand on his own two legs and fight back?

I wasn't without friends in the office. We dried Bob's tears and I promised to re-type his list, which I did.

But at night, every single night, we locked the sheets in a safe, and when the job was finished for the second time, Bob kept them in a safe permanently.

To this day I think that unknown person's venom remains the most appalling, terrifying demonstration of sheer evil I have ever encountered. It was so *personal*. One of the faces I saw every day—and I honestly do not know which one—was capable of destroying a crippled old man's dream, a crippled old man she knew, spoke to, probably joked with. All because a fellow worker had shown her up. What she hadn't counted on was my willingness to do the same job all over again.

The crux of the matter is that nit-pickers and control freaks can't help what they are, and if that means they work harder and/or faster and/or more accurately than others, it's a fact of life. I am just glad that when the mylar sheets were finished for the second time, I moved on and never went back.

A true story, one I haven't embroidered in the least. It isn't necessary to embroider something so horrible.

Now here am I in a wheelchair, not paraplegic, but walking is a pain in the arse, literally. As well as a pain in the hips, the legs and the feet. I can walk a little way pushing a wheeled walker, but it's standing kills me. Not to mention that I've lost depth perception in my vision, so I don't see steps, or jogs and humps in a flat surface. Therefore when I leave the familiar contours of my house, it's wheelchair time.

And no, I'm not whining. That is the prelude to explaining a fate worse than death for a control freak— losing control. I am at someone else's mercy most of the time. Ric's, most of the time. The best egg that ever was, but it is just *awful* not to be in control of one's own locomotion! The ordeal isn't too bad while I'm being pushed forward, but when he turns my chair around and pulls rather than pushes, my heart doesn't know whether to rocket out the top of my head or thump through the soles of my feet. *What won't Ric let me see?* It's a cockroach! A cockroach, it's got to be a cockroach! And if it is a cockroach, I'm stuck in this ruddy chair! It's a cockroach! I know it's a cockroach, he says it isn't but he's got that I-won't-tell-her-about-the-cockroach tone in his voice—it's a cockroach! Oh, please, puh-lease, Ric, don't let the cockroach get me! It's a cockroach!

THE CRUCIFIXION

This essay has been a long time in the writing, and gone through many drafts. Unless a subject be lighthearted or lightweight, I put what I deem a satisfactory draft into a drawer for weeks or months, then look at it anew with a dispassionate eye. And finally, it seems to me, I have shorn away the pretensions that marred the fleece of scholarship sufficiently to view my subject with a true detachment: the detective's conclusions based on scanty evidence.

When I began to amass knowledge of the history of the late Roman Republic and the early Imperium, a question popped into my mind that never seems to occur to those of us nurtured in a largely Christian society: *Why did Jesus Christ die the death of a slave?*

Later on in the Imperium, particularly after its administration passed into the hands of Greek freedmen and other non-Roman civil servants, crucifixion was levied upon free men as well as upon slaves, though it was always a capital criminal's death. No Roman citizen or foreign citizen could be crucified; the common death sentence for Roman and non-Roman alike was beheading.

During the period in which Jesus Christ lived, crucifixion was strictly limited to two kinds of men: slaves and pirates.

Rome did have one exception to this: a Roman convicted of *perduellio* treason. After a ponderous trial heard in the Centuries, a man found guilty was crucified "tied to an unlucky tree"—that is, a tree that had never borne fruit. It was an archaic process of the early Republic, long fallen out of use by the late Republic, but Julius Caesar ran a case for it in the Centuries against one Rabirius Postumus; the trial was abruptly terminated before the vote was fully taken. Caesar used it as a political device to prove a political point. No later case of *perduellio* was ever heard, and Caesar's employment of it was called frivolous.

During the relevant period two instances of mass crucifixion are recorded in the ancient sources. Marcus Licinius Crassus hung 6,600 rebellious Spartacan slaves on crosses along the Via Appia all the way from Capua to Rome. Julius Caesar crucified a large number of pirates on the river flats below Pergamum against orders from the Governor, who wanted to sell them as slaves. Both acts were done to show slaves what would happen to them if they rose against Rome or preyed on Roman shipping.

These parameters didn't change under the emperors Augustus and Tiberius. There are a few other, unconnected instances of crucifixion of inviduals, but nothing that basically affects the reality of the time: crucifixion was the death of a slave.

Why Jesus Christ received the death of a slave is a mystery. Not one thing that has come down to us suggests that Christ was in fact a slave, including his being hied before the Roman prefect for permission to execute him. Were he in truth a slave, his master had no need to apply to anyone for permission to kill him.

The charges laid against Jesus Christ were of treason against Rome; the Prefect of Judaea, one Pontius Pilatus (we do not know his *praenomen*, or first name), dismissed the charges and ordered the prisoner released. Whereupon the members of the Jewish Sanhedrin proceeded to bully and browbeat Pontius Pilatus into reversing his decision and passing a sentence of death by crucifixion on Christ *after* he had been exonerated!

Every fact contradicts other facts, and all of it ran counter to Roman law and practice. Above all, the Romans were in love with their law as well as extremely litigious-minded. Nor were governors or their prefects prone to be intimidated unless their province stood in danger of imminent war or rebellion.

The history of the period in southern Syria was turbulent. To understand the political climate when Christ was sentenced, it is necessary to go back to 69 BC, when Alexandra, the widow of King Alexander Jannaeus, died. The old Queen's two sons, Hyrcanus and Aristobulus, were the last Hasmonaean kings. Alexandra had favored Hyrcanus, whom she made both High Priest and King of the Jews. The sovereignty was not over a land, but a people; even if the land dwindled to nothing, the King's realm was no smaller. Despite which, Judaea was the ancient homeland and Jerusalem the Holy City.

Aristobulus and his sons disputed the succession, provoking revolt and hugely annoying Pompey the Great right at the moment when Pompey was looking forward to spending the winter in Damascus, reputedly a delightful place to spend the winter. Instead, he had to lay siege to Jerusalem, a city he loathed. The result of Pompey's irritation horrified the Jews, but it was too late to retrieve Aristobulus's blunders. Pompey annexed the whole of Syria into a Roman province and made sure the two legions garrisoning it kept a severe eye on Judaea. Rome was suddenly a presence that would not go away.

In 57 BC the Governor of Syria, Aulus Gabinius, literally dismembered Judaea, seeing this as the best way out of his troubles there. He split it into five tiny, geophysically unconnected districts: Jerusalem, Gazara, Jericho, Amathus and Galilaean Sepphora. Each had a Jewish governor, called a tetrarch.

Relations between Rome and the Jews passed into the hands of a crafty, brilliant Idumaean nobleman named Antipater, who had an Arab wife, Cypros, and three sons deemed Arabs under matrilineal law, a Semitic characteristic. Antipater set himself up as the "expert" on Jewish matters to the Roman greats marching through the region in pursuit of civil war; Julius Caesar and Cassius used him and liked him as a man who got the job done.

Antipater's second eldest son, Herod, was an unscrupulous, cruel, murdering individual who, despite his Arab status, set out to become King of the Jews. Further to that end, he married the Hasmonaean princess Mariamne and sired matrilineally Jewish sons. One of the best crawlers of all time, Herod wormed his way upward through Marcus Antonius and then Octavianus, who became the first Roman emperor, Augustus, in 27 BC. Augustus took some of Herod's sons to live with him in Rome to receive a "proper education"—that is, to Romanize them.

Always full of himself, Herod took the title Herod the Great and managed to have Gabinius's five tiny districts joined together again, with the addition of Samaria, Idumaea and the Greek cities of the Decapolis. Alas, a paper tiger! Herod's chief duty was to collect the taxes and tributes for Rome. The only way he hung onto his throne was by murdering any among his relatives, even his sons, who seemed a threat. He was a notorious voluptuary, a characteristic despised by Jews and Romans alike.

Jewish intransigence continued unabated. In 6 AD Augustus gave the Jews a Roman head of state physically present within Jerusalem: the Prefect of Judaea. This executive was junior to the Governor of Syria, but to no one else; by birth he was a Roman nobleman and a member of the Senate. Modern usage, particularly pertaining to schoolchildren, has tended to diminish modern perception of the prefect's importance and power: he had military and civil teeth, and within his sphere his word was law, enforced by the legions and by a cohort of troops permanently garrisoned in his capital— in this case, Jerusalem, possessed of a formidable fortress called the Antonia.

With the Kingdom of the Parthians on the far bank of the Euphrates River, Syria was of vital military importance, and Judaea a perpetual Roman headache. Its prefect was always a very capable, carefully chosen man.

Here I introduce the hypothesis of an impressive classical scholar of the 1920s and 1930s, Robert Graves. Nowadays Graves is best known to the public as the author of two novels, *I, Claudius* and *Claudius the God*. Among many other works in a serious vein is a book entitled *King Jesus* that postulates that Jesus Christ really was the King of the Jews, and that the Sanhedrin knew it.

Graves contended that Christ's mother, Mary, was a slave in the Great Temple and was the heiress of the House of David. The phrase "temple slave" may be true or, in our eyes, a misnomer; to the Jews of that time, an irrelevancy. Mary was resident in the temple precinct as a person of high honor. The reason for her detention was to keep her out of the clutches of Herod, who wanted to marry her, sire sons who were by Davidian blood rightfully entitled to the throne. Whereas the Sanhedrin had another choice for husband: one Joseph, a widower and Mary's kinsman. If he were indeed our Joseph, he was from her village, her blood relative, of suitable social status, and with Pharisaical leanings.

Mary was probably all of fourteen years old when Herod's senior son, Herod Antipater, abducted her and fathered her firstborn, the male child we know as Jesus Christ. Herod Antipater was typical of his house: vain, amoral, merciless, hugely ambitious, and intensely jealous of his near male relatives. Poor little girl! She would have married at fifteen, but only after careful preparation and much support from her female kin. This hinted at rape.

What no one seems to have taken into account were Herod Antipater's brazen brand of atheism and his reckless daring. To the Sanhedrin, residence in the Great Temple made Mary safe. It stopped Herod the Great, but not his senior son.

By Graves's telling, the whole business was furtive—had to be, to avoid the wrath both of the old King and the Sanhedrin. Eventually came the flight into Egypt; the entire scheme fell to pieces. Herod the Great murdered his son Herod Antipater and Mary returned with her infant son to Nazareth, where she married Joseph.

Under matrilineal law the husband's duty was to bring both additional wealth and prestige to the woman carrying the bloodline. Which, if one follows Graves's reasoning, would make Joseph an important man of some affluence; he was probably the Sanhedrin's original choice. A widower getting on in years (he is said to have had two grown sons, which would put him in his forties) was not frowned upon as a matrimonial partner for a young girl; he was a made man rather than a man in the making. If Joseph's business was carpentry, it didn't have to be a humble workshop. Certainly Mary seems to have had other children by Joseph, both girls and boys.

When the Emperor Augustus heard of Herod Antipater's murder he was angry and grief-stricken; Herod Antipater had lived in Rome as Augustus's guest when a child, and Augustus had loved him. An imperial command went out to Herod the Great that stopped him in his tracks: there were to be no further reprisals of any kind.

Herod Antipas, a far different man from his stormy elder brother, now moved upward. When old Herod died, he assumed the title King of the Jews and "ruled"—but not in Jerusalem. His Roman title was Tetrarch of Galilaea, where at Sepphora he built a luxurious palace and cavorted far from the jaundiced eyes of the Roman Prefect and the Sanhedrin.

While the historical substrate and some of the events told in the Christian Gospels are accurate, the above on Mary is Robert Graves's hypothesis, one attempt at solving the contradictions inherent in the life of Jesus Christ the man: he was the true King of the Jews.

By this, I hope, the reader has concluded that I am not concerned with the godhead of Jesus Christ, a state of being that has no place in this essay. Like Graves, I am attempting to solve a factual conundrum: I am asking why Christ was crucified rather than beheaded?

Curiously, there had been a worldwide frisson of excitement that had begun in about 35 BC and was to continue until about 65 AD—a total of 100 years.

It was said that a Chosen Child would be born to herald in a Golden Age. For the Romans it began at a time when they were exhausted by a long series of devastating civil wars; the stimuli were the pregnancies of Octavia, Augustus's sister, by Marcus Antonius, and Scribonia by Augustus himself. Virgil hymned it for one. But when both babies were girls—oh, *darn*! Neither Antonia the Elder nor Julia was hailed as the Chosen Child, but the rumors did not die down. The Chosen Child and the Golden Age were still coming. Gaius Caligula believed himself the Chosen Child.

It took three generations for the talk to die away. The Hellenized (Greek-influenced) world expected the New Dionysus, who would change water into wine and make every day an unadulterated orgy of joy and pleasure. Marcus Antonius and Cleopatra cashed in on this. Jewish anticipation was of the Messiah, not by the Sanhedrin, but in regions like Galilaea, a hotbed of Messianic rumors, and other rural districts.

The Jews at this time were not entirely religiously united. Most Jews appear to have had Pharisaical inclinations, among them a belief in a life after death, angels, and a Jewish nation. However, there were many Sadducees; as they pinned their hopes on prosperity in this life, up to and including gentile habits, they did not believe in a life after death or a Jewish nation. The common folk were Pharisaical, especially in rural areas, but both sects contained persons of liberal mind as well as conservative and orthodox persons. The Sanhedrin was dominated by Pharisees who tended to be orthodox *and* conservative.

Though Samaria was a Jewish land, its interpretation of sacred scriptures was so different from the Jerusalem line that Samaritan Judaism was deemed a schism—a state of religious being that gave it some clout. Whereas up-country Galilaean beliefs were scattier and regularly produced wild men, prophets and hermits who proclaimed themselves the Messiah or the trumpet sounding the clarion of his arrival. The result was deemed a heresy and had no clout at all.

I gain an impression of a vital, vigorous, ancient religion, sternly monotheistic, that was often debated and always in a state of flux. All the more interesting, then, that the arrival of Jesus Christ on the religious scene inspired such opposition. Galilaea was the home of heretics, and presumably these men made little

27

impact upon society beyond Galilaea: what then was so different about Jesus Christ? Did his importance lie in his heretical teachings, or was it because he was believed by many to be the rightful King of the Jews? Or did he also claim to be the Messiah?

It is difficult to decide whether at this stage I should go on to discuss Jesus Christ the man himself, or whether I ought first to discuss early Christianity. My previous efforts have dealt with the man and his crucifixion first, so here I will take the other tack and discuss the rise of Christianity. If the reader knows the genesis of the new religion, it may be easier to reach warming conclusions about the man and his death, however inadequate.

I must be one of very few from the Christian world to have walked the long, wildflower-strewn grasses of an utterly deserted place in far northeastern Turkey named Ani. It lies on the lip of a great gorge; far below flows the river the ancients called the Araxes, and on the far side (at the time of my visit) there bristled fences of barbed wire, guard towers and soldiers. For the far side of the gorge was Russian Armenia. A lone army helicopter clattered down the gorge, then vanished to leave Ani to the whirring peace of birds and insects.

Ani is the oldest purely Christian community extant, though no one has lived in it for centuries. Its brick buildings stand as shells, some still vaulted by roofs; some are humble, some more imposing. Almost every interior of every building is adorned by wonderful frescoes that depict early Christianity, an illustrated story whose predominant color takes the breath away—a rich, intense, vivid ultramarine blue. I presume that there was a deposit of lapis lazuli in the neighborhood that, ground to pigment, provided the artists with the chief glory of their palette.

But there is tragedy, too. In obedience to the laws of Islam, every face has been gouged off every human or angelic or godly figure, leaving its blue draperies and the flesh tones of hands and feet. Haloes and remnants of hair survive, and all the non-human details, but no face has escaped. When one religion infringes the tenets of another, there will always be man-made demonstrations of the power of one god over the other; east of the sources of the Euphrates is a fundamental world.

In the Roman mind, Christianity was inevitably entangled with Judaism. From time to time the Imperium was shaken by fears of a pan-Jewish uprising, for no part of the Roman sphere of influence was without a fairly large Jewish population, and the two cultures were at ideological loggerheads. Because of their religion's Judaic roots, early Christians were all too often lumped in with Jews willy-nilly, though after the death of Jesus Christ and his contemporaries, Christianity ceased to have any attraction for Jews. In fact, quite the opposite. Most Jews avoided it as one more burden. This, combined with Roman belief that Christians and Jews were one and the same, only served both to increase and diversify anti-semitism, a great tragedy.

Christianity was never a religion of enlightenment. It was a religion of revelation for the abjectly poor designed to help them bear their unenviable lot. They could neither read nor write. Thus for the first two generations at least the religion was orally disseminated to believers; what was written down by a very few was vestigial and read aloud to gatherings. The importance of the Epistles cannot be over-emphasized, as their writers knew well how unlearned the congregations were.

A hierocracy is natural to a system of beliefs wherein few have learning; those who had it gradually became known as bishops, responsible for instructing more junior ministers, the priests.

However, I don't wish to discuss the Christian hierocracy any further: it is not germane.

★ ★ ★

There are great differences of opinion upon the date when the four Gospels were formally written down. Many scholars argue for a time as close to Christ's death as thirty or forty years. However, one large group opts for a date after the first third of the second century AD as their very earliest; circa 133 AD, a century after the crucifixion. The hypothetical "Q" is said to be at least a generation earlier—if there ever was a Q. The four Gospels, apparently teaching aids aimed at new converts, were written in Greek, an indication to me that if this date is right, it reveals an upward trend in converts toward those who were literate. Q is said to have been written in Aramaic, a pan-Syrian semitic language, but to me Greek sounds more logical for the early Christian writers. It was the lingua franca of the eastern Mediterranean, and the earliest Christians seem to have been Greek-speaking.

What is known is that Christianity made great strides, that its adherents multiplied rapidly, and that by the time Constantine spent his childhood among the barbarian Picts and Scots, they also were converting to Christianity. Jesus Christ's simple credo, with its emphasis on the life hereafter and its promise of a happiness eternal, was perfect for its time.

That today it is dwindling is due to such gargantuan changes in the human condition, at least for western peoples, that its simplicity and promise are deemed antiquated, unappealing rubbish.

Its greatest appeal remains among those peoples who are abjectly poor, under-educated, and politically oppressed. However, there are some prosperous peoples who have found vigorous versions of Christianity robust enough still to offer spiritual comfort. I am not wrong. Godlessness is growing in the Christian world.

Back now to the life of Jesus Christ the man.

The problem is that absolutely nothing about him was written during his lifetime or for a generation after. He lived and died unrecorded in the contemporary annals of either Rome or Jerusalem; the little we know comes from the Epistles, the Gospels, and Josephus, and is not very helpful, for they were not concerned with the man per se. Using these sources, Christ was a Jew from Galilaea who seems from his teachings not to have had much time for the finer points of Judaic religious law, inextricably bound up with Jewish government as it then was. He seems not to have hated Rome or viewed it as anything but a temporal power. He preached tolerance and was not a bigot. He believed in Satan, demons, angels and archangels, in living by the rules of goodness and decency, and, above all, by love. He had a kind word to say about almost everyone, and taught that the most hardened of sinners could be redeemed. His preferred method of teaching was the parable. It was a benign, inoffensive credo that made some inroads in Galilaea and other rural regions. A man of thirty, he commenced three years of fairly limited walks and wanders, often attended by large crowds. Only at the very end of his career did he go to Jerusalem.

Why then did he die? And why was he sentenced to the death of a slave?

Already condemned by a trial before the Sanhedrin, he was hied before the Prefect of Judaea as a traitor to Rome. And, since slaves didn't need Roman permission to be killed, it would seem as a free man. Whereupon the Prefect examined the evidence, pronounced it spurious, and dismissed the charges. After which the Sanhedrin, present, created such a furore that Pilatus Praefectus actually recanted his verdict and authorized Christ's death by crucifixion.

None of it makes a scrap of sense.

The text of the four Gospels as they exist today is so non-specific that various and different assumptions may be made.

The first is that Jesus Christ really was a slave, an assumption I dismiss. If in truth he were a slave, the Sanhedrin was not obliged to ask Rome's permission to crucify him. Whereas only the Roman governor or his prefect could sentence a free man to death, be he a Roman citizen or a citizen of his nation.

Under Roman law any free man, Roman or other, was in full ownership of his slaves, and at complete liberty to kill them arbitrarily. Slaves were as cattle, they had no rights at law.

The second is that Jesus Christ had committed capital murder. This fits better legally, even if he had no criminal history prior to committing capital—premeditated—murder.

Even so, I dismiss it. Nothing in Christ's career as we know it indicates a capital crime. Nor did the Prefect pass a death sentence; he debunked the charges as patently ridiculous. Only fierce and remorseless bullying by the Sanhedrin caused him to reverse his original decision.

Apropos Pontius Pilatus's craven crumbling, Jerusalem had been a nucleus of sedition and rebellion for years by 33 AD, the commonest date attributed to the crucifixion. Pompey the Great's siege was seventy years in the past, but fresh Roman insults to the Jewish homeland came hard on the heels of each revolt, and after 6 AD never were the Jews of Jerusalem without a resident overlord. A son of Aristobulus named Antigonus had even ruled Judaea as a Parthian puppet; there were still Jews known to favor Parthian to Roman rule. If the legion of southern Syria was not in Jerusalem's vicinity during that Passover of 33 AD, Pilatus may well have thought the cohort (600 men) garrisoning the city was not militarily capable of putting down open revolt. I imagine the sheer violence of the Sanhedrin's reaction to his decision came as a terrific shock to Pilatus, and, for all he pitied this poor wretch, he wasn't prepared to risk a fragile peace. That at least is feasible and understandable.

What if Jesus Christ really was the genuine King of the Jews?

Robert Graves's treatise fascinated me from the time of first reading forty years ago; it was one answer to some of the most puzzling questions as to why Jesus Christ had to die—and why the title King of the Jews was bruited during the hearing before Pilatus—and why Pilatus tried to defuse the situation by holding Christ up as a figure of fun—and why a note was fixed to the top of Christ's cross announcing that here hung the King of the Jews, a slave with grand pretensions.

When Christ entered Jerusalem riding on a donkey he was hailed as King of the Jews, and even by some as the Messiah. If his mother was the heiress of the House of David, her firstborn son, no matter who his father, could claim to be the King of the Jews. If Graves is followed, the identity of his father was known, increasing his claim, but anathema to the Sanhedrin. If they had to have a Herod, better by far to have the torpid Antipas, as apolitical as he was corrupt.

At this distance in time, it isn't possible to know without better evidence how word of Christ's regal identity would have reached the ordinary residents of Jerusalem, but according to the Gospels he was met by cheering crowds who strewed the path of the King with palm leaves. Since his entry into Jerusalem seems to have been a public announcement of his kingly status, he may have worn purple—of which, more anon.

Because Graves's answer is the only one makes real sense to me, I am going to postulate that it is true.

Following this line, the treason charges laid against Christ to Pilatus were that he plotted to have himself made King of the Jews and foment rebellion against Rome. The Sanhedrin's argument failed to carry weight with Pilatus, who, if one looks at what is known objectively, seems to have regarded Christ as a crazy man whose lunacy he tried to debunk by flogging, a crown of brambles and a broken reed in one hand as a sceptre. Relevant to later events that will be mentioned in due course, the lash appears not to have broken the skin, nor the crown caused typical copious bleeding of the scalp. "Behold the King of the Jews, ha ha ha!" But the Sanhedrin didn't laugh; to them, this was no joking matter. Whichever way one looks at it, this hearing was not Pilatus's finest hour. Only one thing was going to pacify the Sanhedrin: the death sentence of a slave.

Certainly Jesus Christ seems to have become a threat only after he entered Jerusalem; no important Jew seems to have taken any notice of him during his three years of wanderings outside the city. The reaction among the general populace of Jerusalem must then have come as a shock, particularly if he wore the purple.

If one considers Christ's career as an orchestrated bid to spread his heretical ideas to the people, thus offering them a gentler, more unbiased kind of code that made room for the humble, the poor and the powerless in the scheme of things, then his entry into Jerusalem marked a change. It increased his importance immeasurably, and was perhaps the first step in a peaceful bid for the throne. If he could trace his lineage back to David, he himself would have seen nothing incendiary anent his claim. As a Galilaean Jew, his political thinking was probably naive, at least to some extent; the power plays and intrigues among those at the top of the urban social mix would have been foreign to him.

Religious leaders are rarely done to death at the beginning of their careers; only after they have stirred up the political ant heap do they court extirpation. And in Judaea two thousand years ago politics and religion were intermingled, further complicated by a political overlord in Rome that ran counter to Jewish autonomy of all kinds. Did Christ have kingly plans, they would not have been out of character for the man as I see him: he just wanted a simpler, less materialistic, more tolerant attitude to life and living, which, good Jew that he was, he knew stemmed from God. He disliked theologians and didacticians, religious leaders who interpreted God as rigid, intolerant of human frailty. Christ's view was that all human beings were frail, and God loved them anyway.

Jesus Christ as King of the Jews was extremely dangerous to the established Jewish religious governors, the Sanhedrin. If the Sanhedrin plus Herod Antipas comprised Christ's body of accusers, then there were seventy-two men involved.

Christian leaders throughout the ages have thrown up men who blame the Jews for the crucifixion: a manifest injustice. Equally unjust is the retaliatory allegation that the Romans were to blame. The truth is in the Gospels, at least as we have them: including the Roman prefect, seventy-three men exclusive to that time and that place were responsible. No one else.

One, the Roman prefect, acquiesced unwillingly, yet still he acquiesced, while the other seventy-two would not be cheated of their death even at the possible price of provoking the prefect to a military solution. It wasn't necessary. Pilatus backed down—but were they sure he would? All considered, it reads to me as if they were willing to dare everything to achieve Christ's crucifixion.

Pontius Pilatus had been Prefect of Judaea for six years by 33 AD, and, given the Emperor Tiberius's known policy of keeping nobly born, wealthy Romans on foreign duty for many years, he expected to remain in Judaea for more years to come. As indeed proved to be the case. He was not recalled to Rome until three years after the crucifixion, which negates the contention of some Christians that he was recalled to answer for crucifying Jesus Christ—a ridiculous assertion. Why would Tiberius, senile and living on Capri for a decade by this—or his Greek freedman bureaucrats—care about the death of three Jewish slaves, entered in the books of the Antonia fortress and then forgotten?

Such things were not reported to Rome. No doubt Pilatus wrote a report on the matter of Jesus Christ to his boss in the capital, Antioch—the Governor of

Syria. He would have described a potentially explosive incident nipped in the bud at the price of one Jewish life. That accomplished, it appears the Sanhedrin settled down.

By all accounts a severe and dour man, Pontius Pilatus would have couched the matter in a factual light, neither spared nor praised himself, merely informed the Governor that though his decision had been a prudent one at odds with Roman law, it did the trick: threats of an uprising faded away.

It is not astonishing that we hear no more of Pilatus upon his return to Rome. Within a year of that, Tiberius was dead and Gaius Caligula emperor. My feeling is that a man who, on the whole, had successfully governed a notoriously difficult people for ten years, would have had great sense and remarkable antennae for trouble. The motion pictures that portray him as an effete nonentity are far from the mark.

On the ascension of Gaius Caligula, Pilatus may well have retired to his estates, kept his head down and lived out the rest of his days in peace and quiet. In fact, were it not for the crucifixion of Jesus Christ, Pontius Pilatus's name would have been entered on the *fasti* and utterly forgotten otherwise. I find it a pity that he is almost universally vilified; to him, in that place at that time, to give in must have seemed the best course of action. A goodly proportion of the few Jews he knew personally would have been members of the Sanhedrin, which would have given him a basis for his decision. He knew they meant it, it was written on their faces, in their eyes, their very bodies.

I have come to think that it was Christ's entry into Jerusalem, home of the Great Temple, lies at the bottom of that death by crucifixion. Given the paucity of our sources, it is the most logical possibility. How could the Jewish heads of state defuse the situation Christ had provoked? Clearly the ordinary people knew of him through his preaching and approved of his message, which is best summarized in the Sermon on the Mount—a radical departure from the sterner orthodoxy of the Sanhedrin, and from the traditional concept of a rather unforgiving God. So when Christ entered the city, his reception badly alarmed the Sanhedrin, whom I acquit of worldly motives for their hatred.

In their eyes Jesus Christ was apostate and had to be put down. But how? How could seventy-one men deal with what they had seen on that day of palms? By achieving Christ's death, yes, absolutely, but in such a way that his teachings died with him. These men were wise in the ways of men, even if they were not exactly stuffed with common sense. Social disgrace rather than apostacy had to seem the reason for his death, and the Roman prefect its author.

The Sanhedrin was more than a religious government; it was also the Jewish court of justice, and empowered to hear charges against fellow Jews. Also to levy sentence, save for death, the province of Rome alone. But death by sword or axe was the death of a free man: it would not answer. Crucifixion would. If this man who was thought the rightful King of the Jews was deemed a slave and went to a slave's death, he was branded a pariah— especially if he had pretended to be free, and gathered many ardent followers.

Someone thought of it, but who? And what did they need Judas Iscariot for? Identification of Christ's person doesn't wash; after his triumphant entry into Jerusalem, his face was known. Was it Judas's function to testify before the Prefect that Christ had openly boasted of setting himself up as King of the Jews in a war against Rome? Did Judas testify that he was actively courting the Parthians as allies?

He was paid thirty "pieces of silver" for his services—denarii, I imagine. Not a big sum of money, save perhaps to an impoverished upcountry Galilaean who counted his wealth in mere sesterces, three or four at a time. Maybe he had a small gambling debt; there are faint suggestions that he may have been a gambler.

Or perhaps he secretly hankered for the fleshpots? We will never know, beyond the fact that thirty denarii were enough to buy a despicable betrayal. Gaius Trebonius springs to mind: a man who had been superbly honored by his superior, Julius Caesar, and in gratitude amassed envy, resentment, feelings of impotence. All Caesar's assassins were men he had advanced, and they had hated him for his power to do so. Perhaps Judas Iscariot was that kind of man. Such men hate sourly, implacably, even coldly.

What is certain is that the Sanhedrin needed Judas to further their ends, not identify a face. What, you think every member of the Sanhedrin stayed home that Palm Sunday refusing to set eyes upon a sudden enemy? That's not human nature. They were there, in the crowd.

Crucifixion as a slave it was going to be, and so it was. It's the best of the possible solutions to the mystery, and detracts not in the slightest from the eventual structure that grew out of Christ, his life and slave's death: Christianity.

What kind of man was Jesus Christ, as distinct from his message? Nobly born, that seems evident, but he had one superlative gift that is indeed God-given— charisma. He drew people to himself nigh effortlessly, and once he had them, they remained his. Perhaps uniquely in a misogynistic time, he treated women as his equals, permitted them to follow him, had them among his closest friends, and respected their opinions.

There is nothing in the Gospels that indicates Christ was a poor man, though he abrogated wealth. The two are not the same. Carpenters are not poor men, they have a trade that amounted to a skill, for it included what now would be called cabinet making and the crafting of elegant furniture. Joseph's workshop may have been a large one employing a number of craftsmen. When Christ quit his trade to wander he seems never to have wanted for money, accommodation, sustenance. Whether or not he worked miracles is beyond the scope of this essay, nor does his declaration of his godhead depend for proof upon the ability to work miracles. It is an article of faith, and faith alone.

Were Christ abjectly poor, he would not have presented such a threat to the Sanhedrin; his declaration of kingship would have been dealt with in other ways than a slave's death. If he was in truth of the House of David and backed by a wealthy family having considerable power, the threat was urgent. He had to be dealt with immediately, before the family could rally.

★ ★ ★

When Christ was crucified, the eight legionaries who made up an octet in a century threw dice for his garments. If that is true, it speaks volumes.

First of all, he seems to have been given no opportunity to change his clothes between his sentence and his execution. Why was that? The most logical answer is that a crucifixion death had already been scheduled for two slave criminals. The Romans were very efficient; crosses they had, stored in the Antonia. A third cross came out for Jesus Christ, detained overnight in the Antonia without opportunity to see anyone or send any messages. No doubt the Sanhedrin used the time to spread the "truth"—Jesus Christ was a slave going to a slave's death. Certainly those who had cheered him and laid palm fronds before him were not present at his crucifixion; that was a small crowd, his nearest relatives from his mother to his brothers and sisters, some of his close friends, men and women.

If he had no opportunity to change his clothes, he cannot have been flogged hard enough to break the skin and ruin his tunic with blood. There were no enzyme laundry powders in existence, nor even soap; clothing was washed in a fountain or stream and pounded with stones to loosen the dirt. Nor could the thorns in his crown have done much damage; the blood, flowing profusely from scalp wounds, would have dripped on to his tunic.

Secondly, his clothing—loincloth, tunic and stola— must have been worth having to a legionary. The garb of a man going to crucifixion soaked in blood would have been incinerated as unwearable, unsellable. Legionaries were paid, they weren't poor.

Whether Christ's clothing was that he wore for his hearing before Pilatus or a new, fresh set, it was expensive and unmarked.

Thirdly, it was possible that Christ's clothing was purple in color. When they existed, Roman sumptuary laws were directed at Tyrian purple, so dark it was almost black, yet shot with rich, plummy highlights. Not a color a Roman legionary would find very eye-catching, whereas ordinary purple he would love.

Fourthly, the tunic would have needed to be properly cut and tailored to appeal—darts to define the waist and set-in sleeves—the stola capacious—and the loincloth made, as they were, with some resemblance to modern underpants. They would have been of wool, not unenviable linen; weavers in an ancient era could produce exquisitely fine woollen fabrics, semi-transparent or as sleek to the feel as modern top quality suiting. Sheep kept for wool wore supple kidskin jackets to keep the wool creamy-white in color and free from burrs and detritus.

There is a Christian tendency to regard the casting of lots for Christ's garments as evidence of Roman depravity; whereas the truth is that much of a legionary's life was boring in the extreme; as indeed would this unusual duty have been. I imagine few crucifixions happened. This day's may have been the year's total to date. Dice were the best way to while away the time. Not many gambled their pay; most dice were cast out of natural curiosity as to how the ivory cubes would fall, and who had the luck that day. The pot was as likely to be pebbles. To have the chance to play for something worth winning was rare, so Christ's clothing was an unexpected bonus. No matter what its color, that says it was fine, not the garb of a poor man. Nor ruined by blood.

I discount the story of Barabbas as apocryphal. Pontius Pilatus was a Roman governor, and such men did not turn a solemn event into a crowd-pleasing circus; there were games for that.

It is also highly likely that once Jesus Christ left his audience chamber, Pilatus had nothing more to do with his death. It was more likely to be up to his subordinates to decide when and how Christ would die, and if there were other slaves scheduled for death, the tidy bureaucratic mind saw the solution immediately: all together, as scheduled for the other two.

The Gospels were written in Greek for a Greek-speaking congregation that had no love for either Romans or Jews. Orally transmitted events by definition cannot be rigidly policed; the early Church was rife with doctrinal argument and more influenced in the main by Paul than by Jesus Christ the man. The Gospels were an attempt at the history of Jesus Christ the man, whose life was, unfortunately, not appreciated as the product of its times.

A hundred years down the road, crucifixion was a commoner death and not confined to slaves—the reason why, in all likelihood, the slave question never arose. Converts were not only more numerous, but also of a higher social status, and the interpretation of Christ's teachings was becoming more intellectual. Some parts of the Gospels received scant theological attention, as they neither affected nor influenced the thinking of Christian bishops, beginning to thrust out feelers toward debate on Transubstantiation and the Trinity as well as what Christian living should consist of in terms of ceremony and ritual.

★★★

Why weren't Christ's legs broken? Who decreed it?

Under ordinary circumstances those who were crucified begged to have their legs broken, as it hastened death by literal days. A man tied to a cross by his arms was provided with a small, blocklike shelf on which he could rest his feet, thus taking the bulk of his weight on his feet. What killed him eventually were thirst and exposure to the elements. Perhaps three days. But if his legs were broken, all his weight subsided into his trunk and he was unable to expand his lungs sufficiently to breathe. What killed him was suffocation. Perhaps three hours.

It seems to me that the Sanhedrin would infinitely have preferred broken legs; they had no reason to want an articulate Jesus Christ on their hands for several days. Yes, he would cease to speak lucidly at the end, but he was a man in the full flower of his strength, and he wouldn't give in to death easily. But once the Roman machine took over, the Sanhedrin had no power to influence the grinding of its wheels. They could intimidate the Prefect, yes, but had no leverage whatsoever with his minions, unknown to them. One has to presume that Christ himself chose not to have his legs broken—but whom did he ask? I inclined to think it was Pilatus, but after long thought, I believe it was a choice could only be made at Golgotha, of the head legionary. The man probably thought him mad, but if that was what he wanted—well and good.

Though Christ couldn't fight against his death sentence, if he still had the use of his tongue after he was hung upon his cross, Christ could speak out. Not against the Sanhedrin or Herod Antipas, but to voice the ideas he conceived and perceived as absolutes: in his death he could die for all humanity did he have the breath to proclaim it. His suffering would be to atone with God for the sins of men, and thereby save them.

This he did—but only for three hours. Either in fact his legs were broken and he died exactly on time, which didn't get a mention in the Gospels, or at Roman instigation his life was terminated on time by a *pilum* spear thrust through the chest wall. This termination most likely came as the decision of the chief legionary, either fed up with this duty or moved by pity, as was his right as supervisor of the triple crucifixion. Who was to gainsay him? The weather had turned bad, there was a minor earth tremor, and it had been a tedious day, garments notwithstanding.

But Jesus Christ had lived on his cross long enough.

The small crowd was docile and well behaved. And those who were present carried his last messages faithfully as they disseminated to hold aloft the torch he had lit. Inspired, they proved effective and ardent torch bearers. Peter must have spoken good Greek, to have traveled as far as he did if indeed Christian history is right. So must others among them. They were not untutored oafs, bucolic ignoramuses. The pity of it is that as time went on women were subtracted from the Christian equation, though Christ had treated them as equals. The virgin birth held sway only because it turned Mary into a non-woman, a femunculus. Enough said. The place of women in religions is a sore point with me.

Outside every locus of population larger than a village was the necropolis, in the least intrusive corner of which were the lime pits. In these the bodies of those who could not afford to pay for a funeral were thrown, to be covered with quicklime and soil. And there the bodies of Jesus Christ's two fellow condemned were tossed. To go to the lime pits was an appalling fate: as a result, all sorts of lowly, including slaves, contributed a coin or two every so often to a burial club. It was one of the earliest examples of a time-payment contract.

Such was not the fate of Jesus Christ. His body was given, probably on the tendering of a paper, to some persons, including women, who wrapped it in a fine shroud and interred it in the costly private sepulchre belonging to one Joseph of Arimathaea. Three days later the women found the stone sealing the tomb rolled off, and the tomb itself empty. Soon it was spreading at an incredible rate that Christ had been seen alive, walking and talking. At the end of forty days he disappeared, not to be seen thereafter.

The truth or otherwise of this doesn't matter. Christianity is a religion of blind faith, not to be questioned in its essence, for all that ostensibly good Christians have been questioning its essence for two thousand years. Did they not, there would be but one kind of Christianity, whereas the kinds are legion.

To me, it is of no moment whether Jesus Christ the man lived in the knowledge of his godhead with every nanosecond of that life already cemented in his mind, or whether he seized what came with no foreknowledge, just like the rest of us. Immaterial.

What set me off was a valid question: why was Jesus Christ given the death of a slave?

How real the Sanhedrin's fears about Jesus Christ were is hard to tell two thousand years later, but certainly their behavior during the hearing before Pontius Pilatus says that they were terrified of a living, breathing Christ. For all we know today, Christ's power and influence over the common people may have been formidable indeed; seen from the ivory tower of seventy-one men entrenched in their function and implacably opposed to change, a living Christ loomed as disaster. Were they correct in regarding him thus? To their way of thinking, yes.

He had to be put down. If in putting him down they could simultaneously discredit him, all the better.

I have concluded that the reasons behind Christ's crucifixion death were threefold: religious, political, *and* social. An impressive Judaic heresy was a religious threat; a man believed to be the King of the Jews was a political threat; and that man's popularity among the common people was a social threat.

What more effective device to achieve the Sanhedrin's ends in Jerusalem in 33 AD was there than the death of a slave?

MIDSOMER NO MISNOMER

Why on earth is *Midsomer Murders* so successful? In a fabulous British whodunit world that includes series as brilliant as *Dalziel & Pascoe* and *Lewis* and *Waking the Dead* to name but three out of many, *M.M.* has labored plots and unbelievable characters. It's a box of chocolates. Yet for longevity and loyal fans, it puts even the *CSI* series in the shade, rolling on year after year after year. I am way behind at Series 10, but I have no trouble casting my mind forward to Series 49, released in 2040.

Scene: What looks like Anne Hathaway's cottage in spring. A large camera crew is positioned behind the hollyhocks and a decapitated body lies on the doormat; its head sits on the letterbox.

From a cute little shed made of wattled withies emanates a soft "Brrr-clank! Brrr-clank!" noise.

A man in frayed clothes rushes down the pebbled path between heart's-ease, monk's-hood and baby's-breath, and reaches the cute little shed, panting painfully.

"He's dead this time, Mr. True-May, sir, honest he is! He has fallen off the twig, he is no more, he's gone to that big cop shop in the sky, he's an ex-policeman! What do I do?"

The producer thrusts his head farther out of the bionic iron lung in which he lives; it has enabled him to survive for 183 years, and he's still going. The cute little shed hides the bionic iron lung and has been designed to fit in no matter what outdoor location *M.M.* might be using for a shoot.

"Put the facsimile plastic mask on him, 137, blow him up with helium, and use the new kid with the great Nettles voice," True-May orders between the "Brrr-clank!"s of his apparatus.

"Sir, even dead he's past it! Whatever the oncologist did on his last visit, Superintendent Barnaby's joints have locked stiffer than a dicky on a double dose of Dynamix."

"Oh, bugger! Send on his doppelganger."

"Sir, I can't! He died of old age last Tuesday."

"Shit!"

One-three-seven looks suddenly inspired. "Sir, sir! Mr. True-May, I've found the answer!"

"What answer, young whipper-snapper 137?"

"A perfect Barnaby, sir, only ninety-nine years old."

"Splendid, 137, splendid! You'll get an extra tuppence in your pay packet this year. Walk him through the scene."

"Um—wheelchair him through, sir. He's gaga."

"So's Barnaby, that's perfect. Expect an extra fourpence."

It really does begin to trigger weeny fantasies like the above. Our Joyce Barnaby looks a lot sourer than she used to, and in Series 10 it's obvious that sex is off the Barnaby marital menu—if it were ever on, that is. Joyce has started to wear Tom's pajamas, supplemented by ear plugs and an eye mask. Her waist is disguised by a jacket, but she's spending more on pricier clothes. The daughter, Cully, grows older, no thinner on the hips and thighs but scrawnier in the face, and the viewer rather gathers that Cully's acting career has foundered, in which case she is a drain on the government by living on Welfare. However, Series 10 sees a serious boyfriend—the manager of a rock 'n' roll band, yet. Where *did* Joyce and Tom go wrong as parents?

As for Tom Barnaby—um, well … He's been a chief inspector for ten years, so a promotion to superintendent must be just around the corner. Unless that too requires a written examination, and Tom keeps failing it?

Q. How do you deal with a recalcitrant sergeant?
Be thorough.

Q. How many murders a day do you solve? Be honest.

Q. How many murders a day do you think you could solve? Be as ambitious as you like, but don't forget the corpse in the field between Midsomer Mere and Midsomer Marshmallow.

Q. Draw in the location of *all* public toilets in Causton on a freehand map. Be specific. Extra marks will be awarded for artistic ability but cartography will get you nowhere.

I'm getting ahead of myself.

What distinguishes *M.M.* from its rivals is its relatively huge American audience, but there are reasons for that. Brian True-May, who retains the title of producer against all comers, nutted out the correct formula, something no one at the BBC was smart enough or egalitarian enough to do.

First item on the True-May list: no thick regional accents and, by and large, good diction. This means Americans can understand most of what is said. You can't hope for that with Dalziel, though *Lewis*, with the extraordinary Laurence Fox as sidekick, would succeed were it not so intellectual. Big TV success demands low-brow, no matter what the nationality. The second item Mr. True-May stipulated, I speculate, was some degree of Americanization, so that the cast say "Yeah!" and "Hi!" and call a torch a flashlight. There are times, I add, when this leads to fluffs that must have the Americans in fits of laughter.

Sometimes I think that a great deal of the problem is due to the Americans involved, who, I speculate, belong to a tight little klatch of L.A. television moguls. And L.A. television moguls are utterly ignorant of how a native of Tennessee or North Dakota or Vermont lives, let alone any Britisher. So when we non-Americans watch an American program, it is essential that we keep the ignorance of the producers about their own country firmly in mind. Vermonters or Tennesseeans must grow furious.

I digress. Mr. True-May moved from his verbal to his visual approach, and declared a theme of English village life as remote from a real English village as L.A. is from Waterbury, Connecticut. A decision having every advantage. No filming in big cities. A signpost amid thick trees at night turns the location into anywhere from Hong Kong to the foothills of the Himalayas. PUDONG AIRPORT 3K and it's Shankers. KHYBER PASS 10K and it's dangerously close to the Taliban. I adored the Chinese touch at the PUDONG AIRPORT 3K sign: two small men pedaling bicycles. But ninety-nine per cent of the locations are the villages of

Midsomer, a fictitious county stuffed with thatch, half-timber, stone and Georgian red brick as its architectural theme. In Midsomer, it's charming if it can't be pretty, but usually it's both. The difference between a town and a village? Easy! In a town, the village green has been tarred over and transformed into a huge and very ugly parking lot.

Now, Mr. True-May obviously reasoned, what would Americans most love to see? And top of his list is at least one shot of people riding horses with tiny English saddles: kids riding fat ponies, women riding fat hacks, men riding fat hunters. And oh, please, as often as possible, a horse-and-hounds cross-country hunt! As the fox is now protected, hunts are permissible. Do they use an electric fox, like the electric rabbit at a greyhound track? A Japanese prototype robot fox? A toddler in a fox suit?

Village greens must be enlivened by a cricket match, of course. Hint: always a match, never a game. Games are against, matches are between.

Mansions in parklands, sadly devoid of verdure around the house itself, which must be seen. Thatched cottages galore, with gardens in bloom. Pubs, pubs, and more pubs. Social activities having an Olde Worlde feel, from World War II dances to drama society Shakespeare or Shaffer. Receptions at the Big House. And—how could one forget them?—fairs, fetes and festivals on the village greens or in the grounds of a manor.

The plot, Mr. True-May surely decided, was best kept utterly implausible. Who wants to be reminded of reality, equally bitter on both sides of the Atlantic? Therefore, over-the-top situational plots replete with larger-than-life characters are the thing.

The characters are either stock, or wildly eccentric. You know from his or her occupation and appearance what the personality is going to be. A farmer, for example, is foul-tempered, boozy and irascible, and may have a totally intimidated son. His scenes are always shot in a horribly primitive kitchen to show the American viewers how primitive a kitchen can be. At the other end of the scale is the execrable cook Joyce Barnaby's kitchen, wasted on her. Few British kitchens are so fine.

Everything thus far is mere window dressing.

Window dressing? you ask. Yes, window dressing for the dead bodies, almost all of whom have been murdered.

A boring episode features two miserable corpses, whereas a real rip-snorter of an episode will have up to five or six corpses, including one or two you prayed feverishly wouldn't die. I best remember the poor woman who was left utterly alone in the world, even her beloved son murdered—and in such a cavalier way that you know the silly scriptwriter forgot there was a dead son. I detest the persons who perish screaming in hellish flames, and wish the scriptwriters were less addicted to this most horrible of all deaths.

It does occur to me from time to time that the death rate in Midsomer County should prompt a socialist government at least to call for a Royal Commission, after which it could declare the soil of Midsomer County toxic, and evacuate the Midsomerians to Welsh Snowdonia or Scots Orkneys and set them up in a cottage industry, *Murder Inc.*, provided their victims are not too close to home. I can see some valuable export figures if the project were managed with True-Mayan efficiency.

It's on about the fourth episode and the nineteenth corpse that the viewer realizes the ultimate purpose of everything: to harbor a dead body. Village greens are for dumping dead bodies on or around—poor material compared to woods, wherein schoolkids can take short cuts to discover dead bodies, couples can frolic nude to discover dead bodies, couples can have sex on blankets and wind up dead bodies, as well as hang, strangle, stab or shotgun blast other people into dead bodies. Streams are wonderful—lots of trout fishing as well as dead bodies. Ponds and lakes allow skinny dipping and serenely sailing swans as well as dead bodies. Tumbledown barns are more than just picturesque: they contain disused farm equipment to reward the viewers with the grisliest dead bodies. Someone drove a car full tilt into a tractor trailer loaded with logs. Occasionally horses are framed for heavy, hoofy murders that were done by the village blacksmith with his hammer and/or anvil. That nightmare booth called *Punch & Judy* can hide more than police puppets.

However, the best venue for murder is undoubtedly the lovely old Norman village church, God's gift to a scriptwriter befogged by plotter's block. The belfry is useful for chucking persons off of, or donging to death with a bell, or squashing by the two-ton bell, or strangling with a bell rope, or breaking the neck in a fall down the winding stairs. Either apse or aisle is ideal for a blunt instrument death or flaming phosphorus or being suspended from the rafters in a copycat *The Silence of the Lambs* murder.

And when all else fails, there is always the baptismal font for drowning in, as they are the size of bath tubs. Nowadays they're mostly kept empty and have a dinky wee basin in their bottoms for the babies; however, if someone demands the full Henrician immersion, it can be done: just fill the font.

Which led to Episode 3,708 of Series 23, the only case that DCI Barnaby never solved. The worst of it was that in the very next episode, 3,709, he got his promotion to superintendent by drawing England, Scotland and Wales freehand and marking in every public toilet from Peebles to Lower Slaughter.

The scriptwriter had been going well, his setup that the dear old vicar had asked the filthy-rich Squire for the money to put a new roof on the church; the Squire had refused with dreadful rudeness—so much so that the entire village of Midsomer Marsh is ready for murder. When Squire is discovered drowned, the list of suspects is a mile long. The next scene, as yet unwritten, is meant to show the Squire's horror when he finds out that unless he has been baptized in the Henrician tradition, he loses the manor and all his money. So he has to go to the dear old vicar and demand a secret Henrician baptism.

But the scriptwriter, a Muslim, is flummoxed. He doesn't know a Henrician baptism is the full immersion jobbie. To go on with, he has another scene already written: it takes place in the Causton morgue with carefully Americanized dialogue.

"Did he drown, George?"

"Yeah, sure he did, but where?"

"The brook at the end of the graveyard, I guess."

"Nope, nah. The diatoms say that's a negative. The water he drowned in contains tiny fragments of faeces, quite a lot of urine, a hint of someone's bedtime mug of cocoa, fourteen cups of strong oolong tea without milk or sugar, and an American gallon of dirty old flower water. It's a bitch, Tom."

"The urinal in Causton Upper High Street? I had that on my superintendent's exam paper—Jeez, it was hard!"

"Nope, nah. No scrumpy or other home-brewed cider."

"Where did the diatoms come from, George?"

"Nowheresville. There weren't any."

"Bath water!"

"Nope, nah. No dead skin, no methane from farts."

"Then where—?"

"No idea, except you'll never guess what else I found in the cadaver's left lower lung lobe."

"What, George? For Pete's sake, *tell* me!"

"An imposing nodule of shed nasal mucosa—for our esteemed American viewers, a booger."

"Then where—?"

"No idea, Tom. The where is your department. I'm just a Home Office pathologist whose role has gradually increased until it looks like Mr. True-May might give me my own crime series, so piss off, you antiquated has-been!"

In a frenzy because he thought Henrician referred to a fowl roost, the scriptwriter leaped from the belfry just before he wrote the scene where the dear old vicar toils to fill the font, so desperate in the end that anything liquid he can find goes into it. When the disgusting Squire appears at midnight for his secret Henrician baptism, the dear old vicar holds his head under and drowns him, then manages to drag the body to the brook at the bottom of the graveyard. The font is covered, the dinky wee basin put on top, and the dear old vicar forgets all about the events of the night.

Going back now to real life, the scriptwriter is dead at the foot of the belfry. As they were running late that year and a cameraman's toddling child had eaten two beads off the abacus Mr. True-May was using as a calendar, the episode stayed in. No viewer noticed that DCI Barnaby failed to divine the drowning; the new scriptwriter covered it up by having another body discovered in the bottom of a freshly dug grave. As it was two series since they had used this ploy, it worked a treat and Mr. True-May was ecstatically happy. No one ever learned why the original scriptwriter leaped from the belfry, but the word "bats" was bruited broadly in Badger's Burrow and Baron's Bantling, so the (imported) M.E. put the death down to viral encephalitis.

Dr. George Bullard never did get his own series, as the British term, SOCO, doesn't have the right ring to it unless it becomes, as the True-May Think Tank wanted, *Socko the Socos!* in heavy Roman type. The police unions felt that it was too demeaning and the covey of chief constables felt it was too American. Dr. Bullard protested by burning his scrubs on Midsomer Marsh green and going into private practice as a phrenologist. His discovery of and papers on Bullard's Bump, a certain indication of a killer, have led to fame and considerable wealth. He gets $150,000 for an hour-long lecture, as he speaks perfect American.

I have deliberately left the central characters until last, on the premise that, in order to know your enemy exceedingly well, it is best to know his stamping ground from the adult video shops of Causton to the ladies' sewing circle of Midsomer Mere.

Detective Chief Inspector Tom Barnaby looks like a German U-boat commander—blond, icy-eyed, pink-skinned, on the short side. The two-metres-tall types are hard to find jobs for in an armored army or a navy comprised of toothpaste tubes. Tom is not handsome and he exudes no sex appeal; were he or did he, he would not be a suitable hero. His solve rate is phenomenal, but the viewers have to take his word for it, as little happens to explain the why. He has an offsider, a detective constable or sergeant, to whom at times he behaves with gross rudeness, thus contributing to the U-boat commander image. He's very fond of his homely no-hoper daughter but less fond of his pretty wife, whose very stupidity can cut him down to size.

Barnaby has a large, very sleek black police car, even after it became obvious that the British police had down-sized to what I call pootling machines—they look like pregnant roller skates and pootle along. Clearly the pootling machine did not sit well with the American audience; soon, he and his sidekick were back in their sleek black town car.

No snappy dresser, he wears off-the-rack suits and utterly boring ties; in Series 10, I note, he is suddenly becoming more casual in his garb.

Barnaby never loses his cool, even when people slam doors in his face. Of course the truth is that a real British copper would have your guts for garters if you slammed a door in his face. Our man is not highly sexed; though his life with Joyce seems on the celibate side, he never succumbs to any of the thick-ankled temptresses who loll around the pages of a script. His main domestic woe is Joyce's cooking, but as she appears to ruin expensive ingredients, he should have put his foot down years ago and had the family live on take-out food. As far as I have been able to work out, his patience in dealing with Joyce stems from his guilt at forever rushing off on a case. But a lot of that rushing isn't necessary: Barnaby rushes off because he's bored at home.

I can understand this, as Joyce is no Mensa member, but he gives a wife (I am a wife) the impression that he wouldn't be around when a wife needed him most desperately, like after hip replacement surgery or a long, debilitating illness. He'd leave looking after Joyce to Cully—handy, sometimes, to have an idle, no-hoper daughter. No, Barnaby is *not* a good husband.

It's Barnaby's attitude to his sidekick I used to find the least likeable aspect of his personality. His first two sergeants he treated like dirt; any dog that strolled onto the set got a better reception. Candidly, were I either young man, I would have decked Barnaby if I fried for it. However, the change in attitude with the third opens up certain avenues of speculation.

The first two were much taller and far handsomer than their boss, who gave them orders without a please or a thank you, and even, upon one occasion, snapped his fingers! But now that number three has arrived, it's the smell of roses. Why? Could it be because the young man is a trifle shorter than his boss, and not handsome at all? I am intrigued. The new Tom Barnaby is even pleasant to his offsider! They have a chuckle together. They wear casual clothes together. Is Mr. True-May dealing with complaints? Certainly I used to have a few.

In fact, the level of rudeness in *M.M.* is breath-taking. The lords of the manor are insufferably snobbish, the squires and their wives are arrogant, and almost everybody else has a vicious temper. I understand that in order to have so many dead bodies it is necessary to lard the storyline with lots of dreadful people, but this is one series can go too far. Some of the scripts are excellent, but most are cynical, exploitative and untrue to human nature. They actually fuel trans-Atlantic dislike, among other things.

Scene: Midsomer Marshmallow green on a perfect day—the kind of day the poor Brits live for, yet (until recent climate change, anyway) hardly ever experience. The sun is shining, the sky is cloudless and the temperature warm in the sun, cool in the shade. Perhaps a hundred people are sitting in deck chairs or on folding steel chairs, women and elderly men in the main, with a few children thrown in for good measure.

There is a definite dividing line between the upper-class women, clad in floaty frocks, and the lower-class women, whose garb is—well, more *unsuitable*.

In a little club house on a table are thick china cups and saucers, a huge Salvation Army style teapot, several china milk jugs and sugar bowls, and plates of cucumber sandwiches.

The Toffs Eleven, captained by Sir Eustace Uppity-Smythe, baronet, of Cad's Hall, is playing cricket with the Oiks Eleven, captained by Ted Clodhopper, blacksmith, of Oiks Airfield, the last village before Midsomer becomes Oxfordshire.

A total of twenty-three men are assembled, clad in long white trousers, white cricketing shoes, white shirts with their long sleeves rolled up and their collars unbuttoned, and vee-necked cable-knit white sweaters tied around their waists. Inexplicably, the Toffs' Twelfth Man is missing.

Stumps are set, and the long white pads of wicket keeper and batsmen are propped against a fence that marks the boundary. A massive roller is parked out of the way; a naked, bloody arm is poking out from under it, but no one takes any notice of this. Sir Eustace and Ted are taking the toss: a silver coin glitters in the air, falls to the pitch. The two men bend to see it.

SIR EUSTACE

I say, hurrah! Oh, jolly, jolly D! Toffs win the toss. We'll bat first, Ted.

TED

A sticky wicket, Squire.

SIR EUSTACE

Better sticky than dead in Midsomer, ha ha ha!

TED

Aye—ur—grr—um—vroom! You'll be out for a duck, Squire, on our Bert's googlies, hur hur hur!

A rifle shot cracks. Lady Uppity-Smythe tumbles off her deck chair and sprawls with one leg sticking straight up like a U-boat periscope. Her Oiky rival, Moll Muggins, goes into hysterics. The other ninety-eight persons watching the match continue to watch.

SIR EUSTACE

Oh, bugger the missus, getting shot now! Carry on, Clodhopper. Post your fielders, you ignorant Oik.

TED

Aye—ur—grr—um—vroom! Ron, you're in slips. Dave, you're silly mid-on. Wally, you're silly mid-off—

Clodhopper stops as an authoritative figure steps between him and Squire, hands up to call a halt.

BARNABY

Just a minute!

TED

Here, who do you think you are, in jeans, a sweat shirt, sneakers and a scarf that fails to hide your pot belly?

SIR EUSTACE

Quite so, Clodhopper! Who are you, to interrupt the annual Toffs versus Oiks cricket match when it's been going on since 1940 and the arrival of the Spitfires on Oiks Airfield? We Toffs flew them, those Oiks kept them in the air!

Uppity-Smythe and Clodhopper lift their faces to the flawless sky as the ghostly roar of propeller-driven engines sounds; the black shadow of a formation of Dornier and Heinkel bombers darkens the pitch; comes far-off flak, the pom-pom-pom of Bofors guns and the wail of sirens. Screaming noises of diving Spitfires in a dogfight with Me-109s fills the air; the ninety-eight spectators jump and shiver.

BARNABY

I am Superintendent Tom Barnaby of the Causton Coppers, and there will be no cricket match today. Sir Eustace, stop buckling your pads and put your bat down. My pathologist informs me that Lady Cynthia was shot dead by a hollow-nosed Remington .307 bullet less than one minute ago. All that is left of her looks like a U-boat periscope, which makes me feel all funny inside. Where is the Toffs' Twelfth Man?

The cricketers are stiff with outrage.

TED

This is the first fine day in fifteen months, you clapped-out copper! You reckon we can't play? Well, on my watch we do! Ron, out of slips! Dave and Wally, out of the sillies! Billy! Bob! Eddy, Neddy, Freddy, Reddy and Ceddy, man your ack-acks!

SIR EUSTACE

Cholmondely pronounced Chumley! St. John pronounced Sinjun! Lord Gadzooks! Mellors the gamekeeper! Ralph pronounced Rafe! Adolph pronounced Dope! Gwmrullarufydd pronounced Gareth! To me in my hour of need!

Twenty-three white-clad men converge on the lone, casually dressed figure of Superintendent Barnaby, blotted from sight as his trendy clothes come off. The cricketers forget cricket and form into a rugby scrum, out of which bloody chunks of plump policeman's parts fly in all directions as the Toffs and the Oiks, united as they have not been since the Battle of Britain, tear Barnaby into bits about the size of flesh minced by a Spitfire's cannons.

Barnaby's latest sergeant watches, smirking, from the plush interior of the Rolls-Royce they now drive, as it is the only car in the U.K. bigger than a breadbox. Smiling pleasurably, he tosses the Remington sniper's rifle into the back seat and opens his door. The camera focuses on a white-trousered leg and a white cricketing shoe. Yes, the Toffs' Twelfth Man is present on the field of victory after all!

Sir Eustace will never need to know that Lady Cynthia's unborn child would have been a Bantling— which saves a lot of work for everyone, as Sir Eustace thinks bantlings are baby bantam rooster chicks, and has no fowl run at Cad's Hall. Just a series of foul runs when he left Moll Muggins's bed through a window.

Barnaby might be dog food, but *Midsomer Murders* goes on and on forever. Detective Sergeant Simon St. John Siskin-Spliff knows he has passed his inspector's exams with a brilliant dissertation on the latrines of the pre-Bentham Newgates and Bridewells, and he looks forward to a long, long, long career in Causton C.I.D. At fifty-four years of age he's a mere chicken, even if he's a bantam. I told you, there are no jobs for the two-metres-tall types these days.

UNELECTED POWER

When I was a child in Catholic primary school in Australia, we were taught about something then called the G.N.P.—the Gross National Product. My nun teachers were superlative, but more than merely that: they never pulled their punches when dealing with unpleasant subjects or facts.

The G.N.P., we were told, represented the goods and services of a nation, its total output in terms of work. But (and we could tell that a big "but" was coming!) there was one kind of citizen who never contributed a brass razoo to the G.N.P.: the civil or public servant. According to Sister Immaculata, this slug was a paper-pushing parasite "working" (we could hear the ironic quotes plainly) for the government.

Sister Immaculata proceeded to cull the sheep from the goats by informing us that doctors, nurses and teachers were classified as public servants, but since they produced good health and learning, did not fall within the definition of a paper-pushing parasite. We must always be careful, said she, to categorize correctly any public servants who might stray into our purlieus, as stray they were bound to. Once we had done that, we were at liberty to give any slugs of paper-pushing parasite as hard a time as they were certain to give us.

What, I still wonder, had some paper-pushing parasite done to Sister Immaculata? She was young and beautiful, so perhaps he raped her? Or perhaps, as sometimes chances, he decided that tormenting her family for a few months would keep him entertained? I'll never know. All I do know is that Sister Immaculata, a wonderfully skilled teacher with the gift of making her pupils adore her, hated public servants, and passed on the germ of that hatred to her pupils. All it needed to sprout was contact with one horrible public servant, and what human being has not suffered that? In justice to Sister Immaculata, I should add that her calling the public servant a parasite led on to a fascinating lesson on parasites, from the liver fluke to the immense, stinking flower of the Rafflesia. What a splendid education we used to receive back then—and from a human being rather than a machine. Give-and-take between student and teacher.

Nowadays I can give Sister Immaculata's paper-pushing parasites their proper name: bureaucrats, from the French "bureau" meaning a lockable desk. Hmm … Lockable, eh? That conjures up an image of furtive secrecy—a *public* servant, yes, but the contents of his desk must not be available to the public his function says he serves.

Following my nose, I was awed to find that the *Concise Oxford English Dictionary*, Eighth Edition lists only three adjectives to describe a bureaucrat: "inflexible"—"insensitive"—and "oppressive"—*wow!* Someone who edits the *Concise OED* has been savaged by a bureaucrat! Left, I suspect, de-fleshed to the bone. Here I am, hardly embarked upon this essay, and I am discovering that the whole non-bureaucratic world loathes the bureaucrat!

He is furtive and secretive, therefore he locks his output away in a desk that is the root of his name. And he is inflexible, insensitive and oppressive. The perfect tool for a dictator in government—but also, in himself, the perfect dictator.

Before I go into the history of the bureaucrat and discuss his work as well as his work habits (I use the masculine gender in a generic sense, as "Man" is the name of the species), here seems an appropriate place to regale my readers with three of my many encounters with bureaucrats. All three concern a less well known but immensely important branch of the sub-species: the diplomat, a public servant of his country placed in a foreign country to look after the interests not only of his country, but also of its citizens.

★ ★ ★

A junior bureaucrat of the American State Department once gave me a really bad time—a genuine interrogation that had me shaking and in tears. I was twenty-seven years old and had developed my armor plating, but this turd of a man could have ripped apart the armor plating on a dreadnought. The reason he gave for his sadism was a bus trip I made from Venice to Athens; the bus traveled through the then Titoan Yugoslavia. Lack of money dictated my route, nothing else. I was trying to find my brother's body. The wounds he opened up! Even now, forty-four years later, I flinch. Why was he interested? I was applying for a green card to work at the Yale School of Internal Medicine. Had the interview not been so hard on the heels of Carl's death, I would have survived it better, but people like that man have no yardstick whereby to measure other people's pain. I remember his name still, but will not write it. The verdict of my old age is that he was a hen-pecked husband.

The second of my three incidents is actually the earliest in time; it happened forty-five years ago. Under-paid and over-taxed, I was living in a rather horrible rooming house in London, and was very alone. My brother,

Carl, had gone off along the eastern Mediterranean intending eventually to work on a kibbutz—he admired the Jews of Israel intensely. I couldn't afford a phone, and had no one to call anyway; there was a pay-phone in the front foyer for emergencies. I shared the room with a South African girl whom I didn't know, but she was somewhere on the Continent that September.

About three on a Sunday afternoon someone banged on my door and said there was a call for me on the front foyer phone—a mystery, as the only place that number was written down was in the back of my brother's passport, where he had listed me as his next-of-kin because we were 10,000 miles from Australia.

When I answered, a man's voice sounded, cold and poshly accented, yet unmistakably Australian. That told me its owner had gone to the best Australian private schools and came from the upper echelons of Australian society. He asked if I had a brother, Carl? I said I did. Whereupon his cold voice told me Carl had died on the island of Crete in a drowning incident. Just like that. The posh fellow wasn't pleased; he had been summoned to the office to deal with me, and his weekend was ruined. There was a revolution going on in Greece, the Australian Embassy was closed …

There was no seat of any kind in the foyer. I slid down the wall until I was on my knees while the cold voice complained about the inconvenience. I began to cry—weep is too ladylike. When half of everything your mind and spirit are is amputated, you don't weep. You cry, you howl.

Then the voice said, "What do you want done with the body?" His *exact* words! When I didn't—couldn't—answer, he went on to badger me for an answer. I was the next-of-kin, and there was a twenty-four-hour time limit involved. I found speech, told him that my mother was Carl's next-of-kin. He went into a rage, abused me roundly for misleading him, abused Carl for putting the wrong name in his passport as next-of-kin, and demanded my mother's phone number. I gave it and he hung up, still fulminating.

My mother was not a very nice person, but I couldn't let this atrocious specimen of bureaucrat break the news of Carl's death to her as he had to me. Still crying, I called her collect and told her. It was the hardest thing my life will ever call upon me to do, but at least it was done better than to me.

When my father returned to the house, my mother asked him for the $8,000 necessary to fly Carl's body home for burial. My father refused! No one else in the family could find so much so quickly, but my father had far more than that sum on hand. His reason for refusing? Carl was dead, it was a waste of money.

So my brother was buried in an unmarked grave in an obscure corner of a Cretan cemetery, and we lost him for eight long years.

What more could there be than that?

Six weeks after I learned of Carl's death, marooned in England through no fault of my own—I was to continue marooned for the next year—I had a letter from Carl.

Apparently it was found when his belongings were packed up, and mailed to me: or else he had mailed it himself, and it was inexplicably delayed. It was one of those blue sheets one used to buy at a post office, write inside it, fold it as was directed, lick the sticky flaps down, and drop it in a post box.

I stood holding it in my hand for I don't know how long before I opened it. In effect, a suicide note. I had known he was deeply depressed, and had worried about him, but I had thought his journey of exploration would lighten his mood. Exactly how, having rescued two women from drowning, he had managed to orchestrate his own death, I do not know. He wasn't alone, his best friend was there and participated in the rescue, but Carl never came back. Nor did he drown. He was found by the U.S. Air Force floating face-up fifteen miles out to sea.

Reading his words six weeks too late, I understood that his mood hadn't improved; his determination to end his life was quite unshaken. To him, there was nothing in the world worth living for.

I kept it a secret until now, except for Ric. For all my mother tormented me in every way she could, I would never have told her that, though perhaps, as the decades have worn on, I see that her destructiveness was not entirely aimed at me. Carl had a far different relationship with her, but I suspect, peering through the distorted lens of time past, that he too was tormented.

A novelist is moved to take real family events and, having shaped them afresh, use them in a book. As I used parts of Carl's death in *The Thorn Birds*. Such is the nature of the beast.

The third incident, the third diplomat. Interesting, that these top-of-the-trees bureaucrats, "expert" in human relationships—what a load of old codswallop that is!—are the most inflexible, insensitive and oppressive of all their sub-species.

I gather that the Australian Government stretches its funds for its diplomatic service by putting one embassy in the major of a whole group of nations, as it does with its Swedish embassy in Stockholm, also responsible for the surrounding smaller nations, including the three Baltic mini-states of Latvia, Lithuania and Estonia.

I received an invitation to go to a book fair being

held in Lithuania in February of 2005. Much to the organizers' astonishment, I accepted, even though the function was being held at the height of an eastern Baltic winter. Why? Because I knew that prominent writers never go to these festivals in remote little nations, not major markets. It wasn't ego that pushed me to go to Lithuania. My ego is very healthy, thank you very much, and doesn't require such transfusions. I went to please the Lithuanians, and out of plain curiosity to visit a part of the world I hadn't before. And, I confess, after living for fifteen years in Connecticut, U.S.A., I was homesick for *real* snow and ice.

In Stockholm, the Australian ambassador for the region appears not to have owned the right kind of personality for his job, which leads one to think him a "reward" kind of appointee rather than a professional diplomat; if one is wrong, then he says little good for Australian diplomatic training.

The book fair was a very big event for the Lithuanians who, like all eastern bloc peoples, are avid readers with a thriving publishing industry. If the Australian ambassador had done his homework on his entire sphere, he would surely have assessed the book fair rather differently than he did. Perhaps he was not a reader himself? But that is no excuse for misunderstanding what a book meant to a person of a nationality rigidly controlled by a hated overlord for almost a lifetime. Since I had been consistently published in the old USSR as well as in the new Russia, my books had been available in eastern bloc nations for many years. I was known and loved, in the Lithuanian language as well as in Russian.

The book fair organizers did what they always did when a well-known writer came: they deputed someone to approach the Australian ambassador and inform him that his country's most famous writer, Colleen McCullough, was attending the book fair. Their assumption was that he would do what other ambassadors did in similar circumstances: visit the book fair himself and give a reception in my honor. The Australian ambassador's answer was curt, to give it the softest word possible under the circumstances. Colleen McCullough was *not* an important writer! She produced trashy bodice-rippers and was beneath literary notice, so, no, he would not be coming to the book fair and there would not be a reception in my honor.

The poor Lithuanians were staggered when the person who had done the approaching told his story far and wide, which is what happens when indiscreet things are said to indiscreet auditors. The gossip ball rolls. And rolls, and rolls … All that was necessary was to decline gracefully, pleading pressure of work. By the time the story was repeated to me, it was everywhere.

Not a new story, either. Something similar had happened in Paris some time before, and in other places too. In fact, I wouldn't be bothered recounting this anecdote were it not for the shabby image of Australia these over-confident, hubristic fools inspire. I am sure the various heads of governments deemed this particular fool just wonderful, but there's far more to the art of diplomacy than talks with heads of governments. Walk with kings, by all means, but only a fool has no common touch.

I speak out because I am a patriot and object when those in reputed service to my country demean it.

I had a terrific time in Lithuania, incidentally.

Both ancient Egypt and ancient China were riddled with bureaucracy, though my ribbon for First Prize goes to Egypt; ancient China was fragmented into many small states, and compared to the Egyptian pharaohs, the Chinese emperors are late arrivals who did not rule the whole of China.

Egypt was a land mostly about ten miles wide, but it was over a thousand miles long, and had two wider bits: one was between the Nile and an anabranch and was called Ta-She; the other was the fan-shaped Delta, 150 miles wide where the Nile flowed into the Mediterranean Sea through seven mouths. Its great artery was the river, making it easy to rule as a single entity; the wind blew ships down its whole Egyptian length to the First Cataract, while the current carried ships back from the First Cataract to the Delta, a fretwork of man-made canals. There were river police as well as land police, and petty bureaucrats in every village and town. The central bureaucracy was located in Thebes when Pharaoh lived there, or in Memphis when Pharaoh lived there.

Pharaoh literally owned Egypt, from the smallest grain of soil to the most gigantic building: serfs, wives, children, priests, the army, the navy, crops and flocks, linen and paper, and all else, belonged to Pharaoh. Egypt had a sophisticated banking system that belonged to—Pharaoh. The only item Pharaoh shared was linen; one-third of it was a perk for the priests.

That, half a hemisphere away, the various geophysically discrete regions of China were endeavoring to do the same, should tell the readers a seminal fact: that one of the three or four primal urges in a human being consists in being paid as much as possible for doing as little as possible, and sitting down to do it. No job description is older, save only pimping.

Bureaucrats never stand to do their work! And bureaucrats are never under-paid, because bureaucrats staff and administer the government pay departments.

Bureaucrats are never short of chairs because bureaucrats staff and administer the government department that orders and sees to the delivery of chairs. There is also a small bureaucratically staffed and administered department to keep a vigilant eye on the comfort of all bureaucratic chairs, as well as make sure said comfort is graded according to the official status of the bureaucratic bottom occupying it.

Even six thousand years ago, people hankered to have the ease and security of a government job: once hired, never fired! That is a mind-set leading to inflexibility, insensitivity, oppression—and nothing else. How can it be otherwise? Power fuels the human ego, and the knowledge that it is almost impossible to be fired endows the bureaucrat with a huge sense of power.

I mean, why stand up in order to work? Why suffer hands callused from pushing a plough or shredded from clearing scrub? Why be at the mercy of the natural seasons? Let other, more stupid people grow the food, build the shelter, smooth out the bumps in the road! The good things in life belong to the middleman, and who is a more quintessential middleman than the bureaucrat? If work must be done, let it be at a self-dictated pace and achieved sitting down, and if the hands have to be marked, let it be with water-soluble ink! Nowadays, mere pixels on a screen.

The true *modus vivendi* of the bureaucrat emerged at one and the same time as the sub-species, and may be summarized as the compulsion to perpetuate and increase the sub-species. What starts out small must grow ever larger, preferably under the supervision of a boss the bureaucrat never sees—a pharaoh or an emperor is ideal—and doing work whose purpose is never made clear. Imagine it! You, Nh'mer, seventy-second in line of promotion in the Warehouse of the Linen, picked up a dust-bunny from the path of the High Priest of Ptah. Next day as you went to work on the west bank of the Nile at Memphis, entering between the two monoliths of Rameses II, you were told by the High Priest of Ptah that next year you will be given the task of splitting off the priestly one-third of Pharaoh's linen. You are on your way! You, Nh'mer, will become a bureaucratic star.

Even the Romans, who abhorred bureaucrats, couldn't avoid being entangled in their toils, but once Christianity took over, Europe disintegrated into small principalities loosely linked by Rome in the guise of a papal Vatican. The decline in the level of education among the lower classes was so shocking that the "free" lower classes lost all hope of a bureaucratic career; a scribe class of monk arose to deal with the mountains of parchment and paper Church and State demanded. The scarcity of parchment and paper due to their cost meant they were jealously guarded, used over again once the writing faded, leading to one of my favorite words—palimpsest. That's what it means, written on top of other writing. But between plagues like the Black Death and appalling poverty among the lowly, not much went on in the sphere of bureaucrats for some considerable time.

When the New World opened up, so did bureaucratic opportunities. Untold wealth spewed across Europe, and everybody needed slaves. Kings had to employ bigger staffs, paper came back and proliferated, governors went to colonies and needed staff there too. Wars were fought with more sophisticated weapons. Kings like Philip V of Spain became superkings, and island nations like England developed navies capable of piracy when no war was even hull-down over the horizon. The booty had to be shared around somehow. Spanish torpor led to a concomitant bureaucratic torpor, while England and the Low Countries took to bureaucracy as Elizabeth Tudor did to a well-filled codpiece. The motto of the new age was simple: Bounty Breeds Bureaucrats.

In fact, a new kind of bureaucrat arose: the corporation bureaucrat. The British East India Company (BEIC) is a splendid early example of the private business corporation, powerful enough to influence government and foreign nations alike. The BEIC wasn't even daunted when a nation it lusted to buy from rejected the concept of money, as did the Chinese, from whom the BEIC wanted tea, silk, paper, ceramics, jade, you name it. Some bureaucrat or bureaucrats found the answer, which was to grow opium in Bengal and addict the Chinese to it, then use it as a form of currency. Worked a treat! And did it perturb the BEIC that a whole populace became hopelessly addicted? Of course not. Fat profits, heathen people who had no importance in the scheme of things apart from the goods their skills and labor produced. The day of the corporate bureaucrat had definitely arrived.

My interest is flagging; I feel a dreadful ennui creeping over me: can there actually be an end to the subject, if not the sub-species? Yes, there can—but have I covered every mentionable aspect? No, I haven't. There's a cut-off point, at which my dedication to my subject becomes outweighed by the prospect of a degree of self-punishment excusable only in a flagellant, and that committed I am not.

Suffice it to say that there are tried-and-true techniques whereby a bureaucrat may rise through the ranks. Knowing whereabouts the bodies are all buried is by far the most effective of these leavening ploys, but the art of brown-nosing one's superiors cannot be over-emphasized either. Such are coupled with the sheer genius of a bureaucrat's greatest weapon, haven and vanishing trick—the committee, which generates postponements and delays, proliferates yet more bureaucrats to serve it, and ends in the only result a committee is capable of producing—the catastrophe. For which no one is ever to blame!

There are fashions in bureaucrats too. The fat-cat portly knight with lobster bisque stains on his tie has been replaced by the gym-slim Commander of Australia with leather patches on the elbows of his tweed jacket, artificially aged so it never looks new. Though one thing you can be sure of: he always wears the right tie. Down at the bottom of the hierarchy bureaucratic mice scurry in grimy tunnels, but those at the top of the vast heap don't walk the corridors of power; these are left to the elected representatives of the Herd. Your top-of-the-trees bureaucrat bypasses the corridors of power to dwell, a genuine mandarin, in his ivory pagoda tower.

For be they government or corporate specimens, one thing is true of all bureaucrats: they are *never* elected to their office. Governments and boards of all colors and persuasions come and go, but the bureaucrats who shuffle the pieces of paper that cross the tables of those elected to office never change. They go on forever, leading the elected representatives by the nose. For where else can the elected representative go for information than to his unelected bureaucrats? Which means that if a government be as red as Karl Marx or as Tory-blue as Margaret Thatcher, the behind-the-scenes policies it pursues will be the same-old same-old, set in stone by generations of bureaucrats.

POP GOES THE PUSSYCAT

Ailurophobia, which is the fear of cats, seems to go back to the Middle Ages, when the lone crone in the cracked shack on the outskirts of the village always had a reputation as a witch. If she played her prophetic paraphernalia properly, she was classified a wisewoman and was relatively exempt from the pyre; if she worked through terror, juggled weeny skulls rather than knuckles, she was deemed malign, and went up in flames or down for a permanent dunk.

Be she of either kind, she had a cat, traditionally a black moggie with big round yellow eyes having pupils like slits. The cat, everybody in the village thought, was her medium, the lock on the gates to the spirit world. But no one stopped to wonder if perhaps the old woman was lonely, or saw the cat for what it actually was: company able to sustain itself on rats and mice. Dogs cost.

There is a sexual element involved in liking cats. They are judged feminine because they're enigmatic and they have claws they're not afraid to use. They are deemed incapable of love—what woman is capable of love? On the other hand, dogs are lusty, shove their noses into female crotches, love to the point of self-abnegation. Dogs are masculine. What man is incapable of loving to the point of self-abnegation?

A veterinarian once told me that cats organize their lives like human beings, and fall in love without relinquishing their self-esteem. So whether you like dogs or cats rather depends upon what you want from your beloved: enslavement or something more conditional.

Even in our present "enlightened" third millennium, prejudices against cats continue to thrive. An article in an Australian national newspaper in the year 2007 began thus:

"If you own a cat, you know the smelly truth: they break wind and it's foul. Not only that, it harms the planet."

All right, the readers knows the journalist is an ailurophobe, but the article was, I gathered, more a sling and arrow aimed at the rash of little companies that have arisen to sell people "carbon credits." At first, it may seem to be a magical way to eliminate those carbon footprints our cars, disposable diapers, and heating or cooling bills indicate we use; then it turns out that the carbon credit company makes energy-saving lightbulbs, economical shower heads, or engages in think-tanks to reduce the First World's carbon emissions.

The journalist hastily assured readers that the cat keeps on farting, but that a very small sum donated each week will go to lessening the carbon footprint in less physiologically ironclad ways than farting cats.

What I objected to strongly was the choice of a cat to illustrate the problem involved in six billion farting human beings and billions upon billions of farting animals.

Consider the size of a cat: between 6 and 15 pounds. A Labrador dog weighs between 40 and 80 pounds. And a human male tips the scales at anywhere between 120 and 260 pounds. Meat eaters, all, plus, for the dog and the man, baked beans.

In actual fact, cats and women are not profligate farters. When it occurs, a cat fart goes POP! and emits about 1cc of methane. A Labrador dog, which farts very frequently, goes BLURT! and emits around 20cc of harmful gases. A man's fart, as any wife sleeping in the same bed as her husband can attest, goes RRRRRIP BOOM!, emits 100cc of lethal gas, and fouls up the entire bedroom for about ten minutes with the fan going.

Once on Norfolk Island we had a lady politician who spent $38,000—a huge sum for a small government—

on investigating the possibility of harnessing the fruity foetor of pigs to reduce the gargantuan size of our electricity bills; Pacific islands, separated from each other by thousands of miles, have the highest electricity charges in the world. Anyway, Ma's scheme didn't work, but if it had, she would have been a heroine. My feeling is, she was just a couple of decades ahead of her time.

Farts aside, what the newspaper article set me to thinking about was the present climate of confusion, and certain directions I can see the new religion of Environmentalism taking. One such is a substrate of scientific ignorance on the part of most people, combined with that good old Judaeo-Christian patina of guilt makes people sitting victims for sensationalism of all kinds, as fed by apocalyptic movies, poorly-researched documentaries, and print articles inspiring panic. The world's carbon footprints cannot be obliterated by the efforts of the First World peoples; that is a task requires the co-operation of every living human being on the planet, as well as the not inconsiderable numbers who, having died, cannot be found room to be buried.

Ours is a cat household. We used to have a magnificent 22 pound (10 kilos) marmalade cat who lived to be nineteen. His idea of bliss was to curl up on Ric's knees, but in his fourteenth year he was run over by a lawyer's car and began to fart. No more sitting on Ric's knees, though he was happy to sit at Ric's feet. His successor, a marmalade named Poindexter, was far too dainty to fart. Now we have Shady, a perfect *Felis silvestris libyca* who might have walked into a Mesopotamian peasant hut ten thousand years ago. Shady is fat, and was named after the American rapper Slim Shady.

Ric found Shady the other day hunched over in despair.

"What's the matter, fat boy?" Ric asked.

"I am riddled with guilt," said Shady.

"*Guilt?* Over what, for cat heaven's sake? You do us the most incredible services, Shades!"

"No, I don't."

"Without you, we'd never know when our steak has preservatives in it—your nose is infallible."

"That's not enough," said Shady miserably.

"Oh, come off it! You catch and kill a minimum of three rats a night," said Ric, floundering.

"I am guilt-ridden because my farts are turning my beloved planet into something akin to the swirling methane hell of Saturn, a planet I postulate was once overrun with farting cats."

"How do you know about Saturn? You're a cat!"

"Cats can look at kings, wear Wellington boots, and speak in a sexy Spanish accent like Antonio

Banderas. Though, being a very pedestrian grey tabby Mesopotamian original descended through a line of ship's cats as far as the *Bounty*, I can't aspire to such heights. As a result of my ordinariness, I espoused planetary astronomy as an avocation. If I am polluting my dear planet, it surely behooves me to become an expert on planetary atmospheres," said Shady in his eighteenth-century-ship's cat accent.

"Don't worry your scarred little head about it, mate," Ric soothed. "I haven't smelled any farts when you sit on my knees. I also know the definition of an expert, which is what this carbon-conscious mob thinks it is."

"What is an expert, Daddy?" asked Shady, curious as any cat.

"X is the unknown factor, and a spurt is a drip under pressure. Shed your guilt along with your fur, Shady. Guilt may look very becoming on a dog, but it sits ill on a cat. What do you fancy for your dinner, as the humans are having Col's spaghetti?"

"Green prawns simmered in dry white vermouth."

End of conversation.

PORTRAIT OF A COLONIAL OVERLORD

I had thought that any nation, having endured colonial status under an overlord, would, upon finally being granted independence, adamantly oppose the very idea of colonialism. Certainly, I thought naively, it would view the acquisition of colonies with horror. But in reality it doesn't always seem to work that way.

From that discovery, I progressed to wondering why these emancipated nations would hunger and thirst after colonies of their own, and stumbled upon one of those universal truths that people prefer not to discuss—or even to admit exist. Namely, it is a universal truth that all peoples yearn to have control of other people they can safely look down upon. This is particularly true of governments, and even truer of Caucasian governments. It's like going back to school with a *carte blanche* to be a bully.

Since I have a specific colony in mind, I also have a specific colonial overlord in mind. I will confine my story to them, and if my reader can substitute other places for mine, it will not surprise me. However, not all emancipated nations choose the bullying neocolonial path. New Zealand, for example, behaved as a prospective colonial overlord should, and abrogated the role.

The colony I am going to speak of is the place wherein I have lived for thirty-two years: Norfolk Island.

The colonial overlord is the Commonwealth of Australia.

Norfolk Island lies over 1,000 miles (1,600 kilometres) east of the continent of Australia, in the midst of the ocean—in fact, it is positioned at the junction of three named bodies of water—the South Pacific Ocean, the Tasman Sea, and the Coral Sea. It has no geophysical links to the ancient maxi-continent of Gondwanaland; rather, it is a part of a string of volcanoes that extend from the North Island of New Zealand to New Caledonia, and lies 450 miles south of Noumea, 850 miles north of New Zealand. Only the New Zealand volcanoes are still active, but there have been recent reports of a new volcano rising on the Norfolk Ridge—a giant of a thing that luckily has a long climb to the surface ahead of it. Between the East Australian continental shelf (a narrow one) and the Norfolk Ridge lie, going eastward, an abyssal plain, the Lord Howe Rise, and a trench. Whereas Gondwanaland, which incorporates Australia, contains the oldest land on earth at over *three billion years*, the Norfolk Ridge is at most only *ten million years*—a baby. Geophysically it is connected to New Zealand, not to Australia, which has led to some fairly rancorous debates as to which country owns the oil and gas reserves in Norfolk Island's territorial waters, claimed by the Commonwealth of Australia the moment the hydrocarbon reports started coming in during the early 1970s.

The Island was discovered by Captain James Cook on his second voyage, in 1774, and named after one of his staunchest patrons, the ninth Duchess of Norfolk. It was, he recorded, *terra nullius*—uninhabited. However, what Cook couldn't know was that the isle had been the site of several Polynesian settlements down the centuries since those intrepid sailors took to conquering the mighty Pacific in outrigger canoes. Archaeological finds have unearthed a fascinating past for Norfolk Island. With them the Polynesians brought the red or cherry guava (porpay), the banana (plun) and the Pacific Island rat. All this evidence marks Norfolk Island firmly as a part of Polynesia.

The Island is five miles by three miles, 15 square miles; eight by five kilometres means 40 square kilometres. When Cook found it, it was densely forested by what looked like massive pine trees, though in places he discerned flax plants. He saw them almost as a gift from God: southern latitudes lacked trees suitable for ship's masts and anything that could be turned into canvas for ship's sails.

The Island utterly lacked any kind of harbor, and offered a reasonable anchorage in one place only, on the south-eastern side, where a sea-level saucer of land existed; its highest point was over 1,000 feet, it was surrounded by 300-foot cliffs, and the interior was as hilly as it was forested. A coral lagoon embraced the saucer of flat land, through which a stream of fresh water flowed. Time was to reveal that the Island lacked lizards, leeches and frogs, and had absolutely no mammals. It was a place of sea birds, a native parrot, and whatever bird life blew in, usually to perish. The wedge-tailed shearwater, *Puffinus pacificus*, migrated there each year to lay its eggs and rear its young. Fortune preserved it; the taste was too greasy for white men to digest. Whereas the Mt. Pitt bird, as it was known, was literally eaten to extinction by starving convicts.

A tiny place, Norfolk Island. A mote in the vastness of the Pacific's eye.

The first 113 years of this story do not concern Australia, which did not exist as a nation, or even as a union of colonies. It was a collection of possessions of the British Crown, like to Norfolk Island. Every decision that was made, every action that was taken between 1788 and 1901 was a decision and an action of the British Crown, the colonial overlord of an empire bigger than Rome's. The Crown consisted of bureaucrats who knew how to work provided the work was in the correct purlieu; administration of the Empire was an amazing feat. That the governors and other persons at the top of a particular colonial heap were grace-and-favor appointees or promoted beyond their level of competence was inevitable, and it was due to such men that most of the glaring mistakes were made. An inheritance that, interestingly, was adopted by the new colonial overlord when its turn came.

The penal settlement at Norfolk Island commenced on March 13th, 1788, only six weeks after the First Fleet had arrived in New South Wales to find itself the victim of rogues and scoundrels who had supplied poor quality everythings, from saws and spades to tents and barrels of inedibly rotten salt meat. With better soil, better rainfall and softer wood to saw, Norfolk Island did well when compared to the plight of the settlement in what would later be known as Sydney. In fact, for several years the bounty of Norfolk Island was all that lay between success and failure for this penal experiment; New South Wales was so alien, so inclement that it didn't even have limestone from which to make mortar; that too came from Norfolk Island.

Not that all turned out as planned. The "pine" trees were unsuitable for ships' masts; a species of araucaria, the branches all emerge in a ring around the bole, at which the bole will snap. And not one person knew how to ret flax! An expedition to New Zealand kidnapped a Maori chieftain's son to teach the art, but of course retting flax is women's work: the lad had no idea what to do, and eventually was returned to his people.

But by 1808 it had been decided to close Norfolk Island down. Sydney was beginning to prosper, and a five-day sail to Norfolk Island unnecessary. By 1813 every last person was gone, and the Crown in its wisdom decreed that every building on Norfolk Island must be demolished and burned. Why? To discourage the French, whalers, or renegade convicts.

Norfolk Island lay abandoned until 1825.

In 1825 the situation in Sydney was quite different than it had been in 1788. Many of those transported were now free, genuine free settlers were beginning to come to try their luck in a new land, and the dumping ground function originally intended was now becoming slightly passé. Other penal colonies had been founded: Moreton Bay, Van Diemen's Land. But there could be no escaping the fact that certain convicts were natural recidivists, some of them extremely violent ones. Of course no one stopped to wonder why that was: the impulse was simply to get rid of them. So Norfolk Island was made a penal institution for a second time, its inmates the dregs of Sydney that were not sent to Macquarie Harbour on the wild west coast of Tasmania. This second venture was cruel to the point of barbarousness: men being hanged thanked God for His mercy in giving them death. When the Commandant learned that a chain gang on its way to a place of work each plucked a ripe orange from a laden tree and ate it, he had the tree chopped down. No ray of light or hope was permitted to shine. Women convicts— there were some—were forced to dance naked and drunk before the guards who would then rape them.

A groundswell in England changed all that. "Do-Gooders" were accumulating power in Westminster, and transportation as a punishment was deplored. So were the hideous practices reported as everyday occurrences in Norfolk Island and Macquarie Harbour.

And so, by 1850, it was agreed that Norfolk Island would be closed. The second penal attempt was also a failure.

There were many differences between the relics of the first try and the second. The buildings of the first were uniformly perishable, and had disappeared, whereas the buildings of the second were solid stone, and many. The jails, the barracks, the offices and the stores buildings were all surrounded by high stone walls. There was a herd of cows and a mob of sheep. Swine in sties. Hens in runs. Ducks and geese. The second try had been a huge undertaking, and those who ran it insisted upon good food as well as port, cognac, claret, rum and beer.

There were commodious houses for the officers, and the governor's residence, roomy and well tended, sat atop a knoll with a magnificent view.

In 1850, all that was about to be abandoned.

Time now for an essential digression upon a word that few persons understand, including many who use it regularly. *Indigenous.* Australian bureaucrats and politicians take it to mean a populace resident in a land for 40,000 years, this being the length of time the Aborigines have inhabited the continent of Australia. But that is not its true meaning at all. The Maori, who are indigenous to New Zealand, have only been there for 700 years. One is racially Australoid, the other Mongoloid. So it isn't a question of race any more than it is the length of time a land has been occupied.

In a United Nations convention for indigenous peoples held some years ago in Geneva, I listened, amazed, to the official representative of the Dutch government say that although Holland had no indigenous people, his government sincerely sympathized with their lot. I had to bite my tongue. He sat there, dear man, without the faintest idea that he himself was an indigenous person. He had made all the usual assumptions Caucasian Europeans make about indigenousness: that to be indigenous means you can't be white, or belong to a "civilized" race. You have to be colored, at least slightly primitive, and dispossessed of your lands by the white man. Yet the fact remains that the Dutch are indigenous to the Netherlands. They are the same people who once called themselves the Frisii and the Bructeri, and inhabited the lowlands between the Rhenus and the Amasia Rivers.

The indigneous people of Britain were probably driven in great numbers to Ireland; indigenousness is harder to prove in Great Britain.

The *Oxford English Dictionary* attributes no importance to being the first in a place: it simply says that to be indigenous is to occupy a place *naturally*.

Indigenousness is not dependent upon a people's skin color, or color of hair and eyes; the Sami of Lappland are very blond. A people may not even be the first in a place, but it must occupy that place naturally. The word has no degree: one is indigenous, or one is not indigenous. No middle ground, no shades of grey. Nor, according to the United Nations, can an external authority pronounce upon it. The only ones concerned with indigenousness are those who are indigenous. So a government cannot say a people is not indigenous when (a) it has declared itself indigenous and (b) is accepted as indigenous by its fellow indigenes.

The key word is *naturally*. If the object or purpose of occupying a place previously unoccupied is to establish and run a prison, and if persons desirous of settling in it are not allowed to do so, then that settlement is not natural. Its activities do not revolve around the natural activities of a group of persons settling in a new place. On the contrary. No one in the twenty-first century would attach the word "natural" to any nineteenth century penal institution, or aspect of it.

Neither the first nor the second penal establishment on Norfolk Island can be called natural. The second in particular was artificial in the same way as any other high security prison built in virgin territory, as still happens in California, a place in constant need of more high security prisons. Under no kind of circumstances is a settlement natural when it has only one purpose, to sequester society's pariahs, when its servitors come and go according to orders, and no one dreams of it as a homeland.

By 1850, however, the British Crown had decided that the people of Pitcairn's Island would be given a new homeland, Norfolk Island. It was eminently suited to accommodate a small, yet whole and entire, populace. It had an infrastructure that could at least be put partially to use, and it would cost the Crown virtually nothing while endowing a deserted island with a stoutly British people. All important considerations.

Pitcairn's Island was a very long way away from anywhere. It had been wrongly marked on the charts, which made it an ideal hiding place for a group of renegades. Mutiny on a British Navy ship was the ultimate crime, and carried an automatic death sentence. That the officers and men of the *Bounty* were inflicted with a captain who, later in his life, would have two more mutinies and a history of perpetual trouble and discontent wherever he was, made no difference. Colder men wouldn't have given Bligh a sextant when they sent him off in their largest boat, but these mutineers were young and—worse—desperate for love. They had all formed strong attachments to native women in Tahiti, and were determined to return there.

So, in 1790, a year after the mutiny on the *Bounty*, the mutineer Fletcher Christian, twenty-four years old, with five other mutineers, sixteen Tahitian women and nine Tahitian men, found Pitcairn's Island and decided to stay there. It was to be their homeland for sixty-six years: it was *terra nullius* when they settled there, and they loved this crag as people love a homeland.

It lay 3,300 miles east of Norfolk Island in the south-western Pacific: the closest landmass was Chile in South America and the closest Polynesian settlement on Rapanui—Easter Island. In area Pitcairn's is so small it makes the fifteen square miles of Norfolk Island seem gigantic—two square miles. But here, using what tools *Bounty* had carried, they carved out a place that sheltered and fed them, and in time became a people filled with what the American anthropologist Harry L. Shapiro called "hybrid vigor." They developed a language peculiarly their own, and two astonishingly modern laws: the first, that all women were entitled to vote on an equal footing with men; and the second, that all children must be schooled. They were godfearing, kind, and peaceful. When their presence on Pitcairn's Island was discovered in 1815, they were already full masters of their tiny island world, and when in 1825 the Royal Navy visited them, they were impressive. In 1838 a visiting ship's captain gave them a list of "laws" to which they adhered from that point on; it was, in effect, a constitution.

But by 1850 the settlement on what was now known as Pitcairn Island—the apostrophe and the "s" had been dropped—was creaking at the seams. One hundred and ninety people lived there, and it wasn't big enough to support them.

With Queen Victoria on the throne and Prince Albert behind her, the climate in England was very different than it had been even in 1825. A pseudo-science called eugenics was all the rage, and certain important people suddenly saw, one, the saga of the *Bounty* mutineers as romantic, and, two, an extremely rare chance to observe the evolution of a new people unaffected by modern changes and unacquainted with modern living.

It is referred to in the literature, of which Ric has a room stuffed full, as "the Experiment." As best one can reconstruct its purposes, they were to place this untouched people-in-the-making upon a new homeland as remote and far off the sea lanes as possible. Norfolk Island was the best among the candidate islands considered.

The letters that went back and forth between persons like the Bishop of London and various members of Cabinet as well as colonial governors sigh wistfully for the chance to witness a Pitcairner's first sight of a sheep or a cow, never having seen either, let alone obtained food from it. Romanticism was rampant.

It took at least six years to get the scheme moving, given the distances involved in the exchange of letters, orders, afterthoughts, new instructions.

When the proposition was eventually put to the Pitcairners, "We Accepted" says their motto. Upon the payment by the Pitcairners of £4,000 for a ship, the *Morayshire* was commissioned to take the now-193 persons of Pitcairn westward across the South Pacific to their new home and homeland, Norfolk Island.

The main document was an Imperial Order-in-Council, and it virtually gifted the Pitcairn immigrants with the whole of the new homeland; it also stipulated that they were to be left to govern themselves.

The provisos of the Order-in-Council give the game away, of course; the Islanders were guinea-pigs, and the Experiment was to observe what happened during their ongoing evolution as a people, as a society.

This is a tale of one broken promise after another, including to the present day, 2011. It is a tale of a man or a small group of men neither resident on Norfolk Island nor committed by blood to Norfolk Island, taking the fate of a people and manipulating it for their own ends, never admirable or the right ends. It is a tale of that universal truth: people yearn to have power over another people deemed inferior or insignificant.

The Pitcairners arrived on Norfolk Island on June 8th, 1856, and hadn't dried the sea water off their feet before the promises were being broken. Their most precious piece of paper, the one that gave them all but some landing places, was taken from them— no photocopiers in those days! They were stripped of many hundreds of acres, many of the buildings. I will only say here that the trickery was so apparent that a group of Youngs sailed back to Pitcairn immediately, angry, disillusioned and unwilling to participate in the Experiment. The confiscated paper has never come to light, its existence strenuously denied by the Crown; it was, of course, destroyed. Whether this was as the result of a decision made by the Governor of New South Wales (who now had a second hat, Governor of Norfolk Island), or it emanated from London, will never be known, but it is highly likely to have been a decision by the Governor of New South Wales, who was horrified that Pitcairn women were allowed to vote. For us in our day and age it is nigh impossible to imagine the outrage most men felt at the very idea of letting women vote— they were cattle, inferiors, undeserving of masculine prerogatives. Governor Sir William Denison suffered a degree of umbrage unimaginable to us, and took his ire out on the unfortunate Islanders in every way he could. What he could *not* do was strip Islander women of their right to vote; that was entrenched as part of the Experiment. So he took as much of Norfolk Island's 10,000 acres as he dared.

One hundred and ninety-three people had sailed from Pitcairn: 194 arrived on Norfolk—a baby was born en route. With them, the Islanders brought everything that makes a people a people settling in a place to live there *naturally*. They brought sewing baskets, innumerable relics of the *Bounty* from its rudder to its own sewing box; they brought their pet cats, their prayer books, their slates and teaching apparatus, their few precious books; they brought all their people from oldest to youngest, including that one still *in utero*; they brought their language, their customs, traditions and skills.

Finally, in 1856, Norfolk Island became a homeland. It was a place with a natural settlement of genetically unique people. In 1993 the Norfolk Islanders of Pitcairn stock declared themselves indigenous to Norfolk Island as a homeland, and were accepted into the indigenous community at Geneva.

Despite the malign attitude of a series of Governors of New South Wales, the Islanders thrived in their new homeland, though a second group returned to Pitcairn eighteen months after the arrival due to more broken promises. Always bearing in mind, you who read this, that I am still speaking of the British Crown; New South Wales was a British colony. And always the shadow of the voting women cast its pall across official attitudes to the Islanders. Men? They were undeserving of the name, they were dominated by what one governor, Viscount Hampden, described as "petticoat government." Today, of course, the Islanders can claim without any fear of argument that they were the first European-organized government to give women the vote.

Going back to Pitcairn times, the Islanders earned what little income they gathered from whaling, but in the old-fashioned way that stood in no danger of depleting a species. Their few barrels were sold to passing whalers, and the money was cared for with remarkable shrewdness. It was never spent, just added to. When, for instance, charter of a ship to take the people to Norfolk Island was bruited and a figure of £4,000 was named, the Islanders paid it out of what they had saved living on Pitcairn. Living on Norfolk, it increased faster. The money a family kept for its own use came from selling fresh produce and meat to the ships that occasionally called in.

But gradually it was borne in upon London that the Experiment was being endangered by the warmth and generosity of the Islanders. Sometimes a visiting ship left without one crew member: the Islander girls were gorgeous, though, alas, virtuous. If a man became enamored of an Island girl, he had to marry her and stay on Norfolk Island to raise a family. An Englishman named Rossiter was engaged as a schoolteacher—a cruel one, the stories say—and married an Island girl. Pardon Snell, an American from Little Compton, Rhode Island, jumped a whaler, married, and stayed. Isaac Robinson, whose career was so checkered by the time he arrived on Norfolk Island that he was something of a man of well-traveled mystery, serves as a wonderful example of just how far female suffrage went. Robinson got two Quintal girls, sisters, pregnant, but could only marry one—which one? was the question. So the two girls, Kezia and Hannah, were allowed to decide who would marry this bald, elderly Lothario; they decided that Hannah, only sixteen years old, would need him more. Isaac Robinson duly married Hannah Quintal. Three years later, Kezia died, so the Robinsons took her orphaned child, Alice, as their own.

Bataille was a French horse trader; Blucher was a German. But as the news of these marriages percolated back to London, displeasure reigned. The Experiment was endangered, perhaps ruined, by a constant influx of new blood. Worse than that, the new blood tended to be foreign—Americans, French, God forbid, *Germans*!

Added to which, these foreigners were gifted with land because their wives were Islanders and had equal suffrage, equal rights with men on the subject of land as well as votes.

In 1896, the Governor of New South Wales struck. He stripped the Islanders of their right to govern themselves. From that time on, they were under his autocratic control.

Life became intolerable. One governor sent a friend and his son to administer Norfolk Island; they robbed the Islanders of every penny they could lay their hands on. Complaints fell on perpetually deaf ears. If any emotion surged uppermost in an official breast, it was that universal truth: a whole people to oppress, discriminate against, insult, ignore, and, most of all, despise. Non-men who allowed women to vote!

The Islanders took to sending petitions to London. It was a clever move, in that any petitions sent to London via the Governor of New South Wales were torn up; petitions sent direct were at least read by some persons in London. And, if it did nothing else, it served to remind London that there had been an Experiment, and that its guinea-pigs were bitterly unhappy.

Now we come to the year 1901 and the birth of the Commonwealth of Australia, until that date merely a collection of separately administered colonies existing on a continent three million square miles in extent. New Zealand was supposed to be a part of the new nation, but wisely ended in declining; Western Australia did not want to belong and was talked into it, a decision that many modern Western Australians deplore. Norfolk Island wasn't even mentioned; it continued to be a British Crown colony.

The constitution of the Commonwealth of Australia is a rather peculiar document, given its relatively late genesis: the People are mentioned only once, in its Preamble, and are apportioned no rights. The many clauses all pertain to the rights of states and the rights of parliamentarians. Nor has a bill of rights for the Australian people ever been formulated.

The average Australian citizen knows nothing of the story I am writing, so I would like to point out here and now that when I say "Australia" I do not mean its people. They, like Norfolk Island, are all too often government's victims. I must also mention the city of Canberra, where the Australian federal government resides in splendid isolation. A ziggurat of 350,000 persons, Canberra's sole industry is government, and its population one of civil servants. The average wage in Canberra is considerably higher than anywhere else in the nation.

★ ★ ★

In 1914 a panic flashed through the South Pacific because the Germans had been making colonial inroads in Micronesia and Melanesia. In those days Norfolk Island was urgently strategic: it was the only piece of land between New Caledonia and New Zealand. Even though it had no harbor or safe anchorage, the military possession of the Island's 15 square miles was a threat. As a result, Norfolk Island was placed under the authority of the Commonwealth of Australia as a dependent territory. When Australia asked to annex it into the Commonwealth, the Islanders protested so strongly to the Crown that Australia's request was refused. To this day, Norfolk Island has not been annexed. No matter what fancy name Australia puts upon it, it is still a dependent territory.

From 1914 until 1979, a total of sixty-five years, Norfolk Island was under completely autocratic Australian rule. Not only did this huge and prosperous nation embrace the universal truth and look down on the people of Norfolk Island, it also adopted all the worst features of the colonial overlord. Absolutely nothing was done. The only money Australia spent on Norfolk Island was to keep its Administrator and his imported bureaucrats in great comfort. Most of these administrators were abominable men; the few who were sympathetic met a stone wall in Canberra. For twenty-nine years a law was in place that forbade the printing or publication of anything that hadn't been approved by the Administrator. In the twentieth century! It was repealed in 1964.

Any public works or infrastructure considered urgent were refused outright, or else simply never done. *Nothing was done!*

Despite Australia's position as Norfolk Island's colonial overlord, during World War II it was garrisoned by the New Zealand armed services. The airstrip, which did wonderful duty until the 1980s, was built by the American Seabees.

In 1946, by which date Australia had been auto-cratically administering a non-self-governing Norfolk Island for thirty-two years, the United Nations under Article 73e obliged every member nation to disclose its non-self-governing territories. It was pretty hard for Australia to "forget" Norfolk Island in 1946; Australia administered no other small island dependent territory. The Indian Ocean territories were acquired later. So in 1946, with a Norfolk Island desk in Canberra, Australia denied having any non-self-governing territories. *Australia lied!* Lied to the U.N.! It was as crafty a lie as deceitful, because it removed Norfolk Island from any

United Nations map of the world. To the U.N., apart from its indigenous bureau, Norfolk Island does not exist. The Islanders have no U.N. voice.

In 1955 the Islanders were boiling over a fresh onslaught of injustices; 583 of them petitioned the Queen to return their self-government, but of course nothing ever came of it.

Those sixty-five years of Australian rule, during which the people of Norfolk Island were almost entirely descendants of those who had colonized it, are an indictment of Australia's record as a colonial overlord. To a Canberra mind, it entailed little more than being a cushy job as a reward for some party official: until very recently the job of Administrator of Norfolk Island was one of the "jobs for the boys" and carried a hefty remuneration.

In the early 1970s reports began to filter in that there were big deposits of oil and/or gas on the Norfolk Island Ridge, within the 200-mile territorial waters. In 1979 Australia seized these waters by a unilateral act of its parliament, its excuse that Norfolk Island couldn't look after them. Australia doesn't do a very good job either. The best solution would have been to give the Islanders, still the world's greatest seamen, a fast patrol boat. They would have loved the work and done it well, but the issue wasn't looking after. Possible hydrocarbons was.

In 1979 something very strange happened. The Australian Minister for Territories announced that Norfolk Island would be given a "limited form of self-government." By this, the Islanders were becoming more educated and more sophisticated: they began to ask for their inalienable right of self-determination. One of the caveats attached to this limited self-government was that *no referendum of any kind was to be held*. Another caveat was to the effect that if the Island's parliament got into debt, then self-government would be removed forthwith.

Neither caveat has ever been removed, though neither is legal. Once self-government is given, it cannot be taken away. Not in 2011—though right at this moment a so-called socialist Australian government is about to do so. According to the U.N., self-determination is an inalienable right of a people, yet the Norfolk Islanders have never been offered this right. It is theirs, and every move Australia makes to deny them is disgraceful.

But I get ahead of myself. When one feels strongly, it is very difficult to be detached.

The limited self-government given in 1979 was a unilateral affair. No one on Norfolk Island was consulted about what form it would take, what kind of voting structure would be put in place, what functions it could best do.

Curiously, I arrived to live on Norfolk Island thirty-two years ago, at the dawn of self-government, and have watched the local people learn to govern better, if the truth be known, than Canberra governs. It's easier; there are 2,000 people here, a little more than half of whom vote.

After the Seabees built the airstrip, a tiny tourist industry grew here as Qantas and then other airlines ran flights. The day of the Islander was passing; the day of the expatriate was born. Slowly, slowly, the Island's population began to tilt away from Pitcairn dominance, and some of these Australian expatriates began to agitate for closer ties to Australia. Luckily they have always been in a minority, but Canberra has been helping tip that scale by enacting laws overruling local laws. New Zealanders, of whom there are many, had always voted and belonged to the new parliament when it came along: Canberra took their rights away. Much to the anguish of the people it concerns, those who live on Norfolk Island. But having the power is all, and Australia uses it without adhering to the ways of life extant in this speck of land, so remote, so isolated.

Yes, the injustices and colonial overlording continue.

All the projects and infrastructure deemed unnecessary while Norfolk Island was under autocratic Australian rule became urgent, had to be done yesterday. Australia agreed to put up half the cost of each project; Norfolk Island's two thousand people had to find the other half. Thanks to the frugality and shrewdness of the Pitcairn element in the population, literal millions had been salted away, and the Island managed to keep up for quite a while. It doesn't take a gargantuan brain to work out that Australia's new technique anent Norfolk Island was to send it broke with a series of massive undertakings, then strip all self-government away and annex it, which all who live here know would be the kiss of death for a way of life, and the death of the only Polynesian enclave under the Australian umbrella.

The airstrip has been upgraded three times and now can take 737 jets regularly, as well as military aircraft. The tourist hotel strip and school have been sewered. A new airport and adjunct buildings have been constructed. A garbage and waste disposal scheme is in place. The generators have been upgraded to supply the whole island comfortably. Pontoons to help cruise-ship passengers get ashore easily have been built. The Cascade cliff, a huge undertaking, has been rendered safe. Much of the Island's phone and power cables are now underground, obviating the eyesore of poles, and the work continues. One hundred miles (or 160 kilometres) of road have been tar-sealed. There are national parks and reserves. The beaches are pristine.

Not bad for thirty-two years of self-government, eh? Even if the colonial overlord did pay half. When we ran out of money, Australia agreed to lend us the money interest-free! Interest-free! Isn't that big of them? Everybody else gets gifts. Norfolk Island gets loans. Why is that, do you suppose? Why, because the Islanders are naughty, and criticize! They don't lie down and salaam in obsequious thanks.

Self-government in Norfolk Island is dogged by what the locals call "Standover Committees"—Australian parliamentary standing committees, which are really excuses for parliamentarians to go on nice jaunts away at the public expense and, if visiting Norfolk Island, drive the locals mad with questions that can sometimes verge on the ludicrous, so uninformed are these standover people when they come. More fruits of my thirty-two years on Norfolk Island! Standing committees visit Norfolk Island about twice a year, and cost the Island precious money it could spend on other things. Their reports are made in advance of their visit, and are always, always, always negative.

Isn't it amazing to think that in 2011 there exists a colonial overlord with nothing nice to say about its unfortunate colonies? Just criticism, obstruction and utter negativity. Believe it or not, I am an Australian patriot, and it hurts me deeply to have to say such things of my country. But they're all true.

Of the 1,100 people empowered to vote in Norfolk Island elections, the majority, thanks to Australian meddling, are Australians. The writing was on the wall when the New Zealanders were disenfranchised, but then a new Australian law allowed any Australian present on the Island for five months to vote. Until then, one had needed to be, in effect, a citizen of the Island. Not any more. It is so blatantly slanted, so prejudiced and discriminatory! Yet the Islanders were accused of discriminating in favor of the Pitcairn descendants, and forbidden by Australia to so do. This, despite the fact that they have declared themselves indigenous—has any people ever had greater entitlement than they? No. But anything less than a 40,000-year occupation disqualifies them in Australia's eyes. Which simply says that Australia has no idea what the word "indigenous" actually means.

Our laws, of residence as well as of other things, are fair and equable. Five years earns residence and the right to vote—or used to. I condemn Australia roundly for its discrimination in favor of Australians in a place whose situation and history are not, and never were, Australian. The penal failures belonged to the British Crown, not to Australia. Since 1856, the Island has been the homeland of an ethnically distinct people, the Norfolk Islanders. Norfolk Island is not, nor ever was, a part of the Commonwealth of Australia.

After thirty-two years of admirable self-government at great cost to the heart strings and blood pressure of all who truly love Norfolk Island—and after being forced into debt by a hugely wealthy nation to which these few millions are a pittance—in 2011 it seems likely that Australia has finally won the long battle.

But at what price to Australia? The international reputation of a bully and a tyrant, for starters. In 1987, after three years of self-government, Australia terminated local autonomy on poor Christmas Island, in the Indian Ocean, because the Islanders spent unwisely. Here is the place to reiterate that removal of self-government, once given, is illegal: Halsbury's *Laws of England* 3rd edition, volume 5, page 1202 agrees with me. But I do not think that Australia stops to consider whether what it does is legal according to respected convention. Its attitude is more "Who will stop me?" Power corrupts.

Australia cannot say that all the moneys have been unwisely spent on Norfolk Island. In the over thirty years of limited self-government, huge strides have been made both in improved facilities and in infrastructure. Considering the utter nothing that Australia did during its sixty-five years of total autocracy, self-government in Norfolk Island has been a brilliant success. If there are things wrong with it, some glaring, how is that any different from governments *in* the Commonwealth? What's happening on Norfolk Island is not new: we are vilified for things that go on in Australian governments every day. But if it happens in Australia, downplay it— if possible!

Why then at the start of the second decade of the millennium does the Commonwealth of Australia wish to destroy everything Norfolk Island is? Not to improve our lot, for sure! Go to the internet and look up the web sites of Christmas Island to see what happens to colonies administered by Australia without any local self-government. It is a disaster; so is Cocos/Keeling. Unhappy, overrun by bureaucrats, abysmally lacking in facilities and used as dumping grounds: Cocos/Keeling became an animal quarantine station, and Christmas Island contains a massive concentration camp for boat people. When a woman of Christmas Island has a baby, she is flown to Western Australia to have it. Horribly expensive, yes, but there's more to it than that. If no babies are physically born in a place, it cannot be said to have a native populace of any color or creed.

Australia owes Norfolk Island a hospital; it was supposed to build one in 1969. But does the above mean that no obstetrician will be present on Norfolk Island, and the 155-year-old Pitcairn tradition of having their babies born in their homeland will be taken from them? It's cunning, but it works. There's ample evidence in the literature of Christmas Island that Australia's policy once it took the place from Singapore in the 1950s was to discourage the establishment of a populace that could call itself native to Christmas Island. If Norfolk Island is to be another concentration camp, or a defence base, or any other hidden agenda, the first step is to make the place too expensive to dwell in. Taxation and land rates on top of our huge freight bills and our very real local indirect taxes would kill the Island as a homeland for ordinary, working people.

What Australia never tells us is how much the Commonwealth has pocketed by selling our fishing rights, and how much tax it obtains from businesses established here that also exist inside the Commonwealth. The truth of the matter is that to integrate Norfolk Island into the Commonwealth will cost far more than it can ever bring in. The place hasn't been a tax haven since 1975.

We are a nano-drop in the Commonwealth's bucket. So why this relentless push, no matter what the color of the Australian federal government? There's a hidden agenda. There has to be.

But, alas, we won't know what it is until it's too late.

ANTHROPOMORPHISM

No doubt arising from our animal origins and our animal nature, *Homo sapiens* has always incorporated animals into his (her is implied) life, and in multiple ways. Food and clothing. A sign of the seasons. Company. Knowledge of being prey. Fear not of being prey but of being bitten. Man's early world was one of co-existence with animals.

Just when the supernatural invaded Man's brain isn't known, of course, but logic says it was probably tied to his fellow beasts, particularly those seen as owning power. Big cats, bears, wolves. Each posing a threat to human life and limb, and therefore to be propitiated. Gifts were tendered; if the beast's stomach were already full, it would go away. But what demands propitiation automatically has power, and in the tediously slow evolution of human society this power changed, became invested in certain humans within the tribal structure. The shaman or witch doctor took animal power into and unto himself, having convinced the tribe that he had acquired special knowledge and influence over animal magic. For it was recognized that animals retained some kinds of instinctual knowledge that humans were busy losing.

That loss accelerated with the discovery of an agricultural existence. Instead of nomadic hunting and gathering, the tribe stayed in one place to grow crops and collect meat or milk beasts in herds. Another element than big cats, bears and wolves had to be propitiated: the sky, to deliver rain and keep the river flowing, and though this power was not embodied in the form of an animal, it was sensed to exist. Man's cosmogony, his supernatural world, adapted to his new lifestyle.

The word "power" became the word "god", in those early days just a convenient term to indicate what had no visible form or entity, yet possessed the ability to overturn and ruin the most careful or cherished human undertakings.

Some human brains developed in ways able to imagine that a spirit world went on distinct from the human one, whereas other brains developed in ways that nailed the spirit world to animals, even inanimate things like meteors. It all depended upon the human location and particular situation.

But I am not going there. Instead, I want to stay with animal power, with the animal cosmogony. For out of it comes a phenomenon we still see every day, and will continue to see.

Namely, anthropomorphism. *Such* a long word! Greek-rooted too. Its etymological meaning (that is, its core) is narrower than its customary use, which encompasses the entire gamut of creatures part-human, part-animal, part-imaginary, from the booted cat which speaks with the voice of Antonio Banderas to the sphinx which asked Oedipus its riddle on the road to Megara.

Either one subscribes to Carl Jung's theory of the collective race memory, or one does not. I have always felt that it has merit, given that we have been—and still are—actively evolving, and that our brains contain all the levels of our animal antecedents, albeit atrophied, or malformed, or hugely expanded, or radically changed. Why should there not be a thin sheet somewhere deep down in there that goes back to our beginnings? It certainly answers some of the questions about our abiding attraction for and love of humanizing animals or animalizing humans. The emotions evoked are strong, generate pleasure or fear or even terror. Who remembers a science-fiction film of the 1950s called *Forbidden Planet*? Its script contained a memorable phrase: "monsters of the id." The very good plot hinged on collective race memory and the monsters that bedeviled our origins—and how impossible it is to eradicate those monsters.

Because no one teaches Latin roots anymore, let alone Greek roots, a word like "anthropomorphism" is unintelligible. A quick lesson: "anthro" is Greek for male, "morphism" is Greek for form or shape. So the word should mean having a male form. The Greek for changing something's shape or form is "meta", so when the shape or form is altered, you have a metamorphosis. *Star Wars II* featured an attractive lady assassin who is said to be a "morph"—the script uses the word, but also uses "shape-changer" to make sure the audience gets the message. But, George Lucas, you should have called her a "metamorph" or even just a "meta." However, I rather get the feeling that accuracy is not a high Lucas priority. Did I say how much I loathe Yoda and his pop-psychology? Well, I do. I hate Yoda as much as I love Robbie the Robot.

Myth and culture have always been stuffed with metamorphoses. Ovid (Publius Ovidius Naso) wrote down the stories that were already an integral part of his world in 100 AD to while away a political exile on the Black Sea, pining for Rome.

Perhaps his most famous story is about the beautiful young man named Narcissus, who caught sight of his reflection in a pool and fell in love with it. No matter how he begged and pleaded, each time he stretched out to touch the object of his desire, the beautiful young man in the pool shuddered and broke into a thousand ripples, utterly unattainable. In the end the gods grew tired of listening to Narcissus beg and plead, and turned him into a flower—the narcissus or daffodil. In an unexpected consequence, he donated his name to a modern psychological phenomenon called Narcissism—the love of oneself. It was a metamorphosis, but the opposite of anthropomorphic.

The partial or temporary metamorphosis can be the most fun. Take King Midas, he who loved gold so much that the gods gave him the power to turn everything he touched into gold. Not a wise man, you perceive; food and drink were a real problem, but what drove the lesson home was the chrysmetamorphosis of his daughter into a solid gold statue. Relieved of the godly gift of gold, Midas was asked to judge a musical competition between Apollo, playing his lyre, and Pan, playing his pipes. Of course Midas exhibited his usual execrable taste by declaring that Pan's pipes were far superior to Apollo's lyre. Apollo was so incensed that he devised a punishment to fit the crime: he gave King Midas a pair of ass's ears, which Midas wore ever after, even as a judge in Hades. Clearly the gods adored Midas, I imagine because he was the perfect illustration of how stupid humanity could be.

Like fables, metamorphic tales are always founded in human behavior, but once the species became crowded into cities having little or no contact with the agrarian or pastoral or nomadic origins, they went through a time of relative unimportance. Disease and starvation had more ephemeral causes than of yore, which accounts for the rise of the great monotheistic religions and their provision of more satisfactory answers than cosmogonies built on human-animal connections and mythical stories.

But then there are children, who are natural exponents of anthropomorphic changes.

It isn't even necessary to kick-start the process with fairy tales or nursery rhymes; my brother, Carl, and I were never told any. All that is definite is that we had a pet cat named Kitty, and, as tiny tots, saw the penguins at the zoo.

Penguins are utterly charming. First of all, they waddle, a kind of gait that has immense appeal. Why? Chiefly, I think, because a waddle has a clownish self-importance, and after that, doesn't suggest physical suffering. The waddler is, to the beholder, well-fed, well-housed and well-loved. Added to which, the penguin has a happy face and a splendid costume, black-and-white, tailored, sleek. Witnessing a hundred fairy penguins marching to obtain their food in 1939 obviously impressed Carl and me to the point where, when it came time to select a hero-animal for our stories, Pengy the penguin was more desirable than any other. The heroine of course was Kitty, our cat.

Carl's and my waking lives consisted in keeping out from underfoot and effacing ourselves whenever an adult was nearby. In fine weather we were relegated to the backyard. Each day was something to be gotten through rather than anything pleasurable or exciting. What we lived for was bedtime, when our mother, Laurie, turned out the light and left us in the darkness.

Then the real world slipped away and the world of Pengy and Kitty opened up; we lay, each in a narrow little bed, and told our story. Why was it about animals? The only reason I can arrive at is that animals were no threat, animals were friends, animals led lives independent of human troubles and worries.

We were put to bed at 6 p.m. and aroused at 7 a.m.: far too long a period at thirteen hours! Especially for two night-owl kids, wide awake at 6 p.m. But interesting, that neither of us was afraid of the dark. To us, the darkness meant liberty.

For long into the night, Carl and I talked. Or, actually, wove a story about a penguin named Pengy and a cat named Kitty. All through the boredom of the daylight hours each of us thought about Pengy and Kitty, the direction the coming night's story was going to take.

I don't remember the names of the other characters in the saga, except that I imagine they were as down-to-earth as Pengy and Kitty: Doggy, Horsey, Kanga, while the villains would have been Australian animals like Dingo, Goanna, Wild Boar.

Pengy and Kitty traveled the world. Four-legged animals walked upright. No one rode, no one flew. Birds were never a part of the story, good or evil.

The Pengy and Kitty world was magical as well as wonderful. We lived in a region of arid plain, yet Pengy and Kitty lived in a lush environment, rich in color, surreal in nature. It was forested by gorgeous plants, many of which didn't grow in the manner of plants; they were embroidered, beaded, spangled like a priest's vestments, evidently where the idea came from.

Admittedly we were forward kids who soaked up information, and these were the very serious years of World War II, 1939 to 1945. Our uncles were away fighting, and the women's conversation was often cheerless. But Pengy and Kitty never went to war. They journeyed to meet the fellow denizens of their world, and even Wild Boar and Goanna were relatively benign. They ate rainbow-hued rocks that they shaved in tissue-fine layers to reveal the banks of color; each color had a different taste. And they drank fizzy lime-green soda that gushed out of lime-green tree trunks.

All memory of the content of these years-long adventures has gone, but perhaps what our never-ending story showed was how two bored, bright children endowed their lives with excitement, interest, a fantasy that perhaps saved us from becoming warped, or twisted, or horrible. Not a conundrum I'm equipped to answer, save that the story was very much a give-and-take between us. Carl was as eloquent and inventive as I was.

After years of trying, Laurie finally cured us. Carl was five and I was six when the solution occurred: Laurie moved our grandmother, Nanna, into our room with us.

Nanna was a dear old woman, our sole ally in surviving Laurie, but to have to share a bedroom with her was a cruel punishment. For her, poor soul, as much as for us. But Laurie never counted the cost, even when she had to walk across the bodies. The only thing that mattered to Laurie was winning.

I have used Carl and me as data. We received no external stimuli like fairy tales or nursery rhymes, yet still we were pushed to tell stories that extended human thought and activities to creatures manifestly lacking them. Which says that the human connection to our original world is far deeper, far older than so-called civilization. We are in league with the good animals against the bad ones, and in humanizing them, make them equal partners in the enterprise.

Nowadays a human being's divorcement from his origins is more complete than ever before in most cases; he and his live in cities, may never have seen open countryside, or a cow, or hen, or earthworm. Milk comes in containers, eggs are all the same size, and a square of plastic cheese exactly covers a slice of pre-cut bread. An acquaintance of mine who shall be nameless breathessly confided in me a great discovery: after a lifetime of heating frozen French fries in an oven, he found out that he could make his French fires from *potatoes*. It had never occurred to him that French fries were potatoes.

In such circumstances, is it any wonder that metamorphosis has taken some weird turns in direction? Like Superman? In and out of a phone booth, from milquetoast to alpha male with super powers. Wonder Woman. Captain Marvel. Batman. A latter-day pantheon of demigods fulfilling the role of what used to be the inhabitants of Mount Olympus. The usual phrase is "escapist nonsense"—but that's too trite. The demigod retains his importance long after childhood has been left behind.

But flesh is weak, squashable, easily killed. So now there are the machines: Transformers and their confederates, gigantic, shape-changing, all-powerful, hungering to replace human civilization with a world peopled by machines. Animal power has been conquered. Now the threat comes from the machine. *Deus ex machina* lives.

Only where do we go from Transformers?

HANDSOME IS AS HANDSOME DOES

Once upon a time there was a very conceited pussycat. His family background and his genetic composition were mysteries known only to God, but they had, nonetheless, dowered him with a remarkable and unique beauty. For instance, his hair was long, but the fur lay sleek and close where this looked best, while in other areas requiring a bouffant look it stood up and out like a bunny's powder-puff. From early kittenhood he was enormously fat, but instead of, in the manner of cats, having a huge barrel of a belly slung hammocklike on two skinny hind legs, his belly fur wrapped it like silk, even as the fur on his hind legs stood out in a fluffy mass. And his binny-bag, which was the separate stockpile of fat attached sporranlike between his back legs, was fluffy enough to seem frilly as it knocked around his knees when he strolled along. For what it is vitally important to understand is that from the rear—always a fat cat's visual downfall—he appeared magnificent, his embonpoint seeming of a normal size because of his beautiful fluffy britches and binny-bag, and the plumy tail that waved above them proudly.

Naturally his head was noble. Nor was it, in the manner of long-haired cats, squashed in like a pug-dog's, thereby reducing the brain-pan to the size of a haricot bean and the I.Q. to a level down around a planaria's. No, he was at the very uppermost end of the feline intelligence scale. His eyes were a vivid blue-green and his features smilingly charming, even to a retroussé nose. The color of his coat was a uniform dark grey shot with stunning silver highlights, for every one of his billions of hairs was dark grey until toward its tip, where it became a silvery-white. All in all, this very conceited pussycat had a lot to be conceited about, and saw nothing intrinsically, morally, ethically or philosophically wrong with being conceited. It was his due.

But there is always a fly in the ointment, a black person in the woodpile, a flaw in the indictment. *His name.* Had he belonged to a gay man, he would have been Woodrow Wilson or Pithecanthropuss; an elderly woman would have called him Prince Nanki-poo or Count von Picklegruber; a married couple might have plumped for Gorgeous George or Handsome Harry; and a young man might perhaps have dubbed him Fat Cat or Walrus Whiskers. As his name, however, had been the joint choice of a six-year-old girl and her granny, he became Fluffy Britches. Oh, oh, oh, oh! *Fluffy Britches*! A monicker lacking dignity, impressiveness, or any suggestion of the colossal ego dwelling inside this enormously conceited pussycat. He boiled, he steamed, he simmered, he stewed, he did everything he could think of to repudiate such a ludicrously pedestrian name. With the result that the cute kitten grew into a surly, mean-tempered, rather horrible pussycat who scratched the kids, shredded the upholstery and pissed on the carpet.

At one year of age he had definitely outgrown his welcome, so he was donated to a fortyish spinster lady who didn't like Fluffy Britches either. Despite which, she quailed at going through the agonies of training Fluffy Britches to answer to a new name, as she had no idea that Fluffy Britches was quite intelligent enough to leap at a new name—*if*, that is, he liked it. His new mistress's solution was to drop the Britches entirely and keep right on calling him Fluffy. Except that *She* said Phluphphy.

It burst on Phluphphy in a gargantuan, shimmering, opalescent milky-blue bubble like an explosive rain of jewels, flowers, intoxicating perfumes, Vatican boys' choirs, trills and tra-la-las without end. He was cast into an ecstasy so great that it is fair to say he never quite came all the way down again. Finally he had a name that indicated his uniqueness!

"Phluphphy, Phluphphy!" he chanted over and over as he investigated his new environment. "I am Phluphphy!"

He experimented with ways to say it, noting that every "ph" could assume a different nuance from all others, from huge and hazy blue bubbles to trickles of bubbles near as small as dots. It dripped off the tongue, it slid down the throat, it finally gave meaning to the tonsils.

He stopped scratching people, shredding the upholstery and pissing on the carpet. Instead, he perched on the edge of the toilet seat and did his Number Ones *and* his Number Twos directly into the toilet bowl. His mistress was ravished—um, well, metaphorically so, at any rate. That he didn't flush the bowl was not lack of manual dexterity; simply he thought the task beneath him.

Phluphphy had a favorite room in his new house. Baskets of ferns hung from a glass ceiling and some of its walls were made of insect screening, giving it an outdoorsy ambience that Phluphphy relished, as it carried none of the perils inherent in outdoor living, like bits and burrs in the coat, mud on the paws, and a spooky sense of not being in command. Thus he spent many hours sleeping in one of the big, comfortably upholstered easychairs under the ferny canopy. These were *proper* cat-naps: one segment of his brain was always awake, always listening. For instance, the wakeful part would hear his mistress coming, the signal to roll over onto his back and stick all four legs into the air—another metaphorically ravishing sight. Once She (as he called her) had oohed and aahed at his trick, she always rushed off to fetch him a special treat—chicken breast lightly poached in white wine. In fact, She fed Phluphphy a menu straight from pussycat paradise—chicken breasts, juicy cubes of raw fillet steak carefully trimmed of fat, and king prawns cooked in dry vermouth.

One day about two months after his arrival, Phluphphy thought he heard Her coming, and began to roll onto his back. Then a movement in a basket of feathery fern adjacent to a wall of insect screening caught his eye; he stopped in mid-roll. A pointed little head with two beady eyes thrust itself out of the fern, followed by a slender grey body and an extremely long, naked tail. Fascinated, Phluphphy watched the creature nimbly claw down the mesh wall until it reached the floor. Further progress was impossible: one of Phluphphy's lionlike paws was anchoring the tip of its tail, a movement of astonishing rapidity for what had been judged a dumb, torpid, pampered pussycat.

"Who and what are you?" Phluphphy asked, some atavistic sense telling him that he beheld a food source for pussycats, yet in no way tempted because he could see no taste thrill in the creature to equal a plump poached prawn.

The creature adopted an air of nonchalance, sangfroid, even insouciance. "Namel's Jim, 'n' I'm a rat."

"Oh, for elocution's sake, articulate your words! I can't abide people who mumble!" snapped Phluphphy. "I will permit you to call yourself Jim, but kindly introduce yourself by your proper name, which is James." He bethought himself of something. "Now I know why She has a jar in the laundry labeled POISONED WHEAT."

"It's a crime, you know, what the Sentimentalists have done to toxins," Jim said, perching his haunches on the base of his tail as if settling to enjoy a long, clever, philosophical chat. "I could feed my entire family on the wheat—sixteen in this litter—except that She never puts enough down. As I said to old Sid the cockroach, where would we pests and vermin be if it weren't for the political agitation for milder toxins sponsored by the Sentimentalists?"

"Dead?" Phluphphy suggested.

"Right on! As doornails. Though I've never met a doornail that was alive. Have you?"

"I am glad to say I have never met a doornail, dead or alive. That is because I am neither pest nor vermin. I am top of the trees, ferns, the social pyramid and everything else, and my next question is, where are you going?"

Jim collapsed in an obeisance, nose on front paws. "I admit to all of that," he said obscurely, "but who are you?"

"I am Phluphphy." Opalescent blue bubbles, ethereal rainbows, a glissando so complex Chopin could have played it only if he had ten fingers on either hand, fairy bells.

Jim absolutely groveled. "You have The Name! You are The Emperor! All hail, all hail!"

"Arise, James! You are a very small all, but I will let you live because of your keen perception. To repeat myself—I never will again!—where are you going?"

"Er—um—ah—actually I was going to nick two cubes of your yummy freshly diced fat-free fillet steak, Your Exalted and Imperial Majesty. I nick two cubes every day because you don't notice two missing cubes and because two are enough to round out my family's diet of Sentimentally detoxified poisoned wheat."

"Stealing from your Emperor?" Phluphphy growled.

"Oh, give us a break! How was I to know your name? And the thing is, Your Exalted and Imperial

Majesty, that I can't stop now," said Jim in sickeningly obsequious tones. "The wife and I might manage, but not Maude, Matilda, Maximilian, Erich, Heinrich, Sebastian, Prudence, Suzanne, Patricia, Guiseppe, Pierre, Raoul, Charles, Cynthia, Augusta-Viktoria and Manfred-Maria-Schnuller."

"Sixteen is correct," Phluphphy commented. "Very large!"

"About average. Sid the cockroach has 27,000 children per year—naming them is a nightmare, he says."

"*I* have no siblings," said Phluphphy grandly.

"Of course you don't, Your Exalted and Imperial Majesty! Perfection, once attained, cannot be duplicated," fawned Jim.

Phluphphy removed his paw. "Very well, Jim. You may feed your family two overlooked cubes of my yummy raw, freshly diced, fat-free fillet steak every day—on condition that no other rats enter these premises, and that Sid the cockroach takes his 27,000 children elsewhere. Tell him that if he attempts to remain here, I will moult my hundred billion hairs, suffocating them all."

And so it was arranged. In Jim, Phluphphy had his second subject (She was his first), and She had a relatively pest-free home. Besides which, Jim had the opportunity to turn his fern basket into a sumptuous rodent palace, exactly right for a lord privy seal or chancellor. Since Jim was firm about evicting his children as soon as they were grown, they went forth into the world to preach Phluphphyism, which was the gospel of coming to an arrangement with the human family's pet.

I, thought Phluphphy one day as She came in to find him on his back with all four feet in the air, have become an emperor, but my realm is sorely limited. Despite the opalescent blues and rainbow hues of my name, there is a pit of emptiness at the core of my purrpussa. Vermin like Sid the cockroach I can do without, and I am not foolish enough to allow more than one rodent subject and his family within these walls. Therefore in order to gather additional subjects, I have to cast my net wider. I must do what I dread doing: venture into the backyard.

That night after Jim and his family were fast asleep and She tucked up in her virginal bed watching a DVD of *Pride and Prejudice*, Phluphphy squeezed through the cat-flap in the laundry door and stood assimilating the backyard. No bits, burrs or mud, for sure. Neat as a pin. Reasonably large. Paved with pastel-colored concrete slabs. Bounded by six-foot-high fences of dark green wooden palings dove-tailed into each other. A tiny shed in the back left-hand corner. A circular, crankable-uppable clothesline. Earthen flower beds, a bird bath and a sun dial.

His initial reaction was a wave of despair: this immaculate exterior space held no subjects!

"Hey, ponce-features, take your lily liver back into your house or I'll carve you into cutlets and feed you to Otto!" said a loud, unmusical, aggressive voice.

Unruffled, Phluphphy searched until he found its source, a skinny black feline shape atop the shed, its eyes glowing yellow. All the better to see (and to imbue himself with a certain princely dignity) Phluphphy leaped onto the sun dial.

"A subject!" he said, delighted. "Bow down before your emperor, you unruly, vulgar creature! What is your name?"

"One thing for sure, it ain't Nutless Wonder like you, sport. Me name's Tom." Sidling to the edge of the shed roof, Tom arched his back, hissed and spat. None of which even dented the house cat's monumental conceit. It just sat on the sun dial in all its silver-shot glory and regarded him haughtily.

"Why is it that no one speaks with true erudition?" Phluphphy demanded. "Your proper name is Thomas, but Thomas who? Wolsey? More? Tallis? Boleyn? Tank? Twitchett? Well, no matter. Bow down to your emperor, Tom."

"Nyah, nyah, emperor who?"

"Phluphphy."

"Oh, Jeez, you *are* the Emperor! Pardon, O Exalted and Great One! Pardon, I cry pardon!" Tom said, lying flat and cringing.

"Speak decently and I may forgive you," Phluphphy said, his voice mellifluous. "Incidentally, what is a nutless wonder?"

"Um—well—er—actually it's a sort of a battle cry," said Tom. Then, catching sight of Jim emerging from the cat-flap, he tensed, ready to spring. "Egad! What a fat and sonsy rat!"

"Cease and desist, varlet!" Jim snapped, standing on the sun dial next to Phluphphy, one paw familiarly on Phluphphy's arm. "I am James called Jim, Lord High Privy Seal and Chancellor to the Emperor Phluphphy, and recently invested Baron of the Basket. I am no one's dinner, least of all yours."

"Listen, sport," said Tom, reverting to type, "I am driven by two primal urges—sex and food. It's a week since I've had a woman, and a month since I've had a decent feed."

"Well, you can't have my woman," said Phluphphy. "She's in bed drooling over Mr. Darcy, and matters carnal are not in the province of a sovereign. However, a good ruler must feed his subjects, so I will—no, not *feed* you, precisely, but show you how to feed yourself. In return, I expect to see more subjects turn up the next time I hold court, five nights from this one. Have I your attention, Thomas called Tom?"

"Yes, Your Exalted and Imperial Majesty."

"Excellent! First of all, as we mammalian animals are very telepathic, I serve notice on all my subjects that Court when I hold it will not incorporate vocalization. Think-speech only, which does not mean sloppy syntax, understood?"

"Yes, Your Exalted and Imperial Majesty."

"Excellent! Now, your dinner, Tom. Three doors down from here," said Phluphphy in lordly tones, "is a supermarket that has open display cases of meat. Including sirloins, rumps, fillets and rounds. Or there's lamb if you fancy it, as well as pork, veal and offal. Also, in a separate section, prawns."

Tom had jumped down from the shed roof and was now in a more suitable position, looking up at his Emperor on the sun dial. "That's all very well, O Exalted One," he said, "but as I have no access to the supermarket, what boots me it?"

"Abandon this Tudor complexity!" Phluphphy ordered. "Ordinary but grammatical language will do fine. Speak on, Tom."

"The supermarket meat and prawns may as well be on the Moon."

"Nonsense! The first thing you must do is find yourself a rat-companion as your colleague. Then as you find other cats, each must have a rat-companion. The Lord High Privy Seal's family is about to leave home and will suit your purposes eminently well, as James is their father and they know their Emperor. This will limit your raiding parties to five cats and rat-companions each night, repeating every fourth night."

"This is a boring bit!" growled Tom.

"The fact that you find it boring is why you are starving and I am eating chicken breasts poached in white wine, you foolish cat. There is method in what I say. Jim, which of your fifteen children for Tom?"

"Ned. Fly, spry, eagle-eye."

"Thomas called Tom, I formally dower you with Ned as your rat-companion. Due to his own semistarvation before I came to live with Her, Jim is very familiar with the back of the supermarket, and he will teach all the rat-companions how to get inside it."

"I'd rather eat Ned," said Tom mutinously.

"And fill your belly meagrely *once?* Think, Thomas, think!" Phluphphy cried, frustrated. "Five containers of meat per night, each in a styrofoam tray wrapped in clear plastic. You need your rat-companion's paws to get the meat out of the trays without wasting a single fiber. Left to yourself, you'd leave a trail of plundered trays behind you, and next time you came, it would be impossible to get in. The whole object of this is to feed you and keep you fed, plus feed four of your fellows, and keep them fed. With a small, rat-sized portion for each rat-companion."

"All this detail is incredibly boring!" Tom exclaimed.

"Listen, Doubting Thomas," said Phluphphy in the back of his telepathic throat, "I am outlining a plan—a plan that will enable you and however many other cats I decide will eat well for the rest of their days. The crux of the scheme is that the supermarket should never realize that it is being plundered. Therefore the same amount each night—*never* more than five trays, always taken from the front row of the display case. *Capice?*"

"Boring!" said Tom. "Besides, it's limited to five cats."

"Ah! But how many other supermarkets, fishmongeries, bakeries, butcheries and delicatessens are there in our neighborhood, pray tell me?" Phluphphy demanded sweetly. "Three doors down is just the start, though I recommend that the Court be set at thirty cats and thirty rat-companions. That way, every cat and rat-companion can eat every night, just in different places, according to taste."

"Rat-companions! Tchah!" said Tom.

"They will keep your depredations undetected," Phluphphy said. "Each raiding cat will pull his tray of meat outside whatever building it was inside, then pull it to a secure spot where the rat-companions can speedily and *tidily* unwrap it, and the two together can then dispose of the evidence *tidily* inside a trash receptacle of some kind. *There must be no evidence!* For his invaluable services in finding a way inside each building and also disposing of the packaging, each rat-companion will be given a rightful share of the loot. I have spoken, there is no more to be said," the Emperor concluded grandly.

Tom's attention had finally been caught; he put his head on one side and his eyes gleamed as yellow as a real estate agent's premises. "You are very clever, O Exalted and Imperial One," he said. "Boring, but sensible."

"Just remember the two imperial rules: neat and tidy theft, and unnoticed theft," said Phluphphy severely.

"I hear and obey, O Great One!"

"Once you widen your horizons to the other supermarkets and butcheries and fishmongeries, you will have a deep well in. which to dip your bucket."

"Bucket? Dip—lucky dip?" asked Tom.

"A metaphor, Thomas. I perceive that the quality of my subjects will not always equal their quantity. What I meant, Thomas, is that the more sources of food you find and the more surreptitiously you steal, the better you will eat."

"Emperor Phluphphy, I worship you!" Tom cried.

"Thank you. As my third subject, I hereby create you Chairman of the Joint Chiefs of Staff, and your rat-companion Ned my First Sea Lord. Arise, General Thomas!"

In that way Phluphphy established his Imperial Court. When She realized that he liked to sit on the sun dial after dark, She had the gnomon removed, making it a far more comfortable seat; it was the wrong gnomon anyway, fashioned for England, a good twenty degrees sharper of inclination than the Realm of Phluphphy. Thus Phluphphy could sit looking down into a glowing sea of adoring eyes in rapt faces, for word of his wisdom, his sagacity, his glory, his beauty, his power and his uniqueness had spread, and once a month he held open Court, to which anybody could come. Knowledge of—and participation in—the shop raids was limited to the thirty cats and rat-companions of his official Court, which he convoked every four days as the clock on the Town Hall struck midnight.

It may perhaps be deduced that all was going swimmingly in the Court—and world—of the Emperor Phluphphy, and indeed all did for a considerable time.

Then, on one unforgettable night of sultry heat and cloying humidity, Her wooden paling fence shuddered, bowed, cracked, split, splintered and burst: into Her backyard erupted someone Phluphphy had heard lots about, but never seen—the Doberman/Weimaraner/Alsatian crossbred monster named Otto the Terrible, scourge of postmen, little old ladies, pussycats and chihuahuas.

So great was the fear that no one in the Court, not even General Tom and his rat-companion Admiral Ned, tried to flee; every pussycat and rat-companion sat frozen into a motionless, graven statue. Otto the Terrible shoved his way through the petrified ranks until his head—the same height as the sun dial—loomed in Phluphphy's face. Its lips were peeled back in a shocking snarl, its fangs dripped what might have been saliva, or might have been a smoking acidic venom, and its eyes looked into the depths of a pussycat hell.

"You're the Emperor Phluphphy?" Otto growled.

"I am," said Phluphphy, casually licking a paw.

"Prepare to die, usurper!"

In answer, Phluphphy did a backward flip off the sun dial and landed neatly between General Tom and Admiral Ned—that is, in the midst of the Joint Chiefs of Staff, which hadn't yet recovered enough to semaphore Air Marshal Tiddles and Commander Mike, who had been practising a new technique of flying leaps to get at one shop's elusive cache of Japanese export rib-eyes— Air Force stuff.

There Phluphphy pirouetted with a couple of entrechats thrown in, while his subjects, finally galvanized, scattered just enough to give their Emperor room.

Very strange things began to happen. Phluphphy seemed to grow in size until he looked like a spiky stainless steel tiger, and out of his soft, pampered feet there issued immensely long claws that gleamed like brushed chrome. His ears flattened against his head and his mouth opened in a snarl that made Otto's look like a beneficent smile. After which, very carefully, one leg at a time, he began to advance on Otto, all the while emitting a frightful screech that zoomed at the speed of light into a vestigial part of Otto's brain that God had stamped "utter disaster" and hitherto not opened once. Now it opened.

Phluphphy kept advancing: Otto stood paralyzed.

At a yard between them, Otto spoke: "Shit! Oh, shit!" And broke and bolted for the fence, where he fought and scrabbled to find a passage through the wreckage.

The screaming Phluphphy bounded in pursuit as his Court cheered resoundingly.

★ ★ ★

"That wretched dog Otto broke into my backyard last night," She said to a friend over morning tea and scones in her conservatory, "chasing a cat, apparently. And would you believe that my Phluphphy put him out? A terrific racket came from my backyard, so I got up in time to see the whole thing—I was staggered! Who would ever have dreamed that my diddums-widdums could act with so much flair, élan, panache and positive éclat? Truly amazing!"

"He's too fat," said Her friend. "Feed him scraps and kibble, like everyone else."

Phluphphy opened one eye to glare at the friend. Interfering sadist! She was always trying to undermine his position.

"After last night, I'd feed Phluphphy caviar if he wanted it," She said firmly. "The vet says fat cats don't live one day fewer than thin cats. Your trouble, Doris, is that your Maurice uses a litter box, whereas my cuddums-wuddums goes in the toilet."

Unanswerable, thought Phluphphy complacently as he lay charmingly posed on a chair at the same table. My chicken breasts and prawns and fillet steak are safe. Last night was sheer bluff on my part. Not, mind you, that I wouldn't have given a good account of myself if Otto had grabbed me. He's a shake-and-break exponent: grabs the victim by the scruff of the neck and shakes to break it. But if he'd done that to me, all his jaws would have closed on would have been fur, fur, fur. In the meantime I would have had one of his eyes and a good chunk of nose.

Still, bluff is the way to go whenever possible. Wiser, smarter, longer lasting. Without getting a drop of Otto's spit on my beautiful coat, I have ascended into the aether of myth and legend as far as all my subjects are concerned, and I am now the Emperor of Her city. Hmmm … I will have to increase the size of my bureaucracy so that not all my ever-increasing number of subjects arrive in Her backyard on one and the same Court night. A good job for the entire twelve in Jim's latest litter … I do wish he understood contraception, but he says he's just doing what comes naturally. Where would he be without Me?

A rhetorical question; every member of the Imperial Court was well aware of the answer. That life was never boring lay in the strategies and tactics necessary to keep everybody fed so well that bodies were plump, coats shiny, noses moist, and eyes sparkling.

One month after the night of Otto's invasion, Her friend came to morning tea and scones again, agog with news.

"You'll never guess!" the friend cried, smiling all over her face. "Otto has lost a leg, and old man Grouch is going to put him down because he's useless as a guard dog anymore."

The charmingly posed Phluphphy fell off his chair in shock.

"What happened?" She asked; She rather liked Otto.

"Chasing a truck. Honestly, that wretched dog has every bad habit a dog can have."

"But I don't understand! Why didn't the vet just put him down at once, if that's what old man Grouch wants?"

"Oh, his kids adore Otto, and begged the vet to save him. Now the bill's arrived, and old man Grouch says it would have been cheaper for him to have his leg amputated. If he could, he'd put the vet down, but as he can't, the dog's his victim."

"Can't his kids coax him out of his mood?"

"Old man Grouch? You're joking!"

That night Phluphphy called an emergency meeting of the Court, thirty cats and thirty rat-companions.

"Finally we have a mission of mercy," he said from the sun dial. "That is the one aspect of imperial rule I have not had a chance to exert. We are going to rescue Otto the Terrible from sentence of death passed on him by his owner, old man Grouch, because he has lost a leg and is as useless as expensive."

Such was Phluphphy's thrall that not even the resident chronic grumblers, Merv and rat-companion

Bert, protested. Every head nodded solemnly, every pair of loins visibly girded for the fray.

"Where does Otto live, General Tom?" he asked.

"One block down, half a block over, O Exalted One."

"Traffic?"

"From now until dawn, virtually none."

"And the air is clear," said Air Marshal Tiddles.

"And the pond in the corner park is deserted," said Admiral Ned.

"Then we start out in military mode," Phluphphy ordered. "The Chiefs of Staff send out rat-companion scouts, while we, behind the Chiefs, move as a mass packed densely together. If any dog should try to challenge us, whoever is nearest does the bluff while his neighbors sneak up on either side and go for the eyes. When we reach old man Grouch's, I expect the scouts to have found Otto. They will lead us straight to him."

"What if he's inside?" asked Merv the grumbler.

"Pish! Tosh! Rubbish! Otto will be in the backyard, he's not a house pet. Now march!"

Down the side passage, out the front gate, onto the footpath, and down the sleeping street they went, the Emperor Phluphphy escorted by thirty cats and thirty-one rat-companions, the front rank appearing, disappearing, materializing, dematerializing as scouts went out and scouts returned. Even the most whispered telepathy never bobbed to any mind's surface: this was a silent mission! No sleeping dog, ferret, gerbil, mouse, bunny-rabbit or hamster could be inadvertently aroused by a drifting wisp of thought.

It turned out to be easy. The Grouch residence was sprawling, poorly fenced, and had a huge backyard liberally dewed with rusting car bodies, washing machines, motors and old house bricks.

Otto was lying on a hessian bag in front of his kennel, on his side, three legs resting on the ground, and where the left hind leg should have been was covered in grimy, bloodied dressings. His head was stretched out, his eyes closed.

"Too late!" said General Tom.

"Dead as a doornail," said Jim.

"Pish! Tosh! Rubbish!" said Phluphphy, pushing to the front and standing next to Otto's head. "Wake up, you fool hound!"

The eyes opened, the head lifted; Otto heaved a huge sigh. "Oh, shit," he said. "Come to gloat, eh?"

"Gloat? I? Never!" said Phluphphy bracingly. "What is this nonsense? Why are you lying here defeated?"

"I've lost a leg. I can't run or even walk again—I can't earn my keep," said Otto on a whine. "Tomorrow I'm going to get a dose of terminal lead poisoning in the left ear."

"Pish! Tosh! Rubbish! Get up, you silly specimen! Haven't you ever heard of a tripod?"

"I can't get up, and I've never heard of a tripod!" Otto yelled, his head thrashing up and down. "Go away and leave me alone!"

"Pish! Tosh! Rubbish! Get off your side, Otto. Lie on your belly and stick your front legs out. Come on, do it! None of this misery-wart defeatism! Your name was Otto the Terrible—do you want to be remembered as Otto the Sook, Otto the Weak, Otto the Pusillanimous? *Do it!*" And while he spoke these unsympathetic words Phluphphy's eyes roved across his Court. Ah! There! "Lew and Stew, front and centre with Terry and Jerry!"

Two big, sturdy ginger cats came forward, their rat-companions particularly large, sleek, and well-manicured.

"It's a month since the operation, you must have healed," said Phluphphy. He peered at the dressing, whose corners were lifting. "It's a simple disarticulation amputation, no real stump, so if Terry gets on one side and Jerry gets on the other side, they'll be able to pick the dressing off. Air! Air will complete the process of encrustation and soon the scab will fall off."

And while he spoke in these crisply lordly tones, Phluphphy kept nagging Otto to lie on his stomach. Poor Otto was utterly terrified, but Phluphphy's never-ending spate of "Pish! Tosh! Rubbish!" finally irked him so much that he obeyed, astonished to find himself in position, and his exposed wound much as Phluphphy had said it would be—uninfected, encrusting nicely.

"At first you will need help getting up, but soon you won't," said Phluphphy. "You have turned from a quadruped into a tripod. Tripods have three legs and are very sacred. My Court needs a tripod. Now Lew amd Stew are going to help give you some traction as you get to your three feet. Push, Lew! Push, Stew! Upsy-daisy!"

Without too much trouble, Otto clambered to stand on his two front legs and his right hind leg. He teetered a little, trembling and shivering, but the Emperor refused to let him even think about falling over.

"Excellent! You are a natural athlete, Otto, which means you will shortly compensate in every way for the loss of your leg. Now home we go," said Phluphphy, this time leading the way. "I *knew* a pair of Court acrobats would come in handy! Giancarlo, climb on Marcello's back, which will make the pair of you tall enough to serve as a crutch for Otto if Marcello walks under the vacant leg. Hey-ho, and off we go!"

An hour later the exhausted but self-ambulant Otto was in Her backyard, lying on a flat cushion that belonged to Her sun lounge, and wolfing down a tray of gravy beef a small raiding party had obtained from the supermarket.

"Every Court," said the Emperor to his subjects, "needs a true and proper religion, and a high priest to administer it. Otto the Tripod, I hereby ordain you Pontifex Phluphphus."

It was remarkable what a difference having an official religion and a high priest to administer it made to the Court of the Emperor Phluphphy! If the Reverend Otto found a religious reason for this law or that regulation, somehow it made a lot more sense, though it goes without saying that the Reverend Otto's dogmata were lean, sinewy, flexible and stood alone on only three pillars of faith: Phluphphy was, Phluphphy is, and Phluphphy always will be.

"I didn't have a choice," She said to her friend one morning over tea and scones, tickling Phluphphy's tummy and pulling one of Otto's silky ears through Her fingers. "Phluphphy was in the backyard cuddled against Otto, washing Otto's face! I had to give both of them a bath. When I phoned old man Grouch, he disowned Otto as useless. But would you credit it, not an hour after that phone call, I had a lout at my front door brandishing a gun! Then this three-legged dog charged out of the side passage, leaped at him, and took a *huge* bite out of his trouser crotch!"

"Stone the crows!" said the friend. "Was it horrible?"

"No!" She said, laughing. "Otto took every layer of fabric but never touched the skin. I could still hear him screaming in horror ten blocks away. So I acquired a three-legged guard dog. He's the sweetest, gentlest baby in the world, aren't you, diddums?"

"He must cost you a fortune."

"I can afford him. He gets best quality braising beef, great big marrow bones, and an occasional small roast turkey or haunch of mutton, though I notice he winces when he spots the mutton."

My Empire is now as rounded as even I could want, said Emperor Phluphphy to himself as he listened. He opened one eye to see Jim sitting on his ferny portico, one arm around Ophelia, nursing again. He's doing very well, is James—a share of Otto's braising beef as well. My very own rat-companion …

"But now," objected the friend, who really disliked happy endings if they weren't hers, "you have gigantic Number Twos to clean up. Not to mention all the places where Otto cocks his leg—I know you, you'd wash them down obsessively."

She sneered. "Otto uses the outside toilet, Phluphphy taught him how, even with a missing leg. And how can he cock a leg that isn't there? He sits down to do his Number Ones. Don't forget that he's tall enough to put his rump on the toilet seat, and his tail is docked, so there's nothing to get in the way."

"Huh! Therefore all you have to do is flush."

"No. It's an overhead cistern with a chain. Otto pulls it himself," She said in gloating triumph. "More tea, dear?"

TIME

Time fascinates me, going all the way back to the days when first I began to struggle with the concept of Spacetime as a continuum, of Time as another axis forcing a fourth dimension upon our comfortable old three-dimensional world. Yet the Spacetime hypothesis has succeeded so well that even the most ordinary, unscientific people now accept Time as the fourth dimension. They don't understand it, but the boffins say it is so, therefore it must be so. I can't pretend to have the mathematical genius to grasp the mechanics of it either, but I do have some ideas, and a theory of Time that I suppose is more philosophical than mathematical. Since philosophers are allowed to question any and all other intellectual disciplines, I am safe.

In this third millennium the string theorists and a few other kinds of particle physicists are starting to maintain that Time cannot be treated as a simple dimension turning Space into Spacetime. Arguments flare about the inflexibly forward direction of the "Arrow of Time", the contention of these physicists being that Time must also be able to flow backward: the Arrow reversed. Without the divorce of Time from Space and a Time also flowing backward, the equations of particle physics cannot be married to the equations of Relativity—a consummation devoutly to be wished. If Time is treated as a separate and reversible entity, the equations fall into place and we look like having that Holy Grail of all physics: the Unified Field Theory.

Unfortunately to liberate Time in this way detracts from Relativity, and the argument is raging fiercely— who *are* these miserably few people want to let Time slip its leash? Why, they're weirdos studying particles that pop in and out of existence! And to compound the multiple insults to Relativity, the state of—um—being wherein the argument rages is the event horizon of a black hole. Nor is Time the object of the exercise. That is Gravity, for around the event horizon of a black hole something called Supergravity appears and Relativity Goes West. Time is a sort of by-product of the general drift of the theory. Time? Poof, pooh! What is Time, after all? Supergravity is the thing! Who cares if Time flows backward near a black hole?

Meanwhile, wherever we look in the sky, the spectrometer betrays a red shift that tells us every galaxy we can see is receding from us, and that this fugitive motion is accelerating. Will continue to accelerate.

Will never not accelerate, until and beyond where the fabric of Space is so vast that every one of its billions of galaxies will be out of range of any other galaxy at any conceivable wavelength.

Naturally the astrophysicists are hedging their bets by announcing that this mad acceleration may suddenly cease for no reason perceived in the equations. But if it doesn't stop accelerating, eventually the speed of the Universe will hit the speed of light, a traffic hump so huge it's a brick wall.

My question is: When the speed of light is attained, will everything come to a screeching halt, perhaps leading the Universe to go out with a bang or a whimper?

I have a second question: When the Universe hits the speed of light, will some utterly unforeseen phenomenon occur that wafts it onward faster than the speed of light, accelerating to infinity? Superluminal. What an amazing word.

Where is Time in all this?

I can't make sense of it.

Time is spoken of as linear—a straight line. Except that nothing in the Universe is straight. Even the straightest line will curve if the person observing it can get far enough away from it. Light bends—Einstein proved it. The lens effect in the most distant galaxies (those farthest back in time) is there in the Hubble photos. So why is Time thought to be straight? Why can't Time be curved?

Some astrophysicists are now postulating that the nigh infinitude of the Universe may be a false premise: that, in fact, the Universe is much smaller than we think. These vastest of all abstractions can, I suppose, only be grasped by those who have such an exquisite mathematical understanding that no one less well endowed has the slightest chance to understand. An insect like me just wonders.

Time is the opposite of Eternity.

In Eternity, nothing moves. Nothing happens. Nothing is. Nothing was, and nothing ever will be. Eternity exists outside the realm of Time, and nothing can exist outside the realm of Time. Time imparts movement, a state of being, a life of some kind even if in no more than the buzzing throngs of particles inside an atom. When Time stops for anything, it ceases to exist. That is not a description of death as distinct from life, but of non-being as distinct from being. As long as there is Time, substance exists. Whereas Eternity has no substance, it is nothing. It begins to sound like a mantra, doesn't it?

★ ★ ★

Time goes forward, pushing everything in the direction of death, also called entropy, or chaos. What a physicist means by chaos is not Logan Airport in the throes of a blizzard, or an area of devastation after a massive earthquake. To a physicist, chaotic entropy is purposelessness, having no mathematical meaning.

We have three words to delineate Time: yesterday, today, and tomorrow. The past is yesterday and the future is tomorrow; what lies in between is the present, today.

Think about the present. The last breath our lungs drew in is already in the past, and the next breath our lungs will draw in is still in the future, unbreathed. What lies between is a minuscule pause, the thinnest of all possible interfaces. That is what the present is: the interface between the future and the past. It's next-to-nothing, measured in quadrillionths of one millisecond. The present is so short it cannot be appreciated as a quantity of time. Death lurks in the future, and stops a life in the present; from then on, all an individual thing owns is a past. Yet while its substance lingers in existence, it still is. Thoroughly out of your depth? So am I! That is because, of course, sentient human beings cannot divorce their own selves from the great conundrums: God, life, death, and all intangibles.

★ ★ ★

That Time flows is easy to discern. It marks its passage in externals like greying hair, creaking bones, failing organs. And all around us are evidences of Time's flow—the annular rings in a tree trunk, the layers of fossils in rocks, the ebb and rise of oceans, seas, lakes.

We have but one instrument whereby to measure Time: the clock. But all a clock really measures is itself, or perhaps better to say it simply repeats the same interval over and over and over again. A certain number of repetitions sees the Earth rotate on its axis once, a different number sees the Earth rotate once around the Sun. But the intervals are numerically untidy, which ought perhaps to tell us that Time cannot really be measured. If the clock is fast, does less time go by? If it is slow, does more time go by? I mean, how do we honestly *know*? We can't touch Time, or see it, hear it, smell it, taste it. Time is an imponderable, a genuine mystery.

I firmly believe that Time flows at different rates, that how one denizen of its ocean perceives its passage is as valid as any other denizen's, and that no two denizens will experience it as exactly the same. Nor do I believe that Time has ever heard of mathematics or the Unified Field Theory.

The future does not exist: Time hasn't been there yet. It writes itself at the interface we call today. It's the vehicle takes the Universe on its ride from the present into the past. And we know far less about it than we do about Space or Gravity.

What sentient Earthlings don't seem to understand is that with every breath they suck out of the future's supply, predetermined by our genes and our living habits (both properties of the past), they literally *make* their future. It cannot be predicted because it happens a sliver at a time. The future truly does unfold.

Think of it in galactic terms. About 400 million years after the Big Bang or the Beginning, the atoms of the gas cloud became so squashed together that they fused in a chain reaction that liberated a positron and some raw energy. The stars turned on and began to shine in proto-galaxies. They made a future when they didn't have a future. About 10 billion years later than that, the Sun turned on and planet Earth was born. The Sun made a future for itself, and dragged Earth into it. Now, 4.5 billion years farther along, sentient Earthlings are busy making futures for themselves where no futures had existed. Such an interesting premise, that one can pluck something out of nothing! They say it can't be done, but clearly it can, and is. The whole Universe made a future for itself out of nothingness. One further question: Is the Universe merely a figment of someone's imagination

179

that doesn't exist in anyone's reality? If the sleeper awakes, will there be a Universe?

These days the physicists talk a great deal about dark matter and dark energy. Dark matter consists of ninety per cent of the Universe's total matter. Sentient Earthlings don't see, hear, smell, feel or taste the dark matter, and it responds to no gauge or analytical instrument yet invented. So tenuous and ghostly is its premise that it is mathematically inferred as having to exist. Without dark matter, we are led to believe, the Universe would have undergone the Big Crunch or another Big Bang long ago. Nor do sentient Earthlings see, hear, smell, feel or taste the presence of dark energy. Nothing in the Universe has ever been zapped by a charge of dark energy and had it recognized as such. Dark energy, presumably, confines itself to interaction only within dark matter.

I have to ask it! From whence comes the energy that fuels Time the vehicle on its manic ride? Time performs work, therefore it consumes energy from a stockpile of matter. Tomorrow doesn't become today and today become yesterday without massive pain and effort. Dark matter and dark energy are uniformly distributed throughout the Universe. Nothing else is. Except—Time.

THE SEPIA BLUES

Sepia is a particularly uninspiring brown that lends itself to a neutral palette from its most diluted beige through to the solid pigment, near-black. Cuttlefish and some related species squirt it, turning translucent turquoise water into an impenetrable fog that soon saw these talented tentacular beasties hunted for their ink. Over the ages, cakes of sepia dissolved in water enabled Man to write down his thoughts, calculations, inventions, dreams, sketches and philosophies on paper or parchment. If the ink were properly prepared, Man's symbols on paper would last for millennia. Added to which, sepia became a pigment utilized in the painting of pictures.

So what is sepia? It's the color of the writing on the wall, of skins and skunked skies, of shit and shadows, of pollution and putrefaction. It has no innate personality of its own.

If hemlines can reflect the economic climate, what can colors do? It's my opinion that they point up people's moods, the mental attitude of the populace. Study them and their effects, and the investigator will discover things that have the ability to surprise or even to shock. It is not for no reason that scarlet-red is the color of rage, and also the color of the harlot, who is called a "scarlet woman". Because of the astronomical cost in ancient times of obtaining a dye called Tyrian purple, the color purple became the prerogative of sovereigns. And while the phrase "the blues" to describe depression is a modern one, it has always been known that too much of a vapid shade of blue causes the human mood to flatten: which is why theatres are not painted blue inside—bad for favorable reception of the plays. Being the color of healthy plants, green cheers, and orange implies the destructive violence of flames. Whereas all the shades of sepia have no mood at all. The main reason why they are so popular in interior design: what provokes no emotion cannot be called in bad taste.

Here's an example that really gets the color ball rolling. The colder the climate, the darker the color people tend to wear. Sometimes I used to travel to Hamburg, Germany, all the way from my sub-tropical isle and its jewel colors. Invited out for dinner, I would don an outfit that, if it turned heads at all back home, would generate pleasure. Something made of pure silk, say, beautifully dyed in reds with slashes of acid-green and magenta. When, wearing this, I strolled into the

Hamburg restaurant, all conversation would stop dead as both men and women stared at me in sheer disbelief. My colors shocked them; every woman present wore black, or dark brown, or dark grey, or grimy tweed. I inspired not pleasure but unease, discomfort—not exactly disapproval, more the reception given to someone from Mars. I decided that I was a tropical creature, some brilliantly hued reef fish cast up in the midst of North Sea sardines.

One would think it ought to be the opposite. The colder the climate, the brighter the colors, if only to cheer people up as winter grinds on. However, my example is extreme. Canadians and Americans don't dress so drearily when it comes to color; it seems to be more a European phenomenon. But I freely admit that I deliberately saved my most lurid outfits for dining in Hamburg restaurants. It was such a hoot to still the place.

Now to look at three examples of the same piece of work as seen by creative teams working in three different eras: the 1930s, the 1950s, and the early 2000s.

In 1929 the world was plunged into the Great Depression. Nowadays governments have grown more cunning; they don't tell the people that they're in the midst of an awful economic depression, they simply pass what's happening off as a minor recession and go right on blithely spending money they don't have. Whereas the Great Depression was the first global stock market crash, and government was as ignorant of the phenomenon as were the people. Joblessness was a disaster in a world not geared for welfare payments or pensions; shanty towns mushroomed, and women with families despaired.

In this climate, a beautiful blonde woman named Clare Boothe Luce wrote a play called *The Women* which ran on Broadway for a very long time. It was clever enough to pillory the world of rich women addicted to clothes and gossip, and witty enough that some of its lines went into dictionaries of quotation ("substituting fashion for passion and the analyst's couch for the double bed").

Of course *The Women* was made into a film—black-and-white, as films were in the 1930s. But it did contain a segment shot in a thrilling new process called Technicolor: a fashion parade. Its stars were the biggest female names of the day, and it was ideal material for a time when America was painfully starting to emerge from the worst of the Great Depression. Funny and extremely well acted, it laid bare the lifestyles of the Idle Rich without mercy. The film's makers did something very new by clothing each of the characters in garments that reflected her personality, and the result was extraordinary. I remember Rosalind Russell, who played the bitchy, mischief-making marplot, wearing an outrageous dress appliquéd all over in huge eyes, and a svelte Joan Crawford as the husband-stealing vulgar shopgirl displaying her superb figure in underwear that may have covered more than it would today, but managed to be sexier too. The colors of the crazy clothes in the Technicolor fashion parade were as dazzling as luxurious.

In 1956 the film was remade as *The Opposite Sex*. Why the title change? Who knows, save that the 1950s were the prim and proper era, and the word "women" was—um—well, um—pretty blunt. It suggested human beings with vaginas rather than with pudenda ending in a solid wall, like dolls. The dialogue was still pure Clare Boothe Luce and the film could not but benefit from being in Technicolor from start to finish, including the fashion parade. The clothing in this version was stunning, as were the ladies' figures. It was the era of Monroe—big boobs, tiny waists, swelling hips, impossibly long and slender legs—and not a plastic implant anywhere. The colors were brilliant in every sense of that word: a veritable feast for the eyes.

In about 2006 a third version appeared, its title restored to *The Women*. There was absolutely no other point in common with Clare Boothe Luce's play, as her dialogue had been removed. The script was written by the (female) director, who believed the essence of wit was to have a character say "Shit!" Shit. You stupid director! Need I say the film was atrocious? It was.

Even Clare Boothe Luce's poke at the Idle Rich had gone; third millennial rich women don't dare be shown on camera as *idle*. They can shop until they drop, but not on camera! I mean, the impoverished female herd might get the idea that rich women have more of everything, and we can't have *that*—think how hard it would be to hire a maid! So the heroine, whom I called Mrs. Mops because her hair looked as if she'd stuck her finger in an electrical outlet, works her buns off giving lunches, brunches and munches for charity, and does the cooking herself. The food, incidentally, consisted of a wooden bowl of raw vegetables—gotta watch the figure! My question: what for? No one had a figure to watch. With the exception of Jada Pinkett Smith, the actresses were all overweight.

It was colossally egalitarian, so much so that one had to wonder why any of them wanted to be rich. The entire film was shot in sepia tones, giving the viewer an impression that there wasn't much difference between the vulgar shopgirl (Hispanic in this version, another put-down) and Mrs. Mops the aggrieved wife. Mrs. Mops, it turns out, is more concerned with a secret ambition to be—sssh! guess!—a fashion designer. Wow! After the sepia tones, the inevitable fashion parade (clothes designed by Mrs. Mops) was red, red, red, red, and more red. All it proved was that Mrs. Mops had the money and the contacts to burst upon the fashion scene as she never, never would have were she the penurious daughter of an alcoholic coal miner from Wilkes-Barre, Pennsylvania.

There's no bitchy marplot in this version, which shot the entire opus down in sepia flames. I mean, *The Women* is the tale of how there is always one woman who can't bear to see her pals happy, and how she shifts heaven and earth to destroy all hope of happiness. Was this the director's fell hand, or did the star destined to play the bitch decline to be one? Where did the money to make this awful movie come from? Hollywood must be as stuffed with fools as everywhere else.

The best bit in the film was a shot from behind of the four heroines galumphing down Fifth Avenue dressed in the most ghastly clothes imaginable. The tatty blouse not tucked into the skirt is a terrible look anyway, but the chubby legs and big bottom of a rear view screams danger to any woman of sense. My mother was no great shakes as a mother, but she did give me one immensely valuable piece of sartorial advice: always use two mirrors to see what you look like from behind. The phrase is, "the *back end* of a bus". And there they were, the back ends of three buses. Mrs. Mops was safe, as she was wearing a subfusc granny dress and flatties— hides a multitude of sins. But Kmart, not Saks.

Sepia has crept in everywhere. There used to be an avant-garde little skyscraper on the North Sydney skyline, a building much beloved by many. It was like a stack of children's blocks, each one a sheet of glass framed in brilliant orange. Then at the commencement of the third millennium, it got a face-lift, and turned from orange to sepia-beige. What a blight! What chicken-hearted cowardice! The world was suddenly a drabber place. For that orange-rimmed building was very good of its kind, it adorned modern architecture as so much modern architecture doesn't.

Sepia tones indicate a loss of hope, of optimism, of joy, but in a defeated, passionless way; they belong to bureaucrats and timid souls, to people with feet in a rut and tunnel vision. In the 1950s and 1960s the world genuinely thought that there was a good chance of massive nuclear holocaust; the Campaign for Nuclear Disarmament flourished. Yet that world was stuffed with color. What's happened in the meantime?

Too many people on the planet. Terrorism. Cipherdom. A sense of no new worlds to conquer.

Climates of fear and mental depression breed sepia tones. No one wants to stand out from the crowd, best illustrated by the black dress for women. Black is sepia carried to the ultimate degree, for black is the color that is no color at all. Walk into a black-tie reception, and you walk into a sea of black, black, black. Indistinguishable targets for assassins, crazies, bores.

And so my essay dwindles down; inevitable, when the subject is a neutral palette. Climax is negated, drama is defused.

Oh, but I would like my orange building back!

BELITTLING BILL

In the year 1769, shortly after the 150th anniversary of the death of William Shakespeare, one Herbert Lawrence announced that the Bard could not possibly have written the works attributed to him, as he had neither the education nor the cultural experience their author *must* have owned. It was left to William Henry Smith in 1857, nearly 250 years after Shakespeare's death, to assert that there was only one possible candidate for said authorship: Francis Bacon, Baron Verulam and Viscount St. Albans. And after Smith came the cypher-seekers of the American Baconian movement, who found cryptograms within the works that abso-bloody-lutely *proved* Bacon was the author. Poor old Bill Shakespeare, so long in his grave, was dispossessed of his entitlement to his work.

Elsewhere in these unruly pages is an essay on bureaucrats called "Unelected Power", but nowhere have I discussed a different kind of paper-pushing parasite: namely, the academic scholar. His (her implied, as always) home is among the spires, graciously gothic or rudely red-brick, of institutions of tertiary learning known as universities. Within such hallowed halls there floats o'er all a mantra: *"Publish or Perish!"* From the dissertation and the thesis to the hugely heavy tome, an academician must publish unless he be a very rare bird indeed—a superlative teacher. It's a dog-eat-dog world, it has its stars and its slugs, its seekers after truth and its seekers after coveted position. As in any other kind of institution, the individual's ability to play the political game is paramount to the advancement—or otherwise—of his career.

Yet to make a big academic splash is extremely difficult, particularly outside the sciences and mathematics.

Imagine an eighteenth-century scholar of no moment suddenly visited by an enormous enlightenment about the acknowledged master wordsmith of the language! Plays, poems, an output so varied and world-encompassing that it couldn't possibly, under any stretch of an eighteenth-century imagination, have been the product of a Midlands rustic of scant education and experience. One hundred and fifty years after said Midlands rustic's death, this conclusion was not only reached, but persisted in sufficiently large academic circles to lead a nineteenth-century scholar to come to the conclusion that, of all the luminaries who adorned the late Tudor and early Stuart literary scene, only Francis Bacon had the erudition, experience and sophistication to have been the true author of the works hitherto attributed to that Midlands rustic, William Shakespeare.

Why were these conclusions reached at all? And why, having been made, do they hang around like the odor of skunk cabbage in a swamp to this day, to diminish the achievements of a man whose efforts were not questioned for a quarter of a millennium?

The answer is simple. They were made to fuel some scholar's academic reputation, and they persist because, exactly as in the case with bureaucrats, their perpetuation perpetuates the species. How boring it would be if no one had ever queried Shakespeare's right to be called the author of his works! How trite it would be to blame the phenomenon of Shakespeare on something as ephemeral as genius! How echoing the corridors of Academe, devoid of their more lunatic fringe! It even serves a purpose: a few students, who otherwise wouldn't, read the works of Francis Bacon, whose life, certainly, is fascinating, even if his literary output is a trifle dense.

Envy is worse by far than jealousy. Envy is cold, sour, pale, misshapen, and gives off the putrid greenish glow of rotting things. There is no passion in it, no roaring fire. Ah, but it can provide some lives with motivations far above the quick and mortal thrusts of jealousy! It isn't in the forefront of a mind, it hunches in the background like an unacknowledged monster, and it waits patiently for the opportunity to tear down reputations, ideas, even dreams. Lawrence and Smith were just envious men.

I have loved Shakespeare since I was introduced to him in school, at about fifteen years of age. Neither the plots nor the characters of his plays turned me on at the time; what did was the way he said things. Which I suppose was the instinctive reaction of a potential wordsmith confronted with the outpourings of a master.

The man had a fantastic gift for words, and could express an idea in words as modern as tomorrow, as old as humanity. So often, reading or hearing Shakespeare, the actual words bear no relation to time passed or passing.

"Put out the light, then put out the light."

There will never be a better way to say it, as sinister as it is specific, horror masked yet unmasked. The killer who can't bear to look.

I believe that William Shakespeare existed, that he was a rustic from the Midlands, that he had at least some education from a good if free local grammar school— and that, during the course of his fifty-two years, he wrote the poems and plays credited to him. So close to the Welsh Marches, he may have had Celtic blood, a definite asset when it comes to hearing the music in words. By profession he was an actor, and seems to have prospered at it, especially after he started writing plays. It is common for a creative person to go into the type of creativity that satisfies the drive within him to do new things in the most loved, most familiar medium. As a playwright he will have fully understood the tricks of the trade, known the short-cuts and the dramatic devices, all a great help in building a structural armature for the finished edifice.

He wrote comedies, tragedies and historical pieces, which indicates that his gifts were multifaceted. His earliest poems were in the vein of narrative epics: the young bird flying high and wide. Whereas the bird of the sonnets hovers where the air is loveliest and the view far enough. That he read Ovid's *Amores* and *Metamorphoses* we know, and there can be little doubt that he also read Plutarch's *Lives*, even if he didn't have any Greek. He may have obtained access to some scholar's translation. Latin he would certainly have had, it was all around him. As any good Tudor schoolboy would have, he knew his Kings of England. It is important to remember that the Midlands and the West Country had a far higher literacy rate than did London until the twentieth century. He had a great love for Italy and things Italian; what isn't known is whether this was knowledge gained at first hand, or from reading.

There were long periods of "rest" during which an enterprising man might have read and researched, including the two years of plague that saw the theatres closed. Some great noblemen had impressive libraries, but we do not know enough about Shakespeare to pin his sources of material down with much specificity. Very definitely he prospered, owned property in his home town, but he was also burdened with a bankrupt father.

While reading is well and good, there is one quality any man may have that people tend to overlook: the passion for watching others, of listening to any conversation carried on within earshot, and for tracing all the threads of an event. I mean the kind of curious soul who takes an interest in the doings of his whole world. William Shakespeare was surely that kind of curious soul. It's all stored up in the mind, future grist to the writer's mill, though nary a note may be taken.

Genius is impossible to define, it takes so many forms, beyond stating that it indicates a degree of knowledge, excellence and skill not present in the vast preponderance of human beings. In the sciences and mathematics it is easier to discern, and the farthest pole from that is probably literature. Only four names spring to my mind: Shakespeare, Molière, Cervantes and Goethe (screams of outrage from all sides). Not my catalogue, just the one most mentioned, so it's not my fault. But do you begin to see what I mean? What about Ibsen? T.S. Eliot? Zola? Pirandello? Joyce? Marquez? When does the accolade fall, the laurel wreath settle? Who's plain wacko? It's all in the eye and ear of the beholder, except for the Famous Four, about whom, no argument. They're literary geniuses.

Therefore William Shakespeare was a genius. Certainly that's my judgement too. Everything he experienced he fed into his life's work, from the most trifling conversation to the most appalling tragedy: every word ever read or heard, every face ever seen, and all grafted to a far rarer quality: *empathy*. Whatever he wrote about, he felt the emotions as he wrote about it. So many gifts, all squeezed into one man's skull. It does happen, as it did with William Shakespeare.

Take Francis Bacon. A political animal, if ever there was one. A court creature, to whom the good opinion of the sovereign and the sovereign's favorites was all-important. A lawyer, yet! Related to the arch-bureaucrats of the time, the Cecils. His father, the grossly obese Sir Nicholas Bacon, was Lord Keeper of the Privy Seal; even in 1600, the name Bacon was an old and a respectable one. Two marriages and a plethora of sons saw Bacon's father hard put to establish them all satisfactorily, and he died before his youngest, Francis, was properly provided for. Thus both cheated and exposed from birth to a grand and sophisticated world, Francis Bacon's life was marred by perpetual debt, a series of bitter enmities, and a number of allegations that he could be bribed.

But where, in Bacon's desperately busy life of intrigues, did he find the leisure to write a formidable body of plays? Bacon's life was given over to schemes aimed at improving his economic lot through court appointments, the bench and parliament, as well as to his own academic work, which was of a far different nature than Shakespeare's opera. Poetry can be dashed off, and in fairness to Bacon and Shakespeare both, once a poetic form is mastered, it becomes a mind-set a wordsmith finds easy to dash off. No, it is the plays that are the stumbling block, given that one man was immersed in the theatre as a way of life, when the other man was not.

So for Shakespeare the plays were a natural offshoot of a much loved career; he inhabited the theatrical world, knew Marlowe, Jonson and many other luminaries. He knew how plays worked: what the audience had to be provided with by way of information, as well as how the play should progress on stage all the way to its denouement. For a master of the form in a tearing hurry, it would have been possible to write a whole play in about a month, maybe well under that. Especially were the master wordsmith a genius "on a roll" as we'd phrase it today. Rolls do happen. The words flow out like smoothest syrup, the framework goes up without one strut or bolt wrongly placed, and the characters find speech as profound and perceptive as exactly right for their natures. At other times the roll doesn't happen, so the writer struggles. Any wordsmith would attest that the worst feature of a roll is keeping up with the flow of words and ideas spilling out of the brain. But in order to have a roll, the wordsmith must know his craft more intimately than a man knows the contours of his own body.

Could the debt-harried Bacon, with his grandiose ideas of his own position in life and his high-flown intellectual aspirations in philosophy and the sciences of his time, have written such a stunningly varied and large output of plays? Plays that, no matter what their style or subject, always struck their audiences as true to the life of ordinary thought?

Bacon too was a genius, but of a different kind. His very birth and background shaped his genius to thrill at the concept of breaking new ground in philosophical thought; as well, he hungered to devise an entirely new system that gathered all human knowledge into one gigantic relationship.

That's not a mind could be interested in crafting what were, after all, mere entertainments. I don't think Shakespeare ever regarded his plays as earth-shaking advances in any kind of philosophy: they were, plain and simple, entertainments. Money? What profit the plays made couldn't even begin to dent Bacon's debts. Shakespeare's history is of spending precious hundreds, Bacon's of forever needing an income of thousands. Bacon spent much time securing this boon, particularly from James Stuart, who seems to have both needed and despised him. His own uncle, William Cecil, Lord Burghley, was another who seemed to despise him, as he was never quick to help Bacon and had a tendency to ignore his letters of supplication. It also beggars imagination that no one ever referred to Bacon as a dramatist or dramaturge, if indeed he had visited that world.

When it's all boiled down, perhaps the strongest argument against Bacon as the author of Shakespeare's works lies in the fact that it took 250 years for the allegation to be made at all. What the allegation implies is sheer snobbery: that the mind of one capable of grasping so much about human behavior could not possibly have belonged to a very ordinary man of no real ancestry or importance.

There really is very little more to the Baconian Theory than that, and common sense gives the lie.

Just because we today revere William Shakespeare far ahead of Francis Bacon is no argument, let alone proof, in itself. What matters is the kind of world *they* lived in, and it would be hard to visualize two men more different than they. One was a court creature, the other an entertainer: that was the social contrast. But a Francis Bacon, with his dreams of devising a new way to catalogue all human knowledge, prostituting his education and his apirations to write *plays*? It doesn't bear thinking of!

Our trouble—even the trouble of Mr. Lawrence and Mr. Smith—is that we have hindsight. We can see Shakespeare's output for what it is, sheer genius. At the time? I imagine that Viscount St. Albans sniffed impatiently, and dismissed it as the prating maunderings of some actor.

In his time, Francis Bacon was extremely important.

COL ON THE WRITING OF HER BOOKS

Geographical accident and an occupation far removed from the writing of fiction combined to produce a fact most people have long forgotten: that Colleen McCullough never did have an Australian writing career. I was an Australian who wrote novels set in and about Australia, but always with a wider audience in mind than Australians. My primary publisher was American.

How did that come to be? Geographical accident certainly played a large part: when I embarked upon my writing career, I was living seventy miles from the world centre of publishing, New York City. My neurosciences had led to a position at the Yale Medical School in New Haven, Connecticut, so when I finished my first novel, *Tim*, it never occurred to me to send it anywhere else than to New York City, a mere two-hour train ride away. I could be a part of the publishing process if it found a niche.

Some writers and their books travel; others do not. This yea or nay depends entirely upon how easily the readers absorb the material in a book, and to illustrate my point I'll use my own book, *Angel Puss*. Of all my works, this one describes the smallest, most individualistic world; even though Melbourne and Perth are as Australian as Sydney, someone from Melbourne or Perth doesn't get full enjoyment from it. *Angel Puss* is a book for Sydneysiders of a certain age. In other words, it doesn't travel. Whereas *The Thorn Birds* traveled the world effortlessly, so much so that it crossed all the barriers of race, creed, color. And most of my books travel; if they don't, I know it beforehand.

Patriotism takes peculiar forms. Because I never lived in Australia after my twenty-fourth year, and given that my present age puts this date in the 1960s, when the world was an extremely different place, my patriotism took the form of trying to make people who didn't know much about Australia see that country's magic, its customs and traditions, its people in their homeland. My work took me elsewhere, but that didn't mean I wasn't homesick, or fleeing from a place I hadn't liked. I loved Australia, and I thought it a marvelous place to set a novel, fresh and new.

But all those years away from home had counted for much: I understood what people in other countries knew about Australia, and what they didn't. Having this grasp of foreign perceptions, I was in a wonderful position to write about Australia. Had I not lived ten years abroad before I commenced to write novels, had I written my first novel still living in Australia, it would have failed to find a foreign audience back then. Homebodies take too much for granted. If the writer is Nobel Prize material, that doesn't matter, but it matters hugely for a writer whose talents and ambitions are less exalted.

I had always written, but purely to entertain myself in my spare time. Always novels; short stories are the province of different minds than mine. It isn't an exaggeration to say that I must have written a hundred novels between my first effort at five and the death of my brother, a total of twenty-one years. After Carl died, I stopped, and the next few years lie unremembered deep down somewhere. Grief cannot be catalogued or described; the closest I can get is that to lose someone loved unconditionally is a spiritual amputation.

Need for additional income kick-started my second writing career, over the far side of the gulf Carl blasted in my life. I belong to that generation of women who was paid exactly half what her male peers were paid; when Yale brought in equal pay, they decreed that it would be only for new female employees—or those confident enough to quit and hope to be reappointed. We none of us were!

The fact that I wrote in my spare time was my secret. The nuns of my high school had known, and elicited a promise from me: that I wouldn't seek publication until I was a mature woman. Their asking this of me arose from Catherine Gaskin, who was a few classes ahead of me at the same school. When she was fifteen she wrote a bestseller called *This Other Eden*, and it seems the nuns felt she would have done better to have waited a few years. As it was, no one except my mother and brother knew I wrote. If you read "Laurie" in this collection you'll understand why it was an ordeal to have Laurie know—the snooping, the contempt, the barbed remarks. Not to mention the burning; having read an effort of mine after unearthing it from its hiding place, she would burn it. Later, after *Tim* was published, I took a leaf from her book and burned all save one of my existing efforts. Our reasons were poles apart: she wanted to hurt, I wanted to make sure nothing existed that was inferior to *Tim*.

Had it not been for my financial circumstances, it is even possible that I may never have written for publication at all. Single women of huge energy who do not live with another person have acres of spare time to devote to "hobbies." I drew, painted, embroidered, wrote and cooked. I was never, never lonely.

★ ★ ★

Having made the decision to write a novel for publication, I went about the business with all the systematic precision of a scientist. As I had published nothing and knew no one in publishing, what kind of novel should this first one be? Easy! Since I was female, it would have to be a love story, the female writer's traditional sphere. The trouble was that personally I found love stories very boring—a sort of fiction I didn't read. However, needs must.

Before I go any farther, I should mention that I had decided to write a different kind of novel each time I embarked upon the next venture. My research had showed me that publishers liked novelists to hew to the same line in each successive book; it makes the product easy to market. It didn't take a high IQ to perceive that writing different books would prove a stumbling block to my ongoing career if I were lucky enough to have one. However, first things first: write the book!

My love story would have to be very different, very unusual. Were it not, the writing of it wouldn't sustain my own interest. I knew I wouldn't win a Nobel Prize, but I knew I wasn't going to be a hack either. I had an excellent education, a scientific mind and a massive tally of reading in almost all genres. And, having plotted out a book, delved into its characters, I so loved the physical and mental act of writing. For, no matter how well planned a book is, the characters still persist in galloping off in directions the writer hadn't counted on. It's no different from sculpting a statue or painting a picture—what will the end result be like?

Space doesn't permit the story of how I arrived at my love story plot, this first novel for publication that had my future career riding on its back. Suffice it to say that I chose to write about how a young, mildly mentally retarded man might have come to marry a spinsterish woman nearly twice his age. The core subject mattered greatly to me, and my neurological career had given me the exposure and the experience necessary to delineate the characters with sympathy and understanding. I called the book *Not The Full Quid*, then found myself a literary agent by writing her the world's most irresistible letter (for so I described it to her!). Shortly thereafter, my novel was accepted by the respected publishing firm of Harper & Row. The year was 1972, and I was thirty-five years old. I had been with the research labs of the Department of Neurology at the Yale Medical School since 1967.

My editor loved the book, which she called the most polished first novel that had crossed her desk in twenty-seven years—except, that is, for its title, which had to go. This was to be the first of many duels about titles; I always lost them, but I'd always be back for another try next time. The book was published as *Tim*. It received extremely glowing reviews, and earned me the amazing sum of $50,000. Five years' worth of Yale pay.

The next one was, I knew, very different from *Tim*. So different, in fact, that I doubted whether Harper & Row would be interested in it. Its early chapters were firmly based in my own family's history, which made a fine jumping-off place for a novel that had a number of phenomena I wanted to explore. One was the habit women have of falling in love with unattainable men. Another was the iron grip the Catholic Church had on rural New South Wales. A third was to investigate the psyche of a kind of woman we all know: the martyr. And a fourth was to paint in big, broad strokes the kind of place rural farming Australia used to be. Its magic too.

All of which dictated that this second novel would be a far bigger book than *Tim*, with more characters, a sense of the passage of time, yet basically only one integral character: the central woman, martyr and lover of an unattainable man. I killed a lot of birds with the same stone. I remember writing much of it with deep snow outside my New Haven window, while my pages reeked of heat and dust. I lived between two worlds, each as real as the other.

My agent loved it; she said it opened like a flower. But when it went to my editor at Harper & Row, I heard nothing for six months. Other writers might have picked up the phone and enquired, but not this writer. I would wait them out, and I did. When my editor did get in touch, she was dubious of the book's merits—it was far too long, and some of its characters ran tangential to the main thrust of the plot. My answer was literally to unborn one character, lift him holus-bolus out of the book, and throw another character into jail. My editor proved right; it was better at a shorter length, and the characters weren't missed. The title I had given it was *The Thorn Birds*, universally despised at H & R. But while the title wrangle was still going on, the book was auctioned for U.S. paperback rights while still in manuscript, and fetched a then world-record sum of $1.9 million. Of which I got half. Then my agent and the tax man got half of my half, to indulge the curious. There are many myths about bestsellers.

I hadn't expected it, nor did anyone tell me what kind of golden egg I had laid. The goose is always a goose. I'd far rather be that than a vulture!

It had taken two years to get *Tim* into print; it took four months to get *TTB* (my shorthand for the book) into print. And it sold hugely, in so many languages I've long lost count. Of course the critics panned it unmercifully, just as if I had never written a book they'd praised; to earn big bikkies automatically means a book has to be trash. Which is a pity, not for the book or its author, but for the critics, who reveal themselves as utterly two-faced. I wish they understood that they can't matter; the only vindication for a book of any kind is the test of time. If it lasts then it can't be all bad. It was published on Friday, May 13th, 1977.

Then came the crunch. *An Indecent Obsession* said loud and clear that I wasn't about to write *Son of Thorn Birds*. I had spent my university years working as a skivvy in hospitals, around the period between 1954 and 1960. Hospitals then were staffed by professional nurses who had never married, and they fascinated me. Though at the time I was too young to know that I too would become a spinster, I had such a horror of marriage (read "Jim" and "Laurie") that I must have sensed my fate. A great deal of my hard labor was done in a veterans' hospital; ward after ward of men, some resident for years. I used to watch some of those nurses in their relationships with their men-only patients, and out of it came *An Indecent Obsession*: the indecent obsession is duty, and personal happiness is all too often sacrificed on its altar.

Harper & Row hated the book. My editor left me over it, and I was never to have a happy relationship with my publisher for the two books I still owed them under contract. I refused to write *Son of TTB*. Poor *AIO*, it died. All because by mischance I had written not *a* bestseller, but *the* bestseller. Why such intelligent and widely experienced people could not, could not, could not get it through their heads that *TTB* was accidental and I was incapable of writing another in the same vein, escapes me. Irving "Swifty" Lazar summed their attitude up when he glared at me with those two pale pebbles lurking at the bottom of a lenticular sea, and said, "Fifteen million dollars! You stoopid bitch!" I daresay I was. But the fact remains that I was the only one came out of *TTB* still the same kind of person I was before it. My feet were still on the ground and my long-term writing plan was unchanged.

Harper & Row continued to hope for *Son of TTB*. I think the chief executives (all of whom I knew quite well as a result of *TTB*) felt that once I'd gotten this peculiar aberration out of my system by writing *An Indecent Obsession*, I'd see the commercial light and settle down into an obedient writer of bestsellers. Then I gave them *A Creed for the Third Millennium*, which I abbreviate as *Creed*. The shit hit the fan in all directions.

If *AIO* had been a radical departure from *TTB*, then *Creed* was a radical departure from *Tim*, *TTB* and *AIO*! Where the hell was I going with my writing career?

It goes almost without saying that I love *Creed*, which was a huge pleasure to write. Of course, in stoutly maintaining that I love the act of writing, that I wallow in it sensuously, keenly, voluptuously, deliciously, I am mortally offending those literati who on principle state that to write *good* books is agony, the hardest work possible. I dismiss the agony: if a career is that punishing, why do it at all? The hard work, yes, but doesn't hard work go into every satisfying career? Why is one not allowed to enjoy hard work? I love hard work, especially cerebral hard work. It galvanizes me, I fizz with life because of it! So when I say that I love to write and relish every aspect of the process, I speak the simple truth. A writer's tools are words, a writer's blueprints grammar, syntax and usage, a writer's prepared ground are form and structure. Surely if the writer is as well versed with his/her equipment as a neurosurgeon is in that arena, then the writing process should provoke the enjoyment any professional feels when working in what is, after all, the *chosen* field.

Creed came out of a deeply rooted conviction I hold—a series of observations—and an intriguing

213

question. My personal conviction: that our planet is grossly over-populated, and every family on its face must adhere to the one-child family for at least six generations. The observations: that with the enormous increase in the price of heating oil, the colder parts of the U.S.A. are dying, downtowns boarded up, factories vanishing, while in warmer regions population keeps on swelling. And the question: if a Christlike man were to emerge at the beginning of the third millennium, how would he manage to get his message of salvation to the people? Because of the question, I couched the book in allegorical form.

Well, poor *Creed* died too, and I was out of my contract.

I think contracts are outmoded. That they exist at all seems to be a businessman's solution as to how to tame and tie down that captious, inexplicable beast, the creative artist. I would like to see a publishing world without the contract for future books; a contract for the one in the publisher's hot little hand makes some sense at least, for both sides. But I have been wangled into some pretty strapping contracts in my time, and deplore them. I am now seventy-four years of age, and there is still no *Son of TTB*. Can you imagine the one I'd write today? The heroine crippled by arthritis, the hero watching his aortic aneurysm, da de da de da. That's why publishers leave me alone at last to do whatever is my thing.

The Ladies of Missalonghi was, in a sense, commissioned. My dear friend Anthony Cheetham had acquired the British publishing house of Hutchinson, which had a centennial birthday coming up. Anthony wanted to celebrate it by a series of novellas from his top writers, each writer's book to fall into a specific category. Mine was the ghost story. I had been chewing a version of the Cinderella myth for many years, and saw how to combine the two. *Ladies* was the result. Classic Cinderella, with a ghost as the *deus ex machina* rather than a fairy godmother.

In one way I can understand why, since well before I became a famous writer, people have nagged and picked at me to write an autobiography. Some people lead desperately dull lives, through no fault of their own; it's just that they were always visiting the ski slopes the day before the avalanche, or the volcano the day before the eruption, or the bank ten minutes before the bloody holdup. There are other people who can hit Panama on the day of revolution and get stuck in the President's palace, or Greece in the throes of the same, and get stuck in the middle of bloody riots in Thessalonika, or get mistaken for the great diva

Joan Sutherland, or get stuck for ten days in a New York hotel during the Blizzard of '96—need I go on? The latter person is I. Things happen to me, and there doesn't seem to be a way out of it. Birds crap on my head. Dogs hump my leg. Rats laugh at me, and don't say rats can't laugh, because they can.

When *Ladies* was published, I was accused of— wait for it!—plagiarism. If it hadn't been such a shock, I would have seen the funny side a great deal more quickly; as it was, newspapers got into the act, and some old lady in New Zealand embarked on a wild vendetta because I had copied her favorite girls' book author, one L.M. Montgomery of *Anne of Green Gables* fame. A bigger load of nonsense would have been hard to find, as my alleged plagiarisms were far from it. As best I could work it out, there had been a very successful TV series on Anne, and perhaps there were further TV series contracts in the wind—the publicity would have been excellent. Nothing came of it because nothing could, and later on I did laugh heartily—the one thing I have never needed to do is copy other writers! I add that any plagiarism involved L.M. Montgomery as much as it did me—we both had a go at Cinderella.

The incident put a wonderful seal on my career as a writer: if it can happen to anyone, it will happen to me.

★ ★ ★

The story of the *Masters of Rome* series of novels I want to save until last, as it is—at least to me—the most interesting and helpful of all my projects as far as other writers are concerned, especially if said writers aspire to historical novels.

The Song of Troy was a factual retelling of the ten years of war between Achaea (Greece) and Troy (Ilium): what might actually have occurred to give rise to the myth. However, I couldn't bear to let go of the myth's most wonderful trappings, from the flight of Helen with Paris to Troy, to the Trojan horse. Good historian that I am, I started my tale with its root causes, and went on through all ten years before tackling the culminating fifty-odd days chronicled by Homer in the *Iliad*. Then told of the fate of those among the heroes who survived the conflagration.

It has one distinction none of my other published works has: I wrote it when I was twenty years old, and didn't destroy it. I liked it too much. Whereas, the day *Tim* was published, I burned the dozens of novels I had written over the years for my own private amusement. That there might be anything in my mother's house I didn't fear for one moment. Laurie was the original burner, and liked nothing better than burning her children's "scribbling".

My only work of non-fiction was a biography of a remarkable man, Sir Roden Cutler V.C. He was everything by accident, a soldier thanks to war rather than profession who won the Victoria Cross for an incredible feat of bravery, and was thrown into a diplomatic career at the whim of a Labor politician who saw his promise. Wherever he went, things happened, and that same coolness and daring that had carried him through his war experiences stood him in good stead.

Getting facts out of him was akin to squeezing blood out of the proverbial stone; I vowed I would never write another biography! But he was such a dear man. He died, aged eighty-six, a true hero. Our book did very well in Australia; it had no international market, alas, though it did see the light of day in the U.K. We donated the proceeds of *Roden Cutler, V.C.* to charity.

The genesis of *Morgan's Run* was interesting. I had always deplored the Australian tendency to play down its convict origins, and found this nowhere more obnoxiously illustrated than in tales of the First Fleet, an occurrence as important for Australia as the Pilgrim Fathers for America. The convicts were passed over in favor of the British naval and marine officers who governed men and women they treated, by and large, at least as badly as slavers did slaves.

My husband, Ric, has a fascinating ancestry; he's descended from two different Marquesses, Ripon and Hastings, from Fletcher Christian, Matthew Quintal and the Tahitians who took the *Bounty* to Pitcairn Island, and from a First Fleet convict named Richard Morgan who, oddly enough, was sent to Norfolk Island, where the Pitcairners too wound up.

Ric has a Robinson cousin, the famous singer Helen Reddy, who had accumulated a huge amount of documentation about Richard Morgan; Ric too had Morgan documents. It had been Helen's ambition to write a book about Morgan, who is the four-times-great-grandfather of both Helen and Ric. But time had not permitted it; when I expressed an interest, she gave me all Morgan's papers. I sent my stepdaughter to England on a further fact-finding mission, and out of this mountain of authentic fact came *Morgan's Run*, the true story of a remarkable man. More satisfying still to me was the fact that it equipped me to write about the First Fleet from the convict point of view, until then, utterly neglected save for a very good non-fiction book by Robert Hughes, *The Fatal Shore*. But Hughes's canvas was far larger, and the two books do not collide.

The novel did extremely well, and continues to prove popular in paperback, though it's years since it was published.

And after that came my least loved book, *The Touch.*

If a drip of water can eventually wear a hole in a skull, then that was what happened to me. I couldn't write *Son of TTB*, but to shut up my editor I wrote a book about another aspect of the Australian historical experience that involved the doings of a man and his family. Because I found it interesting, I chose gold mining, and from there ventured into the infantile petroleum industry. Some of my most respected friends love *The Touch*, but I despise it. Looking back, a good proportion of that despisal is due to its title, which I fought against with might and main for months to no avail. My editor, who shall be nameless but was a powerful man, refused to see its inanity, suggestiveness and misinformation. To him, it was the Midas touch. To me, it was plain awful, and published with an equally awful dust jacket. I couldn't win, and I didn't win. But nor did my publishers.

A book's content may have all the earmarks of success, yet not achieve it. If I had my way, I'd re-issue it as *Alexander's Gold*, which would at least put the emphasis where it should belong instead of upon some groping, clammy, furtive hand up the skirts of a female figure who, if her dust jacket face is anything to go by, is dead.

Actually, a good title would be *Murder by Editor*.

That I write about this kind of thing at some length is to dispel some of the myths that surround bestselling writers, who are deemed all-powerful when they're not. Well, let me modify that: writers who produce the same book over and over do well. It's the mavericks who run afoul of the system. Maybe the true unkindest cut is that, having produced another reasonable candidate for big success, my editor and publisher combined to kill it in a misguided marketing zeal. I find it fascinating that the person who produces the work is the lowest man on the totem pole.

Now we come to *Angel Puss*, which I don't think was published in the U.S.A. My favorite book, a complete self-indulgence that I understood wouldn't travel well, as I explained in the introductory paragraphs of this essay. It's all about women, but what women! Nothing gets them down, nothing fazes them, nothing the entire male sex can do is capable of knocking them out of the game of living. They're the unsung heroines, the salt of the earth.

Angel Puss is a funny, irreverent novel about grotesques and life outside the mainstream that takes a colossal poke at so-called Christian society. Meeting him at a literary lunch, the fearsome editor of the *Sydney Morning Herald* literary section told me that the book was so funny he couldn't catch his breath for laughing. Though on one level it might be seen as a dirge for the plight of women, *Angel Puss* is a paean for the might of women. I just love the book, which contains my favorite of all female characters, Mrs. Delvecchio Schwartz, in her element in a world long gone: Kings Cross in 1960.

Another reason why I love the book so may lie in the fact that a writer rarely gets a chance to laugh at and with her characters, but I did in *Angel Puss*. Long may that book live!

I had never written a true, formal whodunit, and I was determined to do so as my sixties crept onward. Emblazoned in my mind was a veritable toenail-curler of an opening for a scary whodunit, the only time in my writing career that I predicated a book upon an opening page. After ten years in neurological research at the Yale Medical School, I had a perfect Agatha Christie venue for my tale of blood and serial murders: a small, enclosed research unit whose members were all equally able to fit into the killer's shoes. For that reason I plucked the city of Holloman, Connecticut, and the Ivy League university, Chubb, out of the pages of *Creed,* and set my whodunit in 1965–66, an era before DNA and forensics took all the joy out of police detection. My cop was an Italian-American named Carmine Delmonico, and the plot was diabolical. I called the book *On, Off*—a title that so flummoxed my editor that—he? she?—didn't even argue. You have to wait until the last page to find out why it's called *On, Off* into the bargain.

Another symptom of encroaching old age is that all the little ideas you've been toying with idly for decades you suddenly decide to act upon. And one of these crotchets was a dissatisfaction with the most sacrosanct of all lady's novels, *Pride and Prejudice.* Any fool can see that the marriage between Elizabeth and Mr. Darcy was doomed from its beginning; Austen's prose may be lovely, but her knowledge of human nature is pretty shaky, especially when it involves the male sex; the bulk of men may as well have lived on Mars, Austen knew so little about them.

I had hankered to write a sequel set twenty years down the track, and, having the time, I did so. Another aspect of *P & P* that fascinated me was whatever happened to the fifth sister, Mary, she of the atrocious singing voice, which is just about the only mention

Mary gets. Austen clearly says Mr. and Mrs. Bennet had *five* beautiful daughters, indicating that Mary too was beautiful, so why was she so undesirable? An atrocious singing voice is easy to deal with—just tell the offender to shut up. Anyway, I had great fun inventing a life for Mary and in detailing the state of affairs between Elizabeth and Mr. Darcy; the original novel is so improbable that it gives the writer of a sequel carte blanche in terms of probability. *Dependence and Independence* seemed a good name, except that some would think that it involved the American Founding Fathers, so it became *The Independence of Miss Mary Bennet* instead. I had great fun writing it, I add.

Time now to discuss the Roman books. It was my French publisher gave them their collective name: *The Masters of Rome*.

As a part of my assault on the various sorts of novel, I had wanted to write a true historical novel. By that, I meant a book so carefully researched historically that it would have to be ranked with all the scholarly treatises on the subject: an historical work that never departed from what is known about the period as well as the actual subject and persons.

Because I am a people explorer, it had to revolve around an historical personage, so I started looking for candidates. *Not* King Arthur or Merlin or any of that mystical claptrap so beloved of women novelists! I was attracted to Napoleon, but he'd been done to death. No Middle Ages English Kings either. A Renaissance hero? No. China or some other part of Asia? I'm not an oriental scholar. Finally I lit upon Gaius Julius Caesar the Dictator—the great Caesar, in other words. Nothing of moment had been written about him at all. Thornton Wilder had written a small fantasy, but it was hard to find anything else. Right! Caesar it is, I decided. Only much later, snowed under by the research, did I understand why novelists had left Caesar severely alone—the amount of research was crushing.

I live on a five-by-three-mile speck in the middle of the ocean, a thousand miles from any major landmass, so I realized that I would have to acquire my own reference library, complete and all-encompassing. The multi-volume *Cambridge Ancient History* was already on our library shelves; I sat down with the old volumes (the new aren't as good, in my opinion) VIII, IX and X to peruse their bibliographies. Anything I thought I might need, I bought; the services of a professional book searcher are invaluable in this sort of exercise, I hasten to say. As those books came in, I conned their bibliographies, and so it went, on and on, until I had works of scholarship on every aspect of the period Caesar lived through:

everyday life, clothing, food, wine, the toga, domestic pets, the entire military gamut, roads and road-making, geography, climate, agriculture, pastoralism, the ancient names of rivers, mountain ranges, lakes, seas, towns; business and commerce, government and its structure, the law, courts, wild animals, architecture, shipping and shipping routes, ships, Latin obscenities, Roman provinces, client kingdoms, children, schools and education, rhetoric, furniture, brickwork, stone masonry, glass, ceramics, tools, machinery, and literally half a hundred other aspects of Caesar's world. The habits of a resident of Rome as against a resident of a Roman town or a foreign town—attitudes of mind were as important as objects and people. I wanted to be so soaked in Caesar's world that I felt more at home in it than I did in my own world.

I used a computer for nothing, probably because when I embarked upon the research, the PC was a novelty, and once I had a method worked out, it was easier to keep going than change horses in midstream. The object of everything was memory reinforcement. As I read a book for the first time, I took copious notes by hand on to pads. Then some, mainly facts, would be transferred to pink five-by-eight-inch cards, and stored by category, while the same facts as part of a narrative would be transcribed to pieces of paper on a typewriter.

Then other pieces of it, or the same pieces, would be typed yet again because they were also needed in a different category of note. I had, for instance, when the research was done, 300 double-spaced pages on Cicero alone, more than that on Brutus, 200 on Cassius, 200 on Servilia (a tortuous research business), and on Caesar himself, 1,000 pages. Those notes, which I called my biographies, were kept in spring binders. Each war had its own notes. So did each battle. I knew the name of every tribe in Gallia Comata. I had culled Druidism from sources as far removed as Polybius, Caesar and Ammianus.

I estimate that each fact I found was handwritten at least once, but probably twice, and typed in three or four different places. My memory is formidable, and I fed it relentlessly.

When all the books were in, I had about 3,000 volumes, not all of much use; perhaps 100 were invaluable, but not compared to what are called "the ancient sources". These are the writers of antiquity, published in the Loeb Classics, one of the world's most important heritages: the original Latin or Greek is on the left-hand page, and the English translation on the right. I have all the Loebs, and someone gave me a typed translation of Valerius Maximus, not in Loeb. It's in the ancient sources that one does by far the bulk of one's research, ploughing through Pliny on the rose hip for pages looking for his brief digressions, like the stammering pontifex maximus. From Strabo I learned that the Queen of Bithynia's dog bit her on the bum. The digressions are legion, and form the tiny stitches in one's vast tapestry of events.

One needs insatiable curiosity and infinite patience.

The time line was the most difficult—exactly which year did such-and-such happen? I dug and fossicked and burrowed and scrabbled looking for evidence that would give me dates for this, that, and everything. I found them all, or at least my guess was as educated as anyone else's from Mommsen to Badian.

When I was ready to start writing, my time line was better organized, I think, than any I've ever heard of. I started with a huge concertina-folded block of old-style computer paper, and put the end of it into an Olivetti typewriter that had an old-fashioned roller, easier for this kind of task. One of the most important things was that the paper should never, never tear along its perforations. I wanted the finished product a continuously folded block. On the left side of the sheet was a column for the date: the rest of the line and however many following was for a description of the event—in summary. Working from my assiduously assembled notes, I started typing my block at 110 BC and finished at 27 BC. It took just about the entire block of 500 continuously folded sheets of paper, single-spaced during a description, with a triple-spaced gap between each date for visual clarity. The sheets tended to "walk" as I fed them through; I would have to straighten them every three or four pages. However, the result was neat and clear, date after date after date.

Very well! I had my time line block, but how to display it as I worked on my IBM typewriter? Ric made me an L-shaped device twenty inches wide out of hard, thin board. The IBM typewriter sat on the flat arm of the L; the vertical arm towered behind it. At its top this arm had a long, rubber-sheathed spring clamp. I sat my time line block of computer paper behind the L and fed its first page through a slot at the base of the tall L, then pulled it gently up and held it in place with the clamp. As I finished with a set of dates, I lifted the clamp and pulled more paper through with fresh dates, while the used dates fell down behind the L and were re-pleated even farther back than the original block. I have a very broad work area. So that every time I lifted my gaze from my manuscript, I was looking straight at the relevant dates on my time line. Only at the end of a book did I tear the block at that point, leaving me with seven lots of time line block, still neat, still folded.

Preparing the time line block was indeed a lot of hard work, but the finished product and how it served me was excellent, well worth the labor. It moved onward and upward with far less fuss than a secondary computer would have.

When there were parcels of dates all the same but detailing events in different places, I coded them with highlight markers—red for Anatolia, purple for Rome, and so on.

From 110 BC to 27 BC, I never got my dates confused, and they were there in black-and-white for checking.

Maybe here I should re-emphasize that I eschewed computers entirely for this project. As a scientist, they hold no mysteries for me, but I refuse to trust them with my sweat, my blood or my tears. It's too easy to lose what's in there, and the way my mind works doesn't click with the mind-set of a computer programmer. I would have to write my own programs, and life's too short.

The real trouble with a computer is that it's not dumbly obedient. Even worse, it actually thinks it's smarter. Well, I have news for it …

I woke up with a shock of horror mingled with joy when I realized that in order to do justice to this one man,

Caesar, I would have to write at least five novels, starting before he was born and ending well after he died. Seven, it finally turned out to be. For Caesar embodied a far greater theme than his life: he also embodied the fall of the Roman Republic, a timocratic institution that lasted for 500 years and ended for good and all on the day in 27 BC that the Senate gave Octavianus the title of Augustus. The next 500 years consisted of the Imperium.

By now the year was 1988 and the research had been going on for about ten years. Several key facts had steeled my resolve to write however many books the story demanded. One fact concerned history as it is usually taught: the men it studies tend to spring fully formed onto a country's stage as grown, mature men; a second fact concerned the tendency to study a man or group of men as distinct from the times in which they lived, and from the world that shaped them; and a third fact point out that while a deed of a man may be known, all too often the reason why is a mystery. What I wanted to do was show the world the men lived in, first and foremost; then, trace the progress of these men from infancy to the public stage; and, most importantly of all, attempt to furnish reasons why. Whole academic careers have been made on pondering the reasons behind historical deeds. If I did enough research, I told myself, I too could have a valid stab at the reasons why.

I was ready to go, right down to having decided upon a prose style. It would have to be literate, yet simultaneously project a comfortably modern feel; the Romans of the Republic were a remarkably forward-thinking, forward-looking group of men who would not have couched their speech in a convoluted way. Latin is a crisp language, succinct. And the connective tissue of narrative would have to follow the same rules—neither too colloquial nor too ponderous. *Workmanlike.*

What I lacked was a publisher. I had never been published by any save Harper & Row, a most prestigious New York firm, and, being a creature of habit, I had no plans to transfer to another firm. Unfortunately the start of my writing career coincided with the last of the great editors and the last of the publishing chiefs who saw the book first, and the profit second. Also, as told in the earlier parts of this essay, Harper & Row wanted *Son of TTB.*

I had an interview with the Publisher himself. He was filling in as my editor, and *Creed* had bewildered him. I told him about Caesar and the five books—I didn't dare hint that there might be more. Full of enthusiasm! The first book would be about Gaius Marius. *Who?* The second book would be about Lucius Cornelius Sulla. *Who?* The third book would be about Pompey the Great. Oh! Heard of *him*! The fourth and fifth books would be about Julius Caesar. *Now* we're getting somewhere!

He was an erudite, sophisticated, highly educated man, but as the conversation proceeded I began to see that he didn't have the slightest idea what I was really aiming to do: retell the fall of the Roman Republic in a form that would capture people's interest rather than turn them off. Roman history has an undeserved reputation of dryness, boredom, long-winded speeches and too much law. By 1988 I'd done more than enough research to have learned that for every speech there was a battle, for every law a rebellion of some kind, and for every crisis in Rome there was a war. It was riveting stuff, and the men who peopled it were fascinating.

No, said the Publisher when I had concluded, Harper & Row weren't interested in publishing five novels about ancient Rome, even if Caesar was their hero. However, said he craftily, if I wrote Caesar first in one volume and then followed that up with Pompey the Great, and they were commercially successful, then Harper & Row might see their way clear to publishing Marius and Sulla as—wait for it!—prequels. I was aghast, but had the good sense not to show the depth of my dismay. Once I could speak, I tried to explain that they had to be in temporal order, from earliest to latest, or the history would be lost and the project a travesty.

I ended in flatly refusing to maim my Roman books, and so ended my writing career with Harper & Row. By extraordinary chance, I met Rupert Murdoch on the day I tendered my refusal. Quite unbeknownst to me, Collins, his British publishing firm, had just acquired Harper & Row, which became HarperCollins. After shaking hands with the Great Man and noting that he had a massive cranium not unlike those of Caesar and Cicero, I walked out of the building never to go back; it was the same day Rupert Murdoch walked into it for the first time. What kind of omen is that?

I remember cudgeling my brains as to how I could better have outlined what I needed to do: what the teachers of history did not do, failing to show their students what kind of children or youths the famous men had been. All of us, from Prince Charles through business managers to coal heavers and murderers, are a product not only of our times, but also of our upbringing. Every momentous incident in the life of a five-year-old contributes to what sort of person he or she becomes; as does the success or failure of a first kiss; the unjust beating for an uncommitted sin; some glorious triumph on a sporting field by a child hardly big enough to wield the bat or catch the ball—I could go on, but you know what I mean.

Think of that immortal postscript of Napoleon's to Josephine as he neared Paris and their reunion, always bearing in mind that she was a Creole who loved her bath and her perfumed soap: "P.S. Don't wash." If one wants to know the reason why, look at the Great Man's formative years in a Corsican house that probably had no laid-on water or ablution facilities, surrounded by women who undoubtedly stank of everything from sweat to menses—he was a product of his environment, and adored smelly women.

So too was Caesar a product of his environment, and Pompey the Great, and all the rest. To understand the grown, mature man, it is a great help to know what kind of life he lived as a babe, a child, a youth and a young man. Shrouded in mystery, yet able to be pieced together. Caesar was an Everyman type; growing up in the stew of the Subura would have been a great help in developing this quality, and it would have helped him understand foreign languages too. Whereas Cicero was always conscious of his bumpkin origins, and was an inveterate social climber.

In the end, I realized that I was touting a product nobody would want. Commercial publishing houses would deem the work too scholarly to turn a quick profit, whereas academic publishing houses wouldn't publish fiction by a bestselling writer.

Ric was my only enthusiastic fan, which told me that the Roman books did have popular appeal, at least for men. He's a true critic, in that he says whether or not he likes a work, and waxes more enthusiastic about some books than others. If it's women's fiction, he doesn't like it. But the Roman books? He loves them! No one else did, from agents through to publishers. The world was at best lukewarm. I had tried to explain that they were not designed to turn a quick profit, but that they would always have an ongoing, steady market. Not something publishers want to hear in the third millennium, when a book's shelf life is three months and then it's remaindered. Though, which I find interesting, my books tend to keep selling—small but steady, year after year. What I write doesn't go out of print entirely.

Even more interesting is the number of foreign languages in which I am published—not merely *TTB*, but each book as I write it. I don't know why that is, as my output is so varied. All I can think is that in many countries books continue to be a more important part of life than they are in English.

Carolyn Reidy has been in my life for a long time. She was President of Avon Books, the American paperback house that published me. And she listened. The only problem was, these Roman books were definitely hard cover. The hard cover firm associated with Avon Books was William Morrow, though it leaned toward texts on commerce and finance. Willy-nilly, Morrow were dragged in, complicated by advances that were too big. It's nice to have the money, but paying it back always haunts me, and one can wind up seeing all one's earned royalties debited against unearned royalties on other books. Middlemen are the ones who never lose. Don't be a writer or a publisher: be a literary agent.

Carolyn both understood and believed. I can see no other reason why I had a contract for five Roman books with Morrow and Avon. Not only did she believe; she edited me through *The First Man in Rome* and *The Grass Crown*. What a joy! After some twenty-two books, I have had editors of all kinds, but never one in the same league as Carolyn Reidy— keen, brilliant, merciless, percipient, able to keep the overall picture in her mind even as she dealt with the minutiae. I reveled in being edited by such a professional, someone who was friend as well as the only critic who can ever matter to a writer—one's editor. Other critics see the finished work. One's editor sees the warts, pustules, boils and rashes. And a good editor never suggests how to fix what is wrong, simply points out the faults.

I imagine that Carolyn saw *The Masters of Rome* as I did: not overnight bestsellers, but constant modest sellers for years.

The pity of it was that, as is always true of superlatively gifted people, Carolyn moved onward and upward. I lost not only my best ever editor, but also my support base. Though they were my primary publishers, Morrow disliked the Roman books and did nothing to help each one's progress into print, then their sales force neglected them utterly—why not, when they were interested in selling books on how to make millions on Wall Street?

The First Man in Rome did really well, but before *The Grass Crown* was in print, Carolyn had gone, and things had changed; *The Grass Crown* died. So did the third, *Fortune's Favorites*, though not so badly; of all of them, *The Grass Crown* was the one no one, even the most ardent fans, knew was in print. *Caesar's Women*, about the years Caesar spent inside Rome, did better again, so I looked forward to the fifth and last Roman book under contract to Morrow as able to reach what was a rapidly growing number of fans.

But Morrow was in lemming mood, and determined to wreck whatever chances the fifth Roman book had. Its title had been set in stone for a long time: *Let the Dice Fly*, which was what Caesar said as he crossed the

Rubicon. But Morrow wouldn't have that title. They wanted to call it plain *Caesar*. I argued and battled for months, and let this be a lesson for all aspiring writers: if your publisher takes against a title, they will nag, hector and threaten until the writer gives in. The great argument is always that with the writer's title, the book won't do well, whereas with the publisher's title, it will sell fantastically. And you, the author, thinks of how many other books you want to write, and gives in. Guess what? The publisher's title never does a thing for the book! It would have done quite as well with the author's title. But they have to have their own way, it's a demonstration of power.

So the last Roman book for Morrow came out as *Caesar* in huge letters and, inside on the title page, in small letters, *Let the Dice Fly*. My British Commonwealth publishers left off all mention of *Let the Dice Fly* anywhere, and published it as plain *Caesar*. It did poorly because no one realized it was a new book, so all the progress made with *Caesar's Women* went for nothing, and the volume that saw Caesar conquer Gaul and cross the Rubicon didn't reach its full audience.

Simon & Schuster, which was now Carolyn's firm, took the last two Roman books. *The October Horse*, which deals with the assassination of Caesar, is the best of all the series, but that's hard to say, because they all dovetail so neatly. And the last, of course, was entitled *Antony and Cleopatra*.

But this change of publishers is unfortunate too. The series is split between two houses—houses that have not amalgamated, as well. How am I ever going to see a uniform edition of all seven in a trade paperback size? It's the logical move for *The Masters of Rome* but foiled by circumstances. Were it possible, the books would continue their amble into the far future sure of a small but steady market. The fate I always envisioned.

I can say that with some truth, for since *The Masters of Rome* appeared, Roman history in high schools and universities across the world had found a larger, more enthusiastic student intake. Why did that happen? Because I created a living, striving world correct down to its smallest details; my readers can see how and why men like Caesar and Pompey the Great clashed, why Rome was shaken by a series of civil wars while simultaneously threatened from without by a series of great kings. The best of all books open a new world to the reader, and show it in all its glory and its squalor.

I did all my own maps, by hand. As the books went on, I got better at the mapping, though by *The October Horse* my eyes were failing and the quality went down again. But no one else could have drawn the maps, with their alien names. Some of my editors disliked having maps, but where I'd crumble over a title, I'd never give in over a map.

I gathered photographs of all the ancient portrait busts, and from them drew what look like black-and-white newspaper photographs of Rome's famous men. The busts, bleakly white, with blind bald eyes, were not like that when they were made; they were painted with exquisite attention to detail and color, and looked like a Madame Tussaud waxworks potrait. But with the centuries the paint wore off, leaving us to think this white object was what a Roman saw as he walked around his city. Though my drawings are not in color, they do give the reader a better idea of what Caesar and his contemporaries really looked like.

It took over twenty years to do the research, sometimes having nothing else on hand, at other times squeezing it in whenever I had a free moment, and it went on long after I had started writing the novels. Some women like them, but they appeal far more to men, particularly men of the cloth, men of the courts, and men of the political arena. Some of my fans are famous men in their own right, and from both the far political left and the far political right. That's because, of course, the books deal with politics as a science and an art, and the Romans were past masters at it.

Ric and I went to Turkey, where we hired a minibus, a guide and a driver, and covered 11,000 miles of Anatolia following in the footsteps of Lucullus as he chased Mithridates. We wound up in places no Turk ever visits, let alone tourists, and traveled in the midst of Kurdish troubles; there were seven murders in one remote town near Ararat the night we stayed there, but no one worried us. I add that we came away deeming Asian Turkey the most beautiful country we'd ever seen, and its people the nicest. We saw the pink snow that so terrified Lucullus's soldiers, thinking the gods had stained it with blood: sand from the Sahara. And how stunning the impact of Mount Ararat, white with snow, Little Ararat on its flank. We were in Turkey from mid-April through to the end of May—snow on every mountain, the high passes barely open, the crag of Coracesium rising out of the sea, and lush green grass everywhere. A gorgeous, gorgeous place, especially once we shook off the hordes of leather-coated German tourists who descend on the buffet and leave not a crumb behind. If we saw a promising valley or hilltop, we went there, a marvelous autocracy for tourists. In my "pajama suits" I never offended Muslim sensibilities, though Ric was wolf-whistled by six veiled women in a hotel in Samsun. His face can pass for any Mediterranean nationality, but six-foot-three and a fine physique were more than the ladies could handle, I guess. He smiled at them, and they swooned.

Off the subject of Turkey! I could rave for pages.

Like some statistics about the Roman books?

Three and a half million published words. Given that each book went through at least five drafts, and that I physically typed each one on a typewriter, that's 17,500,000 words. God knows how many carbon and correction ribbons—hundreds, certainly. There were a total of seventy-seven portrait drawings, sixty-four maps, five architectural or other plans, and one table of events.

And, as already said, no computer!

However, I do have a little treasure-trove. I have the originals of all my maps and drawings, apart from a few drawings I have given as gifts. Genuine hand-done work, in my possession. I may be a dying breed, but the satisfaction that one experiences when something is finished is indescribable. *I* did it, not some inanimate assortment of soldered circuitry.

Think what an amazing career I have had!

Twenty-three published works thus far, including one of the greatest bestsellers of all time, and a gargantuan work of true scholarship that even the professional scholars respect. Almost everything I have ever written is still in print. And my books continue to be published in dozens of foreign languages.

At the moment I am writing more Carmine Delmonico whodunits—why? Because I love the genre, and they're both enjoyable and intellectually challenging to write. *Too Many Murders* and *Naked Cruelty* followed *On, Off* and a new one, *The Prodigal Son*, will shortly appear.

I forgot to say that I wrote a cookbook too, for which blame Roger Straus. He was marketing director of Harper & Row while I was still there, and said to me that it was beneath the dignity of a major novelist to write a cookbook. Red rag to old cow! I decided to write a cookbook. I found an elderly vegetarian female friend wondering how she was going to make ends meet in her retirement, and asked her to co-author the cookbook. Her strengths were my weaknesses, and vice versa, so it was an ideal collaboration. The result was called *Cooking with Colleen McCullough and Jean Easthope* and was published in Australia only—all the other publishers chickened out. But the book was well-written and explained many of the mysteries in cooking—what makes bread rise, why the butter has to be cold if you're making pastry, and so on. It did amazingly well, and helped Jean's retirement greatly. I am still being asked to write another cookbook, and who knows? Maybe one day I will.

In the fullness of time, *TTB* will die away into nothing, part of the insubstantial pageant faded. Whereas *The Masters of Rome*, which is a teaching aid as well as a light shone on a different era, will continue. My only unfulfilled ambition? That uniform large-sized edition of all seven volumes.

But not to worry. Time has a habit of solving everything.

The really important thing is that I lived to finish my Roman books. Eat your heart out, Virgil.

List of published works

1974	*Tim*
1977	*The Thorn Birds*
1981	*An Indecent Obsession*
1982	*Cooking with Colleen McCullough and Jean Easthope*
1985	*A Creed for the Third Millennium*
1987	*The Ladies of Missalonghi*
1990	*The First Man in Rome*
1991	*The Grass Crown*
1993	*Fortune's Favourites*
1996	*Caesar's Women*
1997	*Caesar: Let the Dice Fly*
1998	*The Song of Troy*
1998	*Roden Cutler, V.C.*
2000	*Morgan's Run*
2002	*The October Horse*
2003	*The Touch*
2004	*Angel Puss*
2006	*On, Off*
2007	*Antony and Cleopatra*
2008	*The Independence of Miss Mary Bennet*
2009	*Too Many Murders*
2010	*Naked Cruelty*
2011	*Life Without the Boring Bits*
2012	*The Prodigal Son*

ETERNAL STATES

It would seem that, in step with the evolution of the prefrontal cerebral cortex, came Man's terror of dying, and our obsession with the postulated existence of an immortal life commencing when the mortal one here on Earth is over. We break out of our vile and tainted, disgustingly imperfect bodies as out of a chrysalis, to stand forth, exquisite butterfly or foetid cockroach, as an immortal soul.

What is a soul?

Mine is a literal mind, so when I was very young I thought a soul was shaped like the sole of a foot, and was pure white; I even visualized it in motion, undulating up and down like a flat snake through the sea. At about the moment when I might perhaps have transmogrified it into a shimmering, rainbow-hued puff of immortal mist, an old Irish priest told my seven-year-old First Communion class that there was no such thing as evolution. I dismissed the entire religious phenomenon as a load of tired old codswallop, and my interest in the soul perished.

Only relatively recently have I returned to the

contemplation of such things, not really because I now have one foot in the grave and the other on a banana skin; more because in my old age I am allowing myself the luxury of writing essays.

What do I think of a soul today, in my mid seventies?

First of all, that the laws of physics forbid its existence. It doesn't age, or wither, or die. In other words. it is young as well as immortal. Both are impossible states of being when fused into a static package. Leading on from this, as it contains no matter of any kind, the soul must be invisible to every kind of eye, even the eye of a fellow soul. Eyeless in Eternity.

Therefore I do not believe in souls. They are creatures of the imagination conjured up to make dying easier, and should be regarded as a lifelong funeral rite.

That takes care of the immortal soul. Next comes Eternity, which is a state of utter nothingness. In Eternity nothing ever will happen, or ever did happen.

By definition, Eternity is the opposite of Time, the opposite of existence. *Nothingness!*

However, let me suppose that the soul does exist in Eternity. In which case, it must have places to go. There is no point in being alive if there's no place to go, ask any of those dolled-up-to-the-nines young women one sees forming a patient line outside a place to "rave". In my time, raving was something a psychotic maniac did as he swung a bloody axe. Rave, rave, rave. Never mind! Ours is a living language that certainly has an impressive soul. A description that highlights a different meaning for a soul: that divine spark illuminates some human characteristics.

The first rule of an eternal place for souls to go is that it should accommodate only those with similar beliefs, habits and inclinations. This is why each religion varies from all other religions, rather like the pie wedges that septs form in a clan. The faithful flock must be made to feel exclusive, more favored by God than any other favored flock. In fact, most faithful flocks do not believe that any other faithful flocks get a look-in when God strolls around taking a census.

Every religion has a happy place to offer those who live by and obey its tenets, and every religion has an unhappy place for those who do not live by and do not obey its tenets.

Pray pardon me for confining myself to Christianity. I am afraid that I am not conversant enough with other religions to analyze them. The one thing that seems to be common to all religions here on planet Earth is that men invented them and, by and large, still run them. Women may be permitted to be anything from good wives to cattle, but never whole, rounded persons owning fantastically wide educations and running some sort of empire. Which, when one thinks that a man's Y chromosome is really woman's second X with one leg amputated, is hilarious. Though my mother, a truly superlative misanthrope, used to say that men had three legs, growl, snarl, hiss, gnash, roar.

Christianity calls the happy place Heaven.

There are so many Heavens that it's difficult to know where to start—or when to stop. However, the *sine qua non* of any Heaven is perfect happiness, despite the fact that descriptions of what exactly perfect happiness means are thin on the ground—or in the clouds, for that matter. Not helped by exclusivity from creed to creed.

I have this vision of a sky (Heaven is always "up") with one set of Pearly Gates much bigger than all the others, outside which Peter sits at a supercomputer giving the thumbs-up or thumbs-down decision that sends the lucky souls through this outer defence, made of gold and encrusted with gems. Once inside, the souls haplessly wander in search of their Heaven. The red brick gates in a high red brick wall say SEVENTH DAY ADVENTIST and the ones with the Bernini Baldacchino say ROMAN CATHOLIC with, on a signpost headed ATTENTION SCHISMATICS! in smaller script: GREEK ORTHODOX 4 GATES DOWN, RUSSIAN ORTHODOX 37 GATES DOWN, EASTERN RITES 91 GATES DOWN. Other souls have to consult each set of minor Pearly Gates as they come to them under the general heading of HERESIES. Some Protestant sects prefer turnstiles, plain as at sporting venues or designed by luminaries from Eero Saarinen to Christopher Wren. The tartan gates saying PRESBYTERIAN have been boarded up and have a notice attached: CLOSED IN FAVOR OF THE UNITING CHURCH. The Church of England gates are black with gilt detail like the gates of Buckingham Palace; Henry VIII is on duty, chomping his way through haunches of venison while all six wives sigh besottedly, including the two with their heads tucked under their arms.

Rowan Atkinson described Heaven as a place of talking to God, singing in choirs and watering pot plants. A description that comes pretty close to my own idea of what Heaven is like: a very boring place.

Heaven is extremely light on sex, if sex exists at all. One may be joined in it by one's earthly partner, but sex doesn't appear to resume, though the body is young and in tip-top health. Imagine those billions of handsome men sustaining an erection forever, and no sex! Imagine those billions of gorgeous women actually feeling like it, and no sex! It is safe to say that sex is off the menu in any Christian heaven; to Christians, sex is a dirty word. Apropos of one's earthly partner joining one, what happens when the earthly partners have been multiple? Which wife does a husband spend Eternity with? Does it have to be the dumb nurse who worked her buns off to put him through medical school, or can it be the blonde bimbo he married in his sixties and died on top of just before he came?

There doesn't seem to be any food or drink in Heaven either, I presume because of the voluptuous pleasure superb cuisine can give its devourer. In fact, anything that smacks of gratification for the senses is right out in Heaven. Perfect happiness is a state of mind, it doesn't depend upon the senses, so no sex and no fabulous taste thrills. Not even a bottle of Coke or anything else fizzy! I keep thinking of the rapturous look on a little girl's face in Turkey way east of the Euphrates when Ric gave her a handful of candy—now *that* was Heaven!

One thing I know for sure: *God runs a dry operation!* No Glenlivet Scotch or Veuve Clicquot, and, by extension, no kind of recreational substance. Man, just think of it! Finally one lands in a place where there's no such thing as a hangover, and guess what? No intoxicants either!

★ ★ ★

Here may be a good place to introduce the Wowser, pronounced as it is written—wow, sir!—slurred together. The Australians coined it, and I know of no other word to describe the Wowser save terms like "tub-thumper" and the like, but a Wowser can be a Wowser without living a church-bound existence. The word is dying out and it must not be allowed to die out; the species Wowser is anything but dying out. For instance, these days the worst sort of Environmentalist is a Wowser.

The Wowser is a fanatic of a kind. In its old form, the Wowser saw sex as strictly for procreation, wouldn't be in the presence of alcoholic beverages or loose women, ate plain food and used a sheep to mow the grass. Any joke is either dirty or moronic, especially one that offends the obsession: the Wowser sense of humor is vestigial or entirely absent.

The etymology of the word isn't known, nor need it be given a capital letter. Hitler had wowser tendencies.

I ask a pertinent question: *Will there be clothes in Heaven?*

When Michelangelo painted the Sistine frescoes, all the men were—um—well, naked. Then a later pope got the moral heeby-jeebies and ordered that a white cloth be painted over the nether regions of the males, even

253

God's. Adam stayed nude, possibly because his penis is so small it doesn't count. As the pope is infallible, I therefore deduce that in Heaven all men will wear underpants and all women will wear sarongs. The male garment will have to have a little tent sewn into its front to hold the permanent erections comfortably; as Heaven contains perfect happiness, there is no such affliction as lover's balls. Naturally these items of clothing will be dazzlingly white.

Okay! No sex. No food. No drink. No alcohol. No stuff for snorting or shooting up or smoking. White underpants with little tents for men and white sarongs for women. The books will be volumes of sermons and religious treatises and the Bible. No art worth looking at in Heaven, which belongs to the Chocolate Box school. No zoos or zoosters. No pets. No deciduous trees or bushes. No anuses unless they're tucked deep between buttocks. The sun shines eternally, there are no clouds in the sky, and night never falls.

Heaven is all white, with touches of blue and green. All plants are in white plastic pots, and a special process turns potting mix snowy white. Kentia palms are hugely popular, as they don't mind if someone neglects to water them, and the brown bit at the end of a frondlet can be trimmed off with celestial scissors. Rubber plants. African violets. Aspidistras. Ladder ferns. At

Eastertide, potted hyacinths. At Christmastide, potted poinsettias. Potted pot's pots betray their presence by turning a putrid yellow and oozing noisome pus.

There will be music, but choral only, and since Heavenly happiness is perfect, everybody will love the endless repeats of King's College Choir singing Allegri's "Miserere". Handel's "Hallelujah Chorus" will get a colossal bashing, but, alas for poor Beethoven, his Ninth is too pagan to qualify. "Nearer My God to Thee" and "Rock of Ages" and "Onward Christian Soldiers" will be flogged not to death but to eternity. A trillion-name inter-denominational petition to God organized by the Wowsers protesting the bagpipes has resulted in the banning of "Amazing Grace"; the Scots promptly moved en masse into the abandoned premises of the Presbyterians and play "Scotland the Brave" on illicit bagpipes smuggled up from Hell in a haggis.

Heaven does offer special treats. You can be baptized by John the Baptist in person. You can do a brick-by-brick, cobble-by-cobble tour of the Holy Land and be blown up by a suicide bomber, exchanging Christian and Muslim ideas of the perfect happiness awaiting as you fly into bloody little pieces. You can talk to God. You can sing in (some) choirs. You can water pot plants and trim the brown bits off Kentia palms. You can sit somewhere that's simply too, too white with a very sharp knife and keep slashing yourself and watching the blood gush in the perfect happiness of knowing you are not going to die and there's a much-needed touch of crimson in the vicinity. You can take trips to some planet where the ruling species has two heads, or four penises, or propagates by budding; this last is called "Heaven hopping" and is very popular. In fact, you can do what you want, go where you want. Except no sex. No fabulous taste thrills. No intoxicants. White underpants and sarongs. Et cetera, et cetera. You're perfectly happy.

Above the gold and jewel-encrusted Peter's Pearly Gates it says BOREDOM IS BLISS and, below that in smaller script it says WOWSERS WELCOME.

Now I come to the unhappy half of the eternal state.

We may shed this life when we die, but we cannot shed its consequences. If in this life we lied, cheated, stole, foisted other men's children off on our husbands, murdered, indulged in perversions, were lawyers or otherwise offended the tenets of our sex or tribe, we are sent to a place of eternal punishment when our souls stand forth as foetid cockroaches. The generic name for this place is Hell.

In almost all instances, Hell is a seething mass of fire, agonizingly hot. Few indeed are the frozen Hells, probably due to the fact that those being frozen to immortal life go to sleep. Whereas those who burn die screaming every time. Dante wrote of it as layered—like with like. Some, chiefly Catholics of all kinds, have invented a temporary Hell called Purgatory, wherein the agonies are just as bad but have an end, after which the purged soul enters Heaven. Most Protestant Christian sects do not have a Purgatory. Once in Hell, it's for all eternity.

Lucifer the archangel led a revolution in Heaven to topple God, and lost. He was stripped of his beauty, dowered with the most incredible ugliness, and thrown down (Hell is always "down") into a place God created for him—Hell. "Better to rule in Hell than serve in Heaven!" he was reputed to have declared, an angel of his convictions. He is now known as the Devil, or Satan, or Beelzebub, or any of a thousand other names. His best weapon is temptation, but he also brandishes a two-tined, barbed fork, handy for toasting marshmallows. He commands an army of demons and imps. Imps are, I hypothesise, baby demons whose torments are more thoughtless and silly than those of fully mature demons, some of whom spend millennia in diabolical think tanks dreaming up new torments sure to cast the Boss into ecstasies. I mean, it doesn't say anywhere that Satan and his imps and demons don't enjoy their work. One characteristic about the staff of Hell is really interesting: no women imps or demons.

The portals of Hell are el cheapo blow-up gates designed by the same committee who designed blow-up sex dolls. Above them it says ARBEIT MACHT FREI and, in smaller letters, WOWSERS WELCOME.

Satan himself has distinctly Hellenistic pagan elements, as in the Great God Pan. The best visual interpretation of the satanic look is Tim Curry's in a film called *Legend*. Terrific!

Following the tradition of the Christian Heaven, the Christian Hell is an exceedingly boring place.

What is it with Christians, that even their place of eternal punishment is reduced to sameness and monotony? Take a look at a day in the (eternal) life of a soul condemned to Hell. It sleeps in a cockroach-shaped and white-hot coffin, and after passing yet another boring night being smelted with impunity (everyone knows cockroaches will survive anything in the Universe, which makes them carapace-neck-and-snout with lawyers and sharks), it is rudely awakened by a godawful prod from its personal demon's pitchfork.

"What's today's schedule like?" asks the foetid cockroach.

The demon consults a smoking clipboard. "Oh, just the usual, I'm afraid. Flames, flames, and more flames. However, Old Nick does have a weeny treat for you this afternoon. Immersion in a Jacuzzi of lava with Stalin and Gollum."

And that's about it for the Christian Hell. An exceedingly boring place that says beyond a shadow of a doubt that there is nowhere interesting for a Christian soul to go in the next life. So why bother to incorporate a next life into what can be in its finest form an excellent code of ethics for this life? If I am offered my druthers after death, I'll go Julius Caesar's route and opt for an eternal sleep. Many and many are the times when that fate spells a perfect happiness.

Here's my idea of what Hell should be like.

It's a place for satiating the senses, but, this being Eternity, they can never be satisfied.

The liquor is hundred per cent alcohol and is flavored with chili, always chili. It causes an indescribably monumental hangover. The food is delicious, but so much chili is stirred into it that the soul can't taste anything else, this being chili's most irritating characteristic. The menu features Testicles on Toast, Turded Tomatoes, Braised Buttocks, Toe Jam, Dead Dermis Decoction, Pickled Penises, Forced Faeces Fondue, and Seared Scrotums.

Hell's dining rooms are stuffed with souls calling for one more little *wafeur*, and there's a bucket beside each table. The urine is a wonderful vintage, impudent, glandular and just a soupçon banausic—if the chili didn't ruin it.

Sex is freely available, but must be conducted in view of a jeering audience. Another infernal rule permits sex only with virgins, who screech in pain every time the hymen is torn, then sniffle miserably until the act is over. Further infernal rules permit sex in the missionary position only while wearing an inch-thick condom. The virgins are imps in disguise.

There is music in Hell, but it is on speakers that no one can escape, even inside a cockroach-shaped coffin. There is only one tune, Ravel's "Bolero" played on the bagpipes. After Satan discovered that a group of Wowsers smuggled bagpipes Upstairs in a haggis, Ravel's "Bolero" is played at double volume for every last Wowser—and there are billions of them.

The worst—or best—feature of my Hell is its propensity to pick activities for souls that the souls loathe doing. They are, however, varied: marathon runs for fatties whose inner thighs chafe; idle sprawls on sun lounges for workaholics; long ocean voyages in ships without stabilizers for those who get seasick on a mill pond; minding a thousand toddling kids for souls who detest children; permanent barbecue duty for those who hate to cook; and missing the tie-breaking goal for Manchester United playing at home. There are endless possibilities.

Hell is every shade of red plus black and shit-brown. Its chairs make one's bum sore, its tables are either too high or too low, the drawers on its bureaus stick, its beds were designed by Procrustes, and the floor is one heaving mass of cockroaches. It is a hotbed of gossip, if you'll pardon the pun.

"The bastard dobbed me in to Central Headquarters!"

"She sold her sexual favors to Ugh for a new coffin!"

"I saw both of them smarming up to Hitler!"

"Huh, think that's bad? I saw them smarming up to Osama!"

What a wonderful place is Hell!

The Catholics, possibly because they've been going a lot longer, have yet another Eternal State: It's called Limbo.

In Limbo, happiness is *almost* perfect. All it lacks is the presence of God. Now God I can live without. Having to talk to God is surely the most boring aspect of a Christian Heaven; it must be incredibly tedious trying to make conversation with a being so omniscient there's not one flavor of quark he doesn't know because he invented all flavors, threw in spin, and loves popping them in and out of existence. To him, there's nothing fresh to discuss.

In Limbo the Old Boy withholds himself as too exclusive for the inhabitants. That probably means no choirs and no pot plants to water, and it may permit cuddles. It's easy to live without sex, but cuddles are a different matter. I love cuddles.

Limbo is the place for truly good people who don't like the Christian God. Translated into Catholic terms, Limbo-ites are the souls who weren't baptized. In which case, I refuse baptism absolutely. Never happened!

Limbo has a stupendous book library, the Universe's biggest collection of comics, and every film or TV program ever made in its DVD library. It takes a microsecond for the book or disc to appear in one's hand. And its music library boggles the mind, from Bach and Beethoven down to the Beatles and boogie. Music's colors are on full show and the aether is a perfect medium for their transmission.

The weather is whatever you fancy without the damage part; when night falls, the entire Universe is spread across the vault, every star named, every planet known. You can wade through two feet of snow and emerge on a tropical beach. Its plants are all beautiful, its sights, smells, tastes, sounds and sensations a constant joy and pleasure. Pet animals are freely permitted, though not compulsory. In fact, nothing is compulsory, which tells me that Limbo contains no lawyers, politicians, bureaucrats or failed schoolteachers.

The gates of Limbo are anything you want them to be. Above them it says GOOD BUT GODLESS and, below that, WOWSERS NOT WELCOME.

You now know as much as I do about the places where immortal souls go. They all exist in Eternity, a place where nothing happens because nothing exists. Which is tantamount to saying that they live inside our brains and are simply a part of the mechanisms that govern life.

If there was a God, why would it spare so much time on *Homo sapiens*? Are we so important? I cannot think it. If God exists, it made this particular Universe, then moved on. God is not an entity in our meaning of that word. Heaven and Hell are with us on Earth through every second of every minute of every hour of every day. Life is a mixture of both. As Shakespeare said, "Our little life is rounded with a sleep."

POPULATE AND PERISH

No one has any courage these days, and I can't work out why. Is it a genuine blindness to what is happening, or a deliberate closing of the eyes? One issue above all others screams out to be trumpeted far and wide, yet no one has the guts to do it.

The other night I watched a documentary called *Earth*, narrated by a Scots scientist named Iain Stewart. It was better than most of its kind, particularly as Dr. Stewart concentrated upon the physical forces at work making planet Earth what it is. His attitude was unfailingly cheerful as he dealt with the cataclysmic disasters Earth has suffered every few hundreds of millions of years, and that is the proper attitude: not doom and gloom, but the good side of seeing whole living populations wiped out, for only when that occurs can evolution take a giant leap forward to produce different and better (if not bigger) species to replace the vanished.

Easily the most transparent of Dr. Stewart's speculations concerns the species *Homo sapiens*, which he thinks will wipe itself out to be replaced by a new species having a better chance of making a go of living on Earth. And he's happy about it! He's one of the few TV scientists I've encountered with the curiosity and detachment to see Man for what Man actually is—a species breeding itself into extinction.

Even so, ending his hours-long dissertation at the island of Madagascar, Dr. Stewart didn't dare utter The Forbidden, for all that he hinted at it heavily throughout. And I found myself wondering if, as seems likely given the man's pragmatic and lucid Scots temperament, he was firmly told by the financiers of his series that he only got the money to make it if he didn't so much as breathe the word "over-population".

A few years back I flew into Changi airport in Singapore on the first day it reopened after a weeks-long closure due to vast palls of smoke from Indonesia as peasants, in defiance of their central government, burned millions of acres of rainforest to clear it for desperately needed farmland. What must those weeks have been like? I asked myself as my plane touched down in a thick brown fog that reeked of burning organic matter.

Third World peoples don't set fire to millions of acres of rainforest because they're vandals. They do so because there are too many of them to exist on the land already cleared, and as population exponentially rises, the situation grows exponentially worse. Most of the new mouths are either Muslim or Roman Catholic—two massive religions that forbid contraception, let alone abortion. Religions whose administrators and higher-ups think the world too bounteous ever to be threatened by a landslide of human mouths. Or that some frightful plague is sent by God when its cause is over-population. The day of reckoning has actually already passed, but no one will admit it's even on the horizon. The rainforests and other forests go to make room for the new mouths that must be fed, be they burned or bulldozed down. And few of the people who do the felling are trained in conservation or scientific farming, so the topsoil is blown or washed away.

No one speaks of over-population, as if to do so is to utter a blasphemy. No, it is not a blasphemy! It is a fundamental truth so important that all of us should be speaking about it incessantly. *Make* our politicians and religious leaders admit that it exists, rather than pretend there is no such thing. Why won't the world's leaders speak of it? One day, not very far in the future, they will be forced to.

Why won't they speak of it? They are too afraid. Afraid of what? The backlash, among other things—a backlash no one can predict as to size, content, passion. Politicians see a loss of votes. Religious leaders see a loss of worshippers. And the new religion, Environmentalism, has managed to side-step the issue as adroitly as politicians and religious leaders.

In fact, glancing through women's magazines, I would have to say that the true new religion of the Third Millennium in First World countries is having babies. Once upon a time women thought it unfair to the child to have a baby if no father was at least in the vicinity, but nowadays fathers are an unexpected bonus. Babies are the thing, babies and yet more babies. Film stars are doing it, therefore it's the right thing to do.

As Dr. Stewart implies (I daresay he couldn't be frank), there is nothing wrong with planet Earth, and however huge the mess humankind makes of it, within a million years it will recover and return to normal. It's not planet Earth we should be worrying about, says Dr. Stewart. We should be worrying about the species called *Homo sapiens*: Man. What Man is doing to the planet will, given the effluxion of time, correct itself, whereas Man will disappear as if he/she never was.

Why then is Man in such danger of extinction? A propensity to breed like rabbits, in a nutshell. We have extended the life span of individuals by preserving the old from the diseases that used to carry them off, while simultaneously ensuring that the babies we bear survive to adulthood. That alone causes a huge upward curve in the population graph. But to exacerbate it, three-quarters of the people on the planet are religiously prohibited from limiting the size of their families, though when the religious laws were made, families were ravaged by death. An equally huge upward curve in the graph. China, India, Indonesia, Brazil and Mexico have reasonable urban medical care.

As the song says, something's got to give. The trouble is that no people, once introduced to the magical phenomena of automobiles, motor bikes, air conditioning, gas, electricity, a constant supply of pure water, sewerage, houses that don't fall down, glass windows, comfortable beds, plenty of food, flight from one part of the world to another, decent roads, banks, schools, hospitals and entertainment is ever willing to give them up, no matter how much certain people talk of the damage they do to the environment. So fossil fuels will continue to be used until there are none left, the seas will continue to be fished out, and the forests will disappear. How many people know that most ocean fishing is indiscriminate because it's not done to feed people save indirectly? The fish is used to make fertilizer for growing crops because it's natural and rich.

Without the forests to suck up excess carbon dioxide, we will be at the mercy of the first massive volcano eruption as it pours cardon dioxide and hydrogen sulphide into the atmosphere. Add to that, the methane liberated by a melting permafrost in Siberia, and you've got real trouble. Like all the other mass extinctions, Man will snuff out choking not for air but for oxygen. And all those billions will be as if they never were.

The answer isn't in ceasing to burn fossil fuels. The answer is to slash population drastically—one-child families all over this planet for at least six generations or however many it takes to allow the rain forests to grow back and the consumption of fossil energy to die down to a level the atmosphere finds tolerable. Why are we blaming the planet? More importantly, why are we blaming a relative few? The blame lies in over-population.

In our present blind, stubborn refusal to see the truth, we have allowed for only two ways to reduce population: war on a scale more frightful than in all of history, or plague on a scale more frightful than in all of history.

Surely there are people who can see that it's smarter to push for a one-child family than wait for war or plague? In either of those alternatives, humanity will lose vast numbers of its most educated and gifted persons, for neither war nor plague gives tuppence for qualities like intellect, ability, learning or goodness, and the heroic will perish first because they always do. The best will perish along with the worst, and a mass extinction might end in being a blessing.

Fear for humanity, not for the planet. Man is but a tiny hiccup along the planet's way. If humanity extinguishes itself, the wounds it inflicted on the planet will be healed in a million years. The forests will grow back, the oceans de-acidify, the atmosphere be what it should be. And a new species will arise out of the wreckage. A species, one hopes, less masculinely violent, more femininely gentle. A species less prone to be hoodwinked by those awful old men who lead world religions. A species that believes in education for every baby born, that regards every baby born as truly wanted—for the right reasons.

ONE, POTATO, TWO, POTATO

Good evening, ladies and gentlemen!

This is your host, Goliath Ember, speaking to you from the London studios of *One Fiery Ember* for the last time. In a very few minutes we will have ceased to be, without ever knowing why—and that, ladies and gentlemen, just isn't fair.

For the past week the entire world has been frantically talking about the imminent impact of an asteroid code-named MCC with our beloved, defenceless little planet, Earth. Why can nothing be done to avert this looming Armageddon? Science boffins in their thousands have been assaulting the air waves—but the trouble is, ladies and gentlemen, that as far as you, the general public, are concerned, boffins babble gobbledygook. To compound the mystery, no sooner had the Pentagon announced that Earth was doomed, than it disappeared! I ask you: *Where is the Pentagon?* Who stole the Pentagon? How can we do without the Pentagon?

Getting back to the asteroid MCC, the boffins say that it's happening because the magnetic mu is less than one. In which case, why were we taught so much about pi in school? To hear our physics teachers, pi was the root of everything! And one of what, apart from magnets? A pair of old army boots? A bag of jellybeans? Do cows mu? Or is it cats mu?

Oh, enough of these unanswerable questions!

In an attempt to ease your last moments, ladies and gentlemen, I have invited three people to join me and discuss the asteroid MCC on *our* level. They will blow away the pall of dumbfounded ignorance the Pentagon's shock announcement caused to envelop us like a pyroclastic flow—scorching, impenetrable, terrifying, moving at the speed of an express train, able to leap tall buildings in a single bound, out of no—

FEMALE VOICE

Oh, for Crissake, get on with it!

EMBER

As I name you, milord, sir, and doctor, take a bow! Archibald Teazel, Earl of NFA—Sir Stanley Jam-Butty, boss of the Union of Union Bosses—and Dr. Llow Es Cwnwn Denwymnytufydd, my own scientist for the layman. With a name like that, we will call him Thlow.

ONE, POTATO, TWO, POTATO

FEMALE VOICE

Bugger his name! Why aren't there any women?

JAM-BUTTY

We are 52% women, madam, even if there are but 0.00001% women union bosses. If you want women union bosses, I suggest you emigrate to Australia, which runs on women union bosses.

FEMALE VOICE

I mean on your program, numb-nuts!

THLOW

Not at this time of year, Shirley—it is Shirley, isn't it? Indeed and to goodness it is, ha ha ha! In late May, Shirley, the nuts are just forming on the trees, shrubs, or bushes. Numbness is a quality owned by every nut from brazil to hazel—

MILORD

A *nut* is shelling us from outer space?

THLOW

Outer space is a misnomer, milord, ha ha ha! Asteroids come from inner space, look you. Outer space doesn't kick in until beyond the Oort Cloud, which is a region vaster than the entire solar system full of icebergs that turn into comets. Our MCC is a rock, not an iceberg, though its impact will be titanic, ha ha!

EMBER

Gentlemen, please! Milord, MCC is not a nut coming from inner or outer space! It's a whacking great hunk of rock that looks just like a potato.

JAM-BUTTY

A potato? Washed, or unwashed? Goliath Ember, you middle-class parasite, is this just a ploy to sneer at British working men as the Great Unwashed?

EMBER

Washed, Sir Stanley, of course it's washed! There's no soil in inner space to dirty it.

MILORD

We're being shelled by a *clean* potato?

EMBER

Milord, it's a rock! It just looks like a potato.

MILORD

Why would it look like a potato if it's not a potato? I've seen kumeras and yams when I was H.M.'s Governor of East-north-east-east Igololand, but they're cousins of potatoes. Sometimes I saw things I thought were rocks masquerading as potatoes, but they always turned out to be potatoes.

JAM-BUTTY

What else would they turn out to be, you toffee-nosed git? The only shovel you ever laid hands on in your pampered life was silver-plated, so what's with this digging potatoes with potato shovels?

THLOW

Um—ha ha ha! The nut-potato-rock is officially called MCC!

EMBER

Of course it is!

JAM-BUTTY

Think you're fooling me, eh? Don't want to answer the potato shovel charge, eh? Trying to change the thrust of the argument, eh? We're talking about potatoes and shovels here!

THLOW

Sir Stanley, it is a rock. An asteroid code-named MCC originating in the asteroid belt between Mars and Jupiter.

JAM-BUTTY

Oh, Jesus, *whose* belt? Now you're trying to tell me that there are belts out there as well as nuts and washed potatoes! I refuse to be hit by a belt! You can't eat a belt either.

SHIRLEY

Nyah, nyah, can so too eat a belt! A licorice belt!

EMBER

Usher, throw that woman out!

MILFORD

I learned Roman numerals at Eton, and M is one thousand and C is one hundred. Therefore M plus C plus C equals twelve hundred potatoes. Bet you didn't do any Roman numerals at your slimy school, Stan.

EMBER

A thought! MCC is short for the Marylebone Cricket Club!

MILORD

You mean the shell is a cricket ball?

JAM-BUTTY

A cricket ball? Oh, I see what's going on now! So it's an upper-crust rock, is it? Too good to be a potato, eh? And what happened to the potato shovels, Archie, you chinless wonder?

MILORD

They dug potatoes, you Marxist-Leninist layabout!

EMBER

Gentlemen, gentlemen! We are talking about a rock from inner space—not a nut, not a potato, not a belt, licorice or otherwise, and definitely, definitely, definitely not a hard red leather ball with several rows of ecru stitching around its equator! It is a rock code-named MCC, which doesn't mean twelve hundred in Roman numerals or the Marylebone Cricket Club, curse me for saying that! Thlow, what exactly does MCC mean in Pentagon-speak?

THLOW

Massive Collision Catastrophe.

MILORD

What a ruddy silly name for a potato! Potatoes are an American vegetable we name after their Indian tribes. How about Mohawk Cherokee Chippewa?

JAM-BUTTY

What we call them doesn't count. Americans call potatoes after English sovereigns like King Edward. That would make MCC Matilda Charles the First Charles the Second—what a mouthful! Why not call it BAM? Boudicca Arthur Merlin.

MILORD

Merlin was a king-maker, not a king.

JAM-BUTTY

The Earl of Warwick was the king-maker.

MILORD

What, they taught history in your vile and stinking slum school, did they, Stan? Oh, this is boring! When do we get to eat the potato? With lots of melted butter and freshly ground pepper, please.

EMBER

It is not not not not not *not* a potato! It is a rock code-named MCC for Massive Collision Catastrophe.

JAM-BUTTY

On one point we agree, Archie—MCC is boring, even for a potato. BAM for Bloody Awful Mess.

MILORD

How about BEB for Back End of Bus?

JAM-BUTTY

How big is this spud from inner space anyway, Golly?

EMBER

Don't call me Golly! MCC is a rock, Sir Stanley, not a spud, a murphy, a Pontiac or a King Edward!

THLOW

MCC is a mile wide and half a mile long, the Pentagon said.

EMBER

You mean half a mile wide and a mile long, surely.

THLOW

Who says the width has to be less than the length?

ALL CHORUS

Everybody!

THLOW

Then everybody is mistaken. The Pentagon said a mile wide and half a mile long, and the Pentagon is always right.

EMBER

Turn it ninety degrees and it becomes deeper than it is wide, and its hypotenuse will be longer still. Instead of a vertical or horizontal impact, why not a diagonal one?

MILORD

Then, old chap, it can't possibly be a cricket ball. A cricket ball is round and its impact uniform.

EMBER

No one *said* it's a cricket ball! It is a rock that has the misfortune to look just like a potato.

MILORD

Twelve hundred potatoes.

EMBER

Shut up, all of you! Thlow, answer me the burning question—why does MCC look just like a potato?

THLOW

Matilda Charles the First Charles the Second is but one of five billion rocks floating through inner space looking just like potatoes. Inner space is virgin ground. Any farmer knows that the first crop in virgin ground should be potatoes.

MILORD

I prefer Mohawk Cherokee Chippewa.

JAM-BUTTY

Marx's Communist Creation is better.

THLOW

I vote for Matilda Charles the First Charles the Second.

EMBER

And I am not voting for the Marylebone Cricket Club! It's a Massive Collision Catastrophe.

JAM-BUTTY

What is that racket? Sounds like a gigantic potato whizzing through the air—what are these black grains? Yum! Freshly ground pepper!

MILORD

It's raining melted butter!

THLOW

Smells delicious for a rock.

JAM-BUTTY

Well, this is one disaster we can blame C per cent on the Americans—it's their sodding vegetable.

THLOW

Tuber.

JAM-BUTTY

I don't play a musical instrument, you Welsh idiot!

MILORD

Mashed by mashed.

EMBER

And farewell from *One Fiery Ember*!

Creepy sci-fi music starts as a gargantuan, swirling cloud of dust and smoke envelops the set of *One Fiery Ember*. The camera lifts and lifts, higher, higher, until the whole planet is revealed as a ball of smoke. Hovering on a hawser anchored to the Moon is the Pentagon, which gives a mighty shudder and is exposed as a Klingon Vulture warship. The dust and smoke is being dissipated by an enormous fan protruding from the Vulture's beak. Earth looks much as always—no visible damage. It can now be seen that the epicentre of the impact was London. All the city's old-style, majestic buildings have survived unscathed, whereas every single socialist monstrosity from the Millennium Dome to the anal suppository glass skyscraper has vanished, replaced by gracious old-style buildings, squares and parks. A weeny Klingon fighter is skywriting KLINGONS LOVE PRINCE CHARLES! and PRICK ALL BLOW-UP BUILDINGS!

The camera zooms in on the old *One Fiery Ember* studio, and the sci-fi music diminishes as there comes the unmistakable sound of reconstituting molecules. Two shimmering cylinders form into two Klingons.

KARK and KACK stand hock-deep in mashed potato alongside the corpse of Shirley, a potato pillar with a severely Doric capital. Their phasers are in their hands and set to "stun", but they are quite relaxed.

KARK

You really have to poise your fingers on your forehead wrinkles when it comes to potatoes, Kack.

KACK

Well, Captain Kark, the potato is the best thing the Americans ever gave to the Universe—I mean, we all love turkeys and hamburgers and Imperial measure, but the potato is in a class all on its own. Didn't they teach you about the Great Potato Famine of Kling in your school? I know it was five parsecs ago and you come from Kikstarkikik, but so many Klingons died.

KARK

During my school years on Kikstarkikik, the Famine was utterly eclipsed by the Great Potato Plethora and all the revelations about the graft behind el cheapo blow-up buildings and just whose rectum formed the mould for that frightful rash of anal suppository looking skyscrapers—if it hadn't been for his chronic haemorrhoids, President Klok—say no more!

KACK

I had quite forgotten, Captain. We've been lucky to find a vacant space in this solar system. Fancy the Romulans pinching the green cheese planet Gorgonzola! I heard it turned out to be the wrong shade of green.

KARK

De-phylled their chlorphyll, the fools. Ah, but who could forget towing all those potatoes through hyperspace to make a belt—I ask you, a *belt*? I was a midshipman grade zee-double-zee, and it was my job to keep the tow lines from tangling every time an earwig ate a worm hole. Five billion potatoes! All to make a belt? We midshipmen petitioned Admiral Kork to make a beaded jerkin with ice moon buttons and cloud moonlet detail, but his answer was to chuck us into Jupiter's Great Red Spot. Man, those methane gales! I came out with six extra wrinkles on my forehead. Sexy and pulls the women, I admit, but a pain in the koxkilliuk to keep clean. That's how come I invented Wrinklean. I'm rich from the royalties.

KACK

Do you know why the King of Kling is so set on exterminating Earthlings, Captain?

KARK

They have to go, Kack. They don't even know the difference between a potato and a rock, Kack.

KACK

Or a nut, or a belt, or a Kriket ball.

KARK

I heard it was a licorce belt.

Comes the sound of more reassembling molecules. Two Earthlings form to triumphant sci-fi music. Their phasers are set to "kill" and KARK and KACK go up in smoke. As the air clears, it can be seen that one is a genuine Earthling, whereas the other has pointy ears and the green skin that denotes chlorophyll blood.

KIRK

Goddam Klingons! Scratch the surface of a planet, and it'll bleed Klingons. I note from that potato-smothered lot over there that this planet was populated by Earthlings. Unusual, this far out from Centre Black Hole, but we are a bit like potatoes—proliferate profusely. Have you managed to squeeze Gorgonzola back into place,

Spock? Amazing how much space, inner or outer, a potato can eat. However, our luck that the Romulans mistook Gorgonzola's type of green.

SPOCK

A trifle too much blue, Captain Kirk. It required a millionth power of manoeuvring to fit Gorgonzola in, which has somewhat depleted the dilithium crystals. However, I then found a warehouse stuffed with lithium capsules and dyed them a beautiful shade of peacock—blue in one light, green in another. The response of the impulse engines is remarkable, and Mr. Scott assures me that the warp engines will benefit even more. We have inadvertently put the dilithium mining monopoly on Xaspryxasix out of business.

KIRK

Boo-hoo! Time those heartless exploiters of astral navies got their comeuppance. What did you do with five billion potatoes?

SPOCK

Beamed them to Xaspryxasix to plug up the dilithium mine adits. I took my example from observing potato earwigs plug up worm holes.

KIRK

Then let's split, Splock! Places to go, things to do. A *belt* made of potatoes? I would have made a beaded jerkin with ice moons for buttons and cloud moonlet detail. No imagination, Klingons.

SPOCK

Oh, Jim, how can you say that? The Klingon who dreamed up a Vulture disguised as the Pentagon was inspired. I *adored* it!

KIRK

What are you doing, feeling emotions?

SPOCK

Um—ah—er—gee, Jim, I don't know!

KIRK

I do, you Klingon in disguise!

Kirk's phaser jets a red ray and Spock goes up in smoke. A beam of molecules appears and turns into Mr. Sulu.

SULU

Captain, that's the third potato you've zapped today.

KIRK

That was no potato! That was a Klingon masquerading as Mr. Spock.

SULU

They're growing potatoes in all sorts of shapes, sizes and colors these days, Captain. It was a potato.

KIRK

It was a Klingon masquerading as Spock!

SULU

Who am I, then?

KIRK

Mr. Sulu, navigator of the starship *Enterprise*.

SULU

I am not Mr. Sulu. I am Matilda Charles the First Charles the Second, a potato.

KIRK

You mean Mohawk Cherokee Chippewa.

SULU

That's the name of the potato you keep calling Uhura.

KIRK

I'm the only Earthling here?

SULU

You, Captain, are a potato named the Marylebone Cricket Club, and we are all living on Gorgonzola, the green cheese planet. It lies between Mars, solid rock, and Jupiter, a gas giant, and its gooey yet substantial composition represents a transition between solid and gas. Green cheese. Unfortunately the Romulans thought its microbes were symbiotic with their chlorphyll and would provide the "O" their blood lacks, but they were wrong. It stripped the phyll and left them chlor, poor souls. The only way out was mass suicide.

KIRK

I'm hungry. What's for dinner?

SULU

Mashed marble, roast granite and steamed geodes, all in a lava sauce.

KIRK

Is the granite well done?

SULU

Not a trace of pink, I swear it on a stack of baubles.

KIRK

Okay, I believe you. I hate underdone rock, it's too—potatoey.

SULU

Now come along, Marylebone, old fellow. If you don't get a move on, the sun will fry you into a rock that looks just like a potato.

KIRK

Is that why I don't like underdone? Cannibalism?

SULU

Only if you take to eating earwigs.

ON WOOD AND WARS

Northern hemisphere woodpiles fascinate me, all those perfectly round little foot-long logs stacked in an open porch or against an outside wall, covered by a tarpaulin in case it rains hard. Basically it's indulgence wood for a fireplace; something wonderful to look at while the central heating does the real work.

It wasn't like that in the Australian Outback seventy years ago. The places wherein we lived could suffer stunning frosts in winter, but it was never cold enough for sleet, let alone snow. Our wood was for the kitchen stove, a big, black, cast-iron beast that had to burn every day, no matter how scorchingly hot that day might be. The stove cooked all the meals, baked the bread, kept a two-gallon cast-iron kettle boiling to brew many cups of tea. Coffee was unheard of except as a small square bottle of black syrup labeled CAMP ESSENCE OF COFFEE AND CHICORY that Nanna mixed with boiling milk for a treat.

On Mondays the copper had to be lit; it was a huge, round-bottomed cauldron of copper sheeting mounted on bricks, under which sat a firebox, and it held about twenty gallons of water that had to be heated to boiling point. In it, our mother, Laurie, and our grandmother, Nanna, boiled the sheets, towels, men's trousers and shirts. It was situated down at the end of the backyard, where there was room for the cat's cradle of clotheslines. Not that this was really a backyard. It was simply a cleared open space wherein dwelled the outhouse, the laundry, the clotheslines, the wood heap, the woodpiles, and the woodshed.

The wood for burning came from living trees and was chosen carefully, as all Australian wood seemed as hard as rock. When the Europeans first arrived, they couldn't saw it or chop it. What they had called hardwood was a sponge by comparison. The great pity was that softwood did not exist, thus there was no locally made paper until the cultivation of vast coniferous forests began after the First World War, and then the wait for maturation was decades long.

The wood heap, where all the chopping was done, lay at the foot of the yard in close proximity to the ramshackle shed in which sat the copper and two big tin tubs, plus shelves stacked with little bricks of soap; Nanna made her own. The laundry's water wasn't drawn from the house tanks. It came from the bore drain, was undrinkably hard, and made the washing stiff—clean, but stiff. The wood heap itself was a rough circle about twelve feet in diameter, its floor deep in wood chips too hard ever to rot into humus. In the middle of the chips sat several chopping blocks of various heights; the main one was a huge old tree still rooted in the earth. Its top was defaced by fissures and missing bits, but it never seemed to wear out.

Beyond the wood heap reared two different mountains of logs: one consisted of the raw product carted from the paddocks, and the other of the chunks prepared for the woodshed but too green and sappy yet to burn. Both piles weathered as they sat there awaiting the attention of a family axe; saws were reserved for across-the-bole sectioning to a uniform length—more or less. The family men were awesome with an axe; chopping built muscles even harder than the wood.

The woodshed was on the verge of the wood heap, positioned so that Laurie and Nanna could get wood from it for either the laundry copper or the kitchen stove. They shifted it in an old pram—a baby buggy. The woodshed's framework was disused bits of building timber—four-by-twos or six-by-twos made no matter. Once the frame was up, sheets of corrugated galvanized iron were nailed over it. The result wasn't pretty: some sheets were bent, some buckled, some raggedly cut; but for a woodshed, they'd do.

The wood was stacked inside as neatly as such deformed and misshapen pieces could be, rising up to the roof in each row. The entrance was in the middle of one long side, and all the rows of wood came down to this person-sized gap.

It wasn't as dark inside the woodshed as one might inagine. Thin blue rays filled with dizzily dancing dust fingered out of old nail holes, and a huge golden mist of light radiated from the middle entrance. The rows of wood around this central space had been pillaged first, sitting in steps and stairs made comfy by big hessian sacks, put there in case it rained heavily enough to leak through the old nail holes—a rare event.

If one were inside it, the woodshed held an exquisite peace, quite why is beyond all but the conscious thought of an infant. The wood itself was vividly colored—pinks, reds, rust-browns, oranges, bright yellows, like a Turner sunset. Spiders spun webs, wispy and silvery, slater beetles spilled from under a chunk when it was moved, and the shadows were full of mystery. It vibrated as if on the verge of giving voice to a glorious note.

Lazy people chopped the foot-long segments of log dragged in from the paddocks as they needed them, but that entailed a permanent enslavement to the woodpiles. My family cut the wood ready for the stove or copper twice a year, leaving Laurie and Nanna with only two chores: fetching the day's wood from the woodshed, and chopping kindling out of fruit crates, soft drink boxes, inch-thick slabs of bark. The wood chips from around the chopping blocks were handy too, but soon ran out. As for paper—all we had was the daily newspaper, scarcely sufficient.

The first feminine job of the day was to use the still-glowing embers in the kitchen stove firebox to generate a fresh fire, feeding it kindling until it would "catch" a standard chunk. This would not have been possible were it not that these irregular pieces were smothered in vicious splinters the size of skewers; it was the splinters caught first, transmitted their purgatory to the iron of heartwood. Once the fire was going, the great cast-iron kettle was dragged across the plates until it was right above the flames striking like fiery cobras into the vestibule between the firebox and the stove's surface. There it boiled quickly; breakfast was not breakfast without many cups of scalding, treacle-black tea, the bushman's eternal pick-me-up.

Our mother, Laurie, and our father, Jim, hated each other. That is no exaggeration. In fact, some lexicographer should have coined a new word capable of carrying hatred to unheard-of heights; then it might have fitted Laurie and Jim. Never since I left childhood and "home" behind have I encountered such festering poison as filled the very air around Laurie and Jim. In computer-animated films, there is an occasional character whose head is wreathed is weird lightning; well, the moment Laurie and Jim were together in the same room, that weird lightning played a fantastic lacework around their heads.

As toddlers it numbed our senses, filled us with a panic that, if the battle raged on, led to blind terror. We were not old enough to know what was happening, especially once the terror consumed us. This time our world was sure to end, though even that was a logical thought we probably couldn't have fathomed. How does one describe horrified, terrified, blind panic in very small children?

We did understand one concrete thing: the woodshed. Carl and I would flee to the woodshed, the one place we knew no one would ever think to look for us. And there, clutching each other, howling until the tears and snot near suffocated us, hearts like roaring drums in our ears, shivering and shuddering in awful fear, we waited for the end of all things.

He was such a dear little chap, Carl. Nearly sixteen months younger than I, he was mine to protect, console, shelter, comfort, soothe. I was Carl's big sister, a job I took very seriously, and at no time was my job more important than when Laurie and Jim went to war.

The memories flood back: of Carl's silky little nut under my cheek, of his baby's feet in their red shoes set close together, of his tiny hands hanging desperately onto mine. The first time we found the woodshed, panicked out of whatever reason toddlers have, it was to reach a secure haven in the teeth of pursuing monsters too unspeakable to conceptualize; we crossed a chasm into a foreign land, and were safe.

Of course one can't cry forever, just as the worst battle in a marital war can't last forever. At long last Carl and I would cease our frenzied crying, huddle together on a pile of hessian sacks, and go to sleep. In the house, the exchange of hostilities would peter out until Laurie, in noisy tears, would lock Jim out of their bedroom, and Jim cycled off to the local pub to drink with his mates and heap curses on the heads of all women. Not that he was a drunk. Jim was an expert at leaving just before it was his turn to buy a round.

And Nanna, our gentle grandmother, would sneak to the woodshed and get us out of it before Laurie knew where we were. Nanna never betrayed our bolt-hole. Hers was the laundry.

I can still see the woodshed when I close my eyes: those thin blue rays, the golden mist, silver whiskers of spider web all over alluring crannies, dotted with the deadly black bodies having red stripes down their backs. Odd, that neither Carl nor I was ever bitten. The mosaic of brilliantly colored wood. I can still smell the acrid tang of damp hardwood, the musky aroma of slaters, the mouldy stench of hessian bags.

Though what I see and smell is a combination of a dozen and more woodsheds; we never stayed long in one place.

Nor did Jim stay long. Suffering from battle fatigue, I imagine, he was off to North Queensland and the sugar cane again within six months. Laurie alone wasn't exactly any child's idea of a joyous, attentive mother, but at least there was no Jim to light her fuse.

I wonder what tiny children do for a woodshed if they live in an apartment building? Do they survive, do you think?

JIM

If to call a man "Dad" or "Pa" or "Pop" is to have a father, then I didn't have a father. The man who fathered me was named James—always Jim for short—and to this day I think of him as "Jim." No one in the family, including my mother, Laurie, ever referred to Jim as Dad or Daddy either directly to me or in my hearing, so it was quite natural that I called this relative stranger Jim, the same as everybody else did. Jim never voiced any objection, or asked me to call him Dad. When my brother, Carl, arrived nearly sixteen months after me, he called our father Jim too. Our earliest memories revolved around Jim's physical appearance rather than his personality: his shoes were so huge we spoke of them as "boats" and used to gape up at him with necks craning, he was so immensely tall. Had the Empire State Building paid us visits, I think our reaction would have been much the same.

Like my essay on my mother, "Laurie", which should be read after "Jim", there won't be a strict chronology or even logic to this. The core emotions are not

303

involved because love never entered our perceptions of our father; that awesome skyscraper metaphor has been thoughtfully chosen.

Setting me aside for a moment, Jim never seemed to have any of that inexplicable pride makes a man dote on his son even if he has scant regard for his daughter. Apparently Jim despised his son as a weakling and a—his word—poofter, though Carl was neither. His grounds for doing so? That Carl elected to stay in high school after he could legally have left, that he went to university, that he "wasted" himself by teaching mentally retarded children. As far as Jim was concerned, the mentally retarded were a group of human beings who should be sent to the gas ovens. To Jim, Josef Stalin was the greatest man who ever lived. I suspect he admired Hitler too, but wasn't game to say so. Jim could never see the point of spending public moneys on the kinds of people who showed no useful dividends. Be a person mentally retarded or a drug addict, send 'em to the gas ovens!

The fact that Jim's son was a champion cricketer and field hockey player did not impress the man who had been, in his time, a British Empire cross-country running gold medallist. I add that Jim never contributed a penny to his children's educations, and that the allowance he paid to our mother was as small as it was grudging. Carl and I survived on full scholarships; we also worked during our school vacations as soon as we looked old enough to pass for the working age.

Laurie always held some kind of job, and we had one of those wonderful backups, a resident grandmother we called Nanna.

Laurie's family, a large collection of bachelor brothers, lived with us off and on, and we knew them by yet another strange twist of nomenclature: Tom, Harry, Walter and the rest were just that, never prefaced by the word "Uncle".

Whereas Jim was the only member of his family we ever knew. Both parents were secretive; trying to find out information about either of them was nigh impossible, but at this juncture I will report what I know about James Joseph McCullough before he became an unwilling husband and father.

Jim's family were Orange Ulstermen, imported to Northern Ireland from whichever of Scotland's two Uist Islands was the Protestant one to fight the Irish in William and Mary's time, and they had lived in Belfast ever since. On two or three occasions Jim described the kind of place Belfast was during his childhood and youth: machine-gun fire was so common that on hearing it, pedestrians automatically dived for the ground. The Black and Tans happened. It must have been a fascinating and dangerous existence, but Jim refused to expand upon it. Talking of it seemed to make him edgy.

His father was a foreman in a linen mill, and sired four boys and one girl before a mill explosion blew his side out and he spent however much longer he lived lying on a couch. Jim's mother was Welsh, by name of Hughes—I don't know her first name—and, I gather, a formidable woman who voted dozens of times in the Belfast elections and could add up the grocer's bill quicker and more accurately upside down than the grocer could the right way up. The whole neighborhood was terrified of her. With her husband immobilized (I suspect the mill management wriggled out of paying any compensation—that was the usual story of the time) she dragooned the only girl into becoming her unpaid skivvy, and opened a boarding house for men.

John, the eldest, stayed in Belfast. The other three boys emigrated. Jim's favorite brother, Robert, settled in Durban, South Africa, and one made his home somewhere in North America. Jim (born in 1903) chose the continent in between, Australia. He liked the Outback, where he worked as a station hand, which is very interesting: a city boy, and from a violent city at that, must have been remarkably adaptable to learn rural pursuits from riding a horse to shearing a sheep.

It says he was intelligent, and that his cleverness was well organized.

One of the most intriguing facets of his character was his addiction to extremely hard physical labor. As a result, he was never out of a job, and was, besides, all things to all men; when not being prodded by Laurie's pitchfork or his children's betrayal of his Communist ideals, he was the most charming fellow one could possibly meet.

A stunning-looking man, Jim. Six foot three inches tall, he had a whippy physique and long, very muscular legs; his height was in those amazing legs, which certainly indicated that he might have been a champion long distance runner. His hair, brows and lush lashes were jet black, but his eyes were a startling blue that contained no trace of brown or yellow. Widely set and well opened, they had a permanent look of innocence. By anyone's standards his face was strikingly handsome; he even had one of those noses people are always asking plastic surgeons to give them—the correct term, I think, is retroussé. His nose is one of the few things I inherited from him, but I also inherited his height, five foot ten, and towered over Laurie, at five foot two. How she hated being towered over!

Jim had a picture of his mother—what happened to it I do not know—that revealed one of the most beautiful faces I have ever seen. She had the same black hair and light eyes—blue, I presume. Such a pity there were no color photographs! Perhaps here I can slip in the fact that she died untimely. An undiagnosed diabetic, she broke her leg when she was in her early fifties and suffered the inevitable fate of the Belfast poor, be they Green or Orange: the tissue became gangrenous, and killed her. Jim was broken hearted, it seems mostly because he had never gotten home to see her after he left at twenty-one.

I have no idea how Jim and Laurie met, though I should hasten to say that I did call my mother "Mum"—it simply seems more appropriate in these reminiscences to call her by her given name too. I always liked the sound of it, its look on paper.

From her photos, Laurie was an ordinary young woman, except, I gather, for a mass of wonderful red-gold hair. But her nose was far too big, her mouth liplessly thin, and her expression had worn itself into permanent discontent even as a child. She was thin and flat-chested, but she did have excellent legs, all of which endowed her with the kind of figure young flappers of the 1920s sighed for. Not that Laurie was a flapper. Anything but.

The middle child of a large family, all Laurie's siblings were brothers. Some were older, some younger. She seems to have been spoiled rotten, and my sensitive nose sniffs a hint of Electra in the family. She was deeply attached to her father, who was so possessive of her that he refused to let her take a job. She was still living at home well into her twenties when, somewhere, she met Jim, who I gather was the most desirable young man in the district—at least to look at. His penniless situation was patent to all, but Laurie wasn't sensible enough to incorporate financial prosperity into a marital equation. A man of thirty, his looks and hard-to-catch reputation were sufficient for the twenty-four-year-old Laurie, who would have known of his reputation as a hard worker and presumed this meant they would get on in the world.

Jim probably felt that it was time to settle down, become a family man; that his eye fell upon Laurie is logical for one like him. What he saw was an only girl with heaps of brothers, an inexperienced virgin who had been kept at home to act as the servant of a family of men. An unpaid skivvy just like his own sister in Belfast. Ideal! he would have concluded. A wife who was already broken in as a slave to men, and who would therefore never stand up to him or defy him.

Alas for Jim! He couldn't have been more wrong if he had tried. He married Laurie in 1932 and they went to North Queensland on their honeymoon, 1,500 miles from Laurie's home. Jim was thinking about cutting sugar cane, by far the highest paid of all manual labor. Irresistible!

But when he treated Laurie as a quasi-person without rights of any kind, Laurie returned to live with her own family.

Just how things were during those early years I have no idea; no child was ever more ignorant of the prelude to her genesis than I. Where it happened, how it happened, why it happened—all complete mysteries, since some years had elapsed between marriage and my conception. What I do know is that they never seemed to have lived together, set up house together. Jim spent his time cutting sugar cane in North Queensland while Laurie lived with her own people.

Whatever the answer, Jim must have managed to do the deed around about September of 1936, when Mrs. Wallis Warfield Simpson's grasp on the new king, Edward VIII, was tightening fast, as I was born on June 1st, 1937, under the reign of a different king, George VI. From various remarks Laurie made over the decades, it seems she loathed the sexual act. Perhaps, then, around the New Year of 1938, Jim managed to get her tiddly; Carl was born on September 23rd, 1938. And I suspect that was the end of any voluntary sex on Laurie's part—if there ever had been genuinely voluntary sex at all.

* * *

Though Jim made occasional visits, they continued not to live together through all the sugar cane years—1932 until 1950, when Jim, pockets bulging, retired from the sugar. By this time we had moved to Sydney and were living in a house Laurie's brothers bought, though it was put in Jim's name on the condition that it pass to Carl. This ownership was, so to speak, Jim's fee for permitting the brothers to live with Laurie and Nanna. The brothers had all been soldiers during World War II, whereas Jim took the rural dispensation and didn't fight; to have done so, Jim was always ready to explain, would have meant the abrogation of his Communist ideals.

I wish I knew under what circumstances Jim retired and took up residence in Laurie's bed, but the truth is that I just cannot remember. Save that the Woodshed Wars of our infancy now became the Death Duel— whoever of them, Jim or Laurie, died first, lost the war, and that war mattered to both of them more than we did.

The war involved a lot of bedroom juggling in which I was the perpetual pawn, as mine was the only feminine room in a masculine house. After Laurie broke me and Carl up, Nanna occupied the other bed in my room— until Jim came home for good. At once Nanna received her own room on the glassed-in back verandah and was moved out of my room. Laurie moved out of Jim's bed and in with me. Jim imported a niece from Belfast, moved Laurie back to his bed, and put the niece in with me. Laurie evicted the poor girl, moved out of Jim's bed and back in with me. Every so often Jim would literally order Laurie back into his bed; she would go for a couple of weeks, then she'd be back in with me. Over and over. If I could have laughed, I would have called it a game of musical beds, but I couldn't laugh. Sharing my room with Laurie was unspeakable; whatever tiny bit of privacy I had was shaken and worried like a terrier with a rat, but to understand it properly, my readers will have to plough through "Laurie"—here is not the place to talk about Laurie at length. Apart from the terrible permanent exposure of every aspect of my home life to my mother, she had a habit of waking in the middle of the night to sit bolt upright in her bed and scream, scream, scream. A nightmare, she would explain. From the quality of those awful screams, a vision of Hell, more like.

What kind of man was Jim?

Very intelligent but not a scrap intellectual, he detested all persons of true learning; possession of a university degree turned anyone into an enemy. Politics obsessed him, he could talk about little else, though his poor education made him an ignoramus. His politics were of that peculiar kind that profess ardent Communism, yet simultaneously he managed to reconcile them with his private, voracious appetite for wealth. Everything in the world should be equally divided among working men— except, that is, for his own secret pile. It was as if the two hemispheres of his brain were a Communist one and a capitalist one, and some neurosurgeon's knife had separated all connection between them, thus allowing both of them to exist in a happy state of absolute non-communication. That what results is sheer hypocrisy seems never to occur to people like Jim. He would vote a socialist government into power, then "fiddle" his income tax returns to cheat it; after which he would walk the floor in a frenzy of fear in case he was caught. I suspect a great deal of the fear over being caught was because, were he, the hypocrite would stand forth revealed for all his Marxist-Leninist friends to see.

Jim was very shrewd in business matters. Though it was a side of him I never saw, he could charm the birds down out of the trees, his personality was so beguiling, so fetching. He could sweet-talk his elderly women clients into spending far more than they had intended: this was after he went into business as a master plasterer-cum-renovator of old houses. His little firm—he was too stingy to expand—specialized in the houses of the wealthy. How he spoke to us of his clients I am too embarrassed to recount. Suffice it to say that I didn't like being this unashamed and dreadful hypocrite's blood daughter. The saving grace is that a bad example, if appalling enough, can be a good example. I'd sooner die than behave like Jim.

Jim danced superbly well, no matter what kind of dancing was stipulated: Irish tap, Scots reels and flings, the Russian where they dance on their haunches, Fred Astaire ballroom, and more. In Jim, it was easy to see that the Belfast of his time was a mighty port city that saw all nationalities. He played the poor man's musical instruments: ukelele, accordion, spoons, a saw, any kind of drum you can name. His singing voice was baritone and beautiful, whether he was tackling old laments or a flapper song of the 1920s. So he must have loved music and been very musical. The trouble is that Laurie hated his "performances" as she termed them, so I don't know enough to make a judgement.

Jim the miser. Money ruled him absolutely, I can say that with complete assurance. He loved it. Unfortunately once it came into his possession he was never willing to part with it, and he loved no human being the way he loved money. Laurie's housekeeping allowance was a sum calculated down to the last quarter-pound of margarine; we should not be eating butter, or expensive cuts of meat. Let the brothers pay for it. I suspect that they did, too much and too often. I remember those hundreds upon hundreds upon hundreds of evening meals, the apparently amicable conversations between Jim and whichever brothers were there, and wonder now, looking back, how the brothers ever managed to be so pleasant to the free-loading master of the house, between his ravings about capitalist empires and the oppressed masses. Jim looked down a long, narrow tunnel all his life.

The school leaving age was fourteen years and ten months, and from the day I attained it, Jim nagged me mercilessly to leave school and find a job. I was a big person, but muscular rather than jelly-obese, so his recommendations were always that I should do hard labor for a living. It didn't impress him at all that I was head of my class; I think he felt that space occupied by brain matter was wasted. Besides, I used to cut him down to size occasionally during those hundreds of mealtime conversations, and I could do it wittily. Jim didn't like me.

The Nobel Prize laureate Linus Pauling published a textbook of general chemistry for high school students. It appeared in Sydney at the beginning of 1953, and I thirsted for a copy. On glossy paper, it was profusely illustrated, and so much easier to understand than the dismal textbooks available in Sydney back then. It cost a huge amount—£5—and for that you could buy a Bluebird portable typewriter. I girded my loins and asked Jim to lend me £5 until the next school vacation rolled around and I could work and pay him back. His answer was no.

"I've said it before and I'll say it again—get out and get a job as a mangle hand in a laundry. That's all you're good for—you'll never get a husband, you're too big and fat and ugly."

I was fifteen years old, and I was staying at school if it killed me. Education, I knew, was my only passport out of Jim's and Laurie's horrible world. My uncle Walter lent me the £5—I paid him back—and when my mother gave me £5 to buy my last ever family-funded winter overcoat, I used the money to buy a Bluebird portable typewriter. I wasn't very popular in that quarter either, and had to wear my school blazer until I could afford to pay for my own overcoat. But the Linus Pauling chemistry book and the Bluebird portable typewriter were, in their way, open sesames to careers. Nor did I ever subscribe to the palest pink of all socialist creeds: listening to Jim rant convinced me that no one helps save those who help themselves. I prefer to earn my own way than be grateful to some government for doling out what other people earned. Jim wouldn't even pay his taxes gladly.

By the time the second request for a loan happened, I was living in London, and Carl was away on a long journey of discovery and exploration to Greece, Crete, eventually Israel. Cut cruelly short in Crete, where Carl died rescuing some women from a Mediterranean rip-tide.

We had twenty-four hours to find $8,000 to bring Carl's body home for burial. There were too few uncles left to scrape up so much so quickly, I had nothing, and certainly Laurie didn't have it. Jim did. His business was thriving and he was diddling the tax man with a clear conscience, as the government was a Tory one. His fear of banks had led him to a huge wooden box Laurie called The Thing; it lived under his bed and contained every penny he owned. Many, many thousands.

He refused to pay to have his son shipped home.

"Sentimental rot!" said the admirer of Joe Stalin. "The boy's dead, what the hell does it matter where the body is?"

Carl stayed in Crete, and we lost his body for eight years.

I saw Jim later on, in between England and my taking up residence in Connecticut. Though I don't remember the incident at all, it appears that I physically attacked him, so fiercely that I drove him out of the house into the backyard, yelling abuse at him. He managed to break free of me and ran for his life. Knowing Jim, it's likely that he didn't understand why I went for him.

He continued to live with Laurie, each occupying a bedroom, and they continued to have their screaming matches. His greatest delight, I heard later, was to inform Laurie that she and I would never see his money. He had an innate mistrust of banks, as I have said above; every note of what he had seems to have resided in The Thing. In about 1971 he sold his half share of his renovation business for a lot of money— around half a million, he announced, but that may have been a boast. I don't know.

Literally never having had a day's illness in his life, Jim died in his sleep on the cusp of his seventy-first year, 1973.

Six weeks earlier he had gone to a local doctor— not the family one, who was a Hungarian Jew and therefore anathema to the Jew-hating Jim. Apropos of which, why don't people like Jim seem to comprehend that Marx and Engels were both Jews? To the best of my knowledge, in all his life Jim's exposure to Jews of any kind was minimal, limited perhaps to some of his elderly lady renovation clients; they paid him what he asked without a murmur if Laurie reported his talk aright. No, anti-semitism seems to be a part of the Communist package, certainly as far as Jim was concerned. But I digress.

He had had a pain in his chest, he told the doctor, but upon examination the G.P. could find nothing except an hypertrophy of the heart in keeping with Jim's athleticism. Things like blood cholesterol weren't in a doctor's repertoire in 1973; Jim was given a clean bill of health.

"Hah!" snorted Jim. "I'm positive my bitch of a wife is putting poison in my dinner."

When Laurie found him dead in his bed, she called the doctor Jim had seen. This medical gentleman rushed to the house, viewed the corpse in bewilderment, announced that he wasn't going to sign a death certificate, and phoned the police. When several arrived, he explained that Jim had told him he suspected his wife was poisoning him, and that Jim's death was inexplicable. The next thing, there were police everywhere, Laurie was being questioned, and last night's dinner was going into an evidence container for analysis, along with various edibles from fridge and cupboards.

I had just received a $2,000 advance for my first novel, *Tim*; now I had to fly from Connecticut to Sydney in order to sort out Jim's death. I spent the lot, plus several hundred more, and sighed wistfully for the things I had originally planned to buy with that advance.

There were fascinating mysteries. First and foremost, The Thing had disappeared from under Jim's bed. It had absolutely vanished into the blue, never to be seen again. He had no will, and was presumed to have died intestate. His bank denied having the deeds to the house; his account held a princely $457.

I commissioned a lawyer to find the house deeds, which magically turned up at the mere mention of a lawyer. Jim's name had been rather clumsily altered on them, which prompted the legal gentleman to tell me that this kind of thing happened when intestacy reared its head: the deeds would disappear for months, sometimes years, before the person whose name had been forged on them arrived to claim his property. One of the odd penalties for very inexperienced persons like uneducated widows inheriting the house they lived in. Widows who never thought of commissioning a lawyer. I add that the house had skyrocketed in value since it had been bought in 1949.

My lawyer tidied everything up, Laurie got the deeds to the house, and Jim's $457 went toward his obsequies.

The doorbell kept ringing. When Laurie answered these tintinnabulations, it was to find a stranger or strangers asking to see Mrs. McCullough, as they wished to pay their condolences.

"I'm Mrs. McCullough," Laurie would say.

"No, you're not," the stranger or strangers would say.

Eventually it became

"Am so!"

and

"Are not!"

until it resembled a *Monty Python* sketch after four arguments with four different strangers as to the identity of Mrs. McCullough.

One condoling stranger grew quite hot under the collar, vehemently denying Laurie's right to the title, and describing a much younger, prettier woman.

So by the time I reached Sydney, Laurie was a suspect in all sorts of ways. Jim's body was still in the custody of the New South Wales Coroner; now here were Sydney's eastern suburbs stuffed with Mrs. McCulloughs! After forty-one years of marriage, perhaps the only crime Laurie never accused Jim of was bigamy.

Collaborating with my uncle Tom, a man with a great sense of humor, and in between rolling on the floor with laughter, we worked out that Jim had a different girlfriend for every social club he patronized, and always introduced the lady on his arm as his wife. Who knows how many Mrs. McCulloughs there are, or how many of them he may actually have kept as a wife out of the largesse reposing inside The Thing? For that matter, which Mrs. McCullough inherited custody of The Thing, and what instinct or presentiment prompted Jim to hand custody of The Thing over?

By the time Jim was released for burial, I was back at Yale. All suspicions of Laurie's conspiring to cause Jim's death had been quashed, and I was, to tell the truth, underfoot.

Laurie had Jim cremated, I am convinced so that she would have his last remains firmly in her hands. What did she do with the ashes? I never asked, but knowing Laurie, she flushed them down the toilet, quietly cheering as she did so. The reality of Jim's going would not have impacted until later.

Jim died in 1973. Laurie died in 2005. She won the war by the comfortable margin of thirty-two years.

Her verdict on Jim's enviably peaceful death: "He should have died of cancer of the tongue!"

But for that statement's full effect, you'd have to hear her say it. On paper, so anaemic; it lacks the hiss, the ineffable shock of being articulated through clenched teeth …

If I put all that in a book, no one would believe it.

LAURIE

A dear friend of mine says that I am the most rational person he has ever known. If I can approach this subject with equanimity, it is solely because of that rationalism. One has to be able to sit back and see others for what they really are. I believe that the study of others is the only route to knowledge of oneself, and detachment allied with analysis are the proper tools. But can one stay aloof from core emotions? Let us find out.

Laurie was my mother. I know very little about her background or personal circumstances, and have had to piece the jigsaw together more from the bits that are missing than any that I found. Complicated by the fact that I don't know what is true, and what a tissue of lies. So my rule of thumb has been that if I heard an item from all the members of the family, it was the truth, and if from Laurie alone, there was a good chance a part at least was lies.

Her name, Laurie, is a Scottish one, and rarely bestowed in 1908, when she was born in Ashburton, a village in the south island of New Zealand. As best I know, in her met the English of her mother's stock and the Irish-Scots of her father's.

Many Highland Scots are Catholic, natural in supporters of the Young Pretender, Bonnie Prince Charlie; like Welsh Catholics, they tended to emigrate to the Antipodes rather than to North America. And Laurie's father's Catholicism was of the Scots kind, less dominated by the priests. Laurie's mother was staunch Church of England, and remained so. From which I gather that religion was not an important part of family life.

Laurie had a large number of brothers, some older than her and some younger, but no sisters. Her mother, whom I will call Nanna, had nine living children from twelve pregnancies—a somewhat better average than was common.

The children's coloring veered wildly between black hair and black eyes (Nanna) and golden-red hair and blue eyes (father). From the few photographs I've seen, they were not handsome: big and bumpy noses, small, thin, bitter mouths, round heads and faces on what appear shortish, stocky bodies; all staring at the camera with the huge and frightened eyes of trapped animals.

They were poor. Laurie told me that her eldest brother, Spence, was a bastard Nanna had brought into the union with her; Laurie had discovered

Spence's birth certificate while snooping through Nanna's things: father not stated, date two years before her marriage. I remember the terror Uncle Spence inspired in me when I was a small child—he exuded an air of violence, drank heavily, and beat up his many women, upon whom he battered shamelessly. He was a professional boxer, and a good one.

I told a lot of the early years, thinly disguised, in *The Thorn Birds*: how my grandfather's enormously rich sister had brought him and his family to Australia to work for her and inherit her possessions. But the charming Catholic priest paid court to her, and when she died, she left everything to the Catholic Church. In real life, the family was thrown off the property without a penny's compensation, and that was the end of it. What happened to the priest, I do not know.

Therefore I'm finished with the subject. It wasn't one of Laurie's confabulations because the whole family spoke of it and fulminated; there were too many "Auntie Mary" stories to allow fiction, yarns around the dinner table when the men got going on old Auntie Mary and the priest. And one fact is very certain: I got a great book out of family reminiscences!

The dispossessed family continued their lives of impoverished station hands, moving from property to property around the west of New South Wales. They must have been as good at their jobs as they were hardworking, could sow and harvest crops as expertly as deal with the grazing of livestock. Their pride was colossal; through the years of the Great Depression, they never took the government dole, at times subsisting on pumpkin.

As a child Laurie was atrociously spoiled, the apple of her father's eye. No matter what the family went short of, Laurie was the last to suffer. Her only claim to beauty was a dense mane of red-gold hair that her father insisted she wear flowing loose, carefully brushed into a series of sausage-like curls pulled back from her face by a big bow of taffeta ribbon. Her Sunday-best dress, from those photographs, was finished with expensive lace.

School bored her. She was never a good scholar at anything save reading; history, geography and arithmetic went unlearned. At fifteen she left, wanting to train as a nurse, but her father refused to let her. Laurie was a lady, and nursing was not a job for a lady. In fact, ladies didn't have jobs. They stayed at home until they married. His refusal didn't go down well, and Laurie was no doormat. In retaliation, she cut off her hair in a bob or shingle—very short indeed. Her father (I don't know his first name) openly wept, but wouldn't change his mind; Laurie stayed at home. Truth to tell—Laurie so often didn't—the hair wasn't cut over nursing, though it certainly was cut. Nanna confirmed the fact. From the few remarks Laurie made to me about her long hair, she hated it.

Around the middle of the 1920s the men secured a longstanding agrarian job, and were to stay in it for many years. So they rented a house in the nearby town for Nanna and Laurie, better accommodation by far than station housing.

Oh, this is boring stuff! I can only imagine how it irked the restless, adventurous spirit dwelling inside Laurie, hungry to travel, to see the world, to have money in her purse.

She did have a feral intelligence, undisciplined and crafty, but it wasn't allied to an ability to reason. By that, I mean that she never saw the consequences of her actions bearing down, even scant seconds away from impact. When they hit, she behaved as if they had nothing to do with her.

As Laurie wasn't beaten as a child, I can only think that she caught the habit of lying from the terror that went with witnessing her father take his belt to one of her brothers. No kind of lie was unknown to her, from the flat take-it-or-leave-it statement to the most tortuous tapestry of confabulations, but unfortunately she tended to forget her lies. Her husband, Jim, who never forgot anything, was adept at catching her out, and even I, as a small child, once asked her why she bothered to lie if she couldn't keep her story straight. My legs smarted for a week. How dared I!

The snooping must have started early too. Insatiable curiosity, I suppose, but when that curiosity gets one into shocking trouble, surely it's time to stop? Not Laurie! If someone got a letter, Laurie would find a way to read it. If a bank book wasn't carried on the person, Laurie would find it and blab the balance. If bills went unpaid, Laurie would be the first to know. A compulsive eavesdropper, she could sense the brewing of a private conversation miles away, and zoom! she'd be there hiding out of sight, ears straining.

Twice at least her snooping led to hideous family ructions of the sort that never really heal, though Laurie always remained unshakably convinced that her conduct had been impeccable.

Her eldest full brother, Jack, became engaged to be married to a woman from a different district; the family didn't know Joyce, which was her name. So Joyce came to visit. Laurie's father and Nanna were appalled to see a vulgar slattern with bad teeth and a beer drinker's belly. A snooping Laurie found the letter Joyce was writing to her own family, and produced it triumphantly. There was a screaming row that didn't end as Laurie had confidently expected it would, in Jack's breaking off his engagement. No, Jack took Joyce's part! Years were to elapse before the breach was patched up. Carl and I grew up ignorant of this brother's existence, and never knew we had three male cousins.

The second ruction was of a fairly similar nature, though it happened decades later, when we were living in Sydney and I was about fourteen years old. We had built Nanna a little room of her own on the back verandah and I had looked forward to having my own space—studying in that house was very difficult. But Nanna's bed hadn't grown cold before Laurie moved out of Jim's bed and into my room. There was still powder in Jim's magazine: he promptly produced a niece from Belfast, who was immigrating and needed a place to stay. Back to Jim's bed went Laurie while Cousin May moved into Nanna's bed.

From what I remember, May was a nice girl who used to sit at the dressing-table and lay on makeup with a trowel, which I thought a pity; her skin was beautiful. The poor girl must have been reeling, straight off the boat and into a pot of Laurie's venom. I was the hapless ham in the sandwich, though I am sure I didn't take May's side. By age fourteen, I knew better than to annoy Laurie. Therefore let this be a belated beg-pardon to May—little did she know.

Of course Laurie snooped and found a half written letter from May to her family in Belfast. It was predictably full of unkind remarks about Laurie (and me, no doubt)—well-deserved remarks. The next thing, May was gone. To, I devoutly hope, a happier environment. The vacant bed wasn't cold before Laurie was back in it; Jim had lost yet another battle in the war. As usual, I was collateral damage. I'd rather have shared with May than Laurie, but what I really yearned for was a room of my own. It's no fun to be a bluestocking in a family of jockstraps.

At some point in Laurie's late teens, one brother died in a terrible accident, and not long after, another of the sons died tragically. Then when Laurie turned twenty-one, her father died.

All dreams of an independent life and career were abandoned; Laurie had to stay home and help Nanna. It is probably to this period that Laurie's little jobs belong. There seem to have been a number of them, usually as a receptionist or a clerk, but they never lasted much longer than a week. What I know was gleaned from remarks Laurie made to me during the years when she shared my room, remarks that revolved around unjust dismissals or employers who refused to pay her. One or two such incidents I might have believed, but Laurie recounted a dozen and more. My theory is that she didn't perform her jobs well enough, and was fired. This was certainly true of the jobs she held during my teens, only one of which lasted for any length of time; it consisted of packaging goods in a mail order firm.

Apart from Spence—long gone to a world of boxing and razor gangs in Sydney—and Jack—married to the execrable Joyce and living far away—Laurie seems to have been the only one who hankered for a wider, freer existence.

She continued to cling to the dream of the spinster nurse, talked of its independent power, respectable income, opportunities to go anywhere in the world. Many and many's the time Carl and I heard her perpetual lament: how a husband and children tie a woman down to a life of drudgery with no thanks, and of how she should have been a nurse.

Yet Laurie behaved very strangely for someone who pictured herself a nurse.

If either Carl or I said we felt sick on the stomach, she locked the nauseated one in the bathroom with a bowl until the vomiting was done; then, heaving and gagging, she covered the bowl with a cloth and rushed it to the outhouse. The only time I ever threw up on the floor, she gave me a bucket of sand, a dust pan to use as a scoop, and a bucket of soapy water with a rag in it. Then she left me to clean up the mess myself. I was five years old. She wasn't being deliberately cruel; she simply couldn't bear cleaning up bodily messes.

The dream of becoming a nurse was just that: a dream. Laurie would not have lasted a single day on a ward, especially in the 1920s and 1930s, when nurses were slushies for the first two years of their three-year training period. In fact, I think it is possible that Laurie did start training as a nurse, only to quit because of the messes and the dragons of ward charge nurses.

Most of Laurie's lies were told to conceal her own shortcomings and make herself look really good. It makes no sense that a doting father would have refused to let Laurie go nursing, which was an eminently desirable career for a girl, including ladies. It does make sense, however, that having discovered how unlike her dreams the reality was, Laurie turned her dead father into the villain of the piece.

And Nanna, you ask? What did Nanna have to say? Nanna said absolutely nothing to contradict even Laurie's most outrageous lies. In the end I decided that Nanna had learned her lesson years before I was born, and let Laurie weave her own destruction. I do know that Nanna was extremely afraid of her. The poor old woman was doomed to spend the rest of her life with Laurie, and realized that the only way to survive was not to provoke Laurie in any way. I never remember Nanna as anything but white-haired and wrinkled in the face, but I remember her with great affection. If Carl or I had done something sure to irritate Laurie, we went to Nanna for help; if we'd wet our pants or gotten dirty, we could go to Nanna sure that the wet pants or filthy clothing would be smuggled away and never mentioned. I loved Nanna, but it was never an intimate affection; Nanna didn't hug or kiss or cuddle. To us as children, she was just there, another part of Laurie's furniture.

In her old age she fell down a grease pit in a garage and broke her pelvis. She never fully recovered. Maybe it isn't wrong to say that as far as Laurie was concerned, Nanna had outlived her usefulness: I was seventeen, Carl sixteen when it happened. So her bachelor sons put her in a nursing home and visited her literally every day for years. Nanna loved being in the nursing home; she had her own room and an enviable stream of visitors. She was 101 when she died. I was in Connecticut.

Laurie was a reader who devoured women's magazines and many kinds of novels, particularly those that chronicled exotic events in exotic places. It was an era of sequels; Laurie would wait eagerly for the next one in a serles. Her reading habits were developed independently of the great bodice-rippers; I never remember her speaking of Ethel M. Dell or Elinor Glyn. An Australian writer named Thwaites was her favorite, but the books she read as a child stayed with her as long as she lived: *Little Women, Seven Little Australians* and *East Lynne* were spoken of constantly. A voracious reader when I was a child, I tried to get her interested in historical novels, but she scorned them as too full of men's doings.

Her bodily figure was the perfect one for her time: flat-chested, skinny, and good legs. Passionately fond of clothes, she lusted after a fur so hungrily that her brothers shot dozens of rabbits, tanned the best skins, and had a rabbit fur coat made for their sister. The only makeup she wore was a face powder famous in its day; her almost lipless mouth didn't look enticing when lipsticked. I can still see her pounding away at her nose with a thin velvet puff; someone must have told her that if a nose was in the least bit shiny, it looked bigger. She hated her nose, large and bumpy. Perhaps significantly, her favorite colors were all the browns and beiges through to cream. Vibrant, vivid or delicate colors she detested. Into which intrudes one curious aberration: when Carl and I were toddlers, she dressed us in brilliant scarlet-red, an absolute no-no at that time. The hours I've wasted trying to figure that out!

I haven't said anything about her temper. It was bad but not hot—filthy-mean, Carl called it—the sort of bad temper people wake up in rather than due to the day's events. So the day took on the hue of her bad temper, no matter how potentially good its events were. Grudges she held forever, blown up out of all proportion to the original offence, and she inflated tiny faults into major flaws.

Carl was wonderful with her. No one else ever found the key to the door inside Laurie's mind that shut away happiness, joy, gales of laughter. Once he grew into adolescence he stumbled upon the key, I suppose; once he had it in his grasp, he never let it go. He would sneak up behind Laurie and untie her apron strings whenever her mood was filthy-mean. She'd snap, bark, tie it up again. He'd untie it. This went on until she was ropeable, at which stage he would pull clownish, woebegone faces at her. Finally she would begin to laugh, grab the wooden spoon and chase him. Leading her dances all over the place, he'd go on laughing at her and pulling those faces, she by now breathless with laughter too, until her mood magically blossomed into real happiness. But he was the only one could ever do it.

★ ★ ★

Irrational. Bad tempered. A compulsive liar. An incurable snoop. Ambitious. Vain. Grudge-cherishing. Self-important. Not very bright intellectually. Egocentric. Dictatorial in the extreme. They were the qualities she showed to her family.

Ah, but she was different with outsiders, who universally thought her charming. The change was immediate; let someone other than a family member appear, and she was all over them in her anxiety to please, to have them think well of her. Laurie was the quintessential street angel and house devil, which made it quite impossible for Carl or me to convince people she was a monster. She must have known how thin the veneer was, however, for she never invited strangers or even the neighbors into her house, and Carl and I were forbidden to bring other kids home. That was a rule we dared not break. Of course it meant we were strictly forbidden to go to another kid's house. Until Carl grew into a crack sportsman and I into a scholar in a library, our lives outside of school hours were spent friendless. The other boys and girls couldn't work it out and we could offer no reason that satisfied them.

Pray pardon the digression. Things don't always belong in chronological order.

One might say she wasn't a nice person, yet Laurie must have had assets, character traits that were admirable and fine. Part of her trouble was that her hatreds and resentments drained her of the energy to be nice to those whom she knew too well and saw as anchors, as intolerable burdens: her family.

Physically fearless, she was a natural athlete, a first-class tennis player who yearned to try golf. There's a clue in that: instead of throwing heart and soul into what she did have, Laurie always wanted something she couldn't have. It seems that if she had worked at it, she would have been a champion tennis player—but no, she wanted to be a golfer, economically out of her reach. Her brothers, who all lived their bachelor lives under her roof, didn't help by calling women's tennis the "hit and giggle club".

Sometimes she could think on her feet, save a person from peril just because she had no ability to pause and reason things out. She neither smoked cigarettes nor drank alcohol. Her addiction was to the "cuppa"—tea—which she drank strong enough to look black and without milk or sugar. She despised tea bags as weak apologies for the real thing.

People had a habit of dying in her arms. These strange creatures do exist, and Laurie was one such. In that role she was perfect—tender, compassionate, exquisitely easing away the terror of a looming unknown. I do not exaggerate when I say that there were about a dozen women and men who died in Laurie's arms, and they fared better than most of us do when comes the moment to die.

She did have a sense of humor, strait-laced sexually and set at liberty only by those she considered funny— Carl and her youngest brother, Tom. And one could wind up on the right side of her occasionally for the oddest of reasons: if to champion me, for instance, meant unpleasantness and discomfort for someone she loathed, then Laurie the champion was there at my side.

That Carl and I managed to stay at school wasn't really due to our full scholarships. We were there because Laurie knew how much it irritated Jim to see his children still in school once they attained the age to leave. It would be delightful to think our brilliance pleased either parent, but the truth is far more complicated. No parent relishes being intellectually out-classed by the children.

Laurie loved dogs and cats. As a child she had a pet pig named Midget that wore its trotters down finding her after the family moved. For Laurie's sake I wish that story had had a happier ending, but it seems Midget ended up roast pork. I feel that a great deal of the mountain of love that must have been tamped down inside Laurie was expended on pet dogs and pet cats. Pet animals were no threat to her. I particularly remember a Persian cat named—what else?—Fluffy, as cerebrally stupid as bred animals are but an ideal lap cat. Laurie would spend her "sit-down" time combing Fluffy as it purred on her knees; she carefully collected every strand of its long hair for years, and when it died, she stuffed the hair into a specially made felt cushion that she wouldn't be parted from.

Back now to Laurie at the age of twenty-four, a spoiled young lady shut inside a cage and desperate to try her wings.

That she elected marriage was inevitable. It represented the only escape from her cage. In Jim, she could congratulate herself that she had "caught" the local heart-throb, swooningly handsome and enviably tall. When it came to money he was no catch whatsoever, but by her mid-twenties Laurie had learned that the rich young men of the district married rich young women. If Laurie had been beautiful … But, alas, she wasn't.

Though it is a pure guess, I believe the marriage foundered on the honeymoon, spent 1,500 miles from home in North Queensland. The abysmally ignorant Laurie discovered the phenomenon of sexual intercourse. Not only did she loathe it: she feared it.

Nor was Jim the right man to put in time and effort in persuading his new wife that the act could be wonderful. All too often in 1932 (the year they were married) young women were so sheltered and sexually uneducated that the honeymoon became a horror story. There was no television; motion pictures held one fully clothed kiss; and a book was called "spicy" if the heroine palpitated with something called desire.

The maturing flow of hormones is greatly helped by exposure to the hinterland of sex at least, a thousand-and-one modern aids to sexual readiness that we don't even think of, yet that Laurie's generation plain didn't have. The modern person may object that Laurie was a country girl, inured to rutting animals, and with many brothers sure to talk. But it wasn't like that. Laurie was never let go near rutting animals, while her brothers were so shy and sexually inhibited themselves that, except for Jack and Spence, they never had girlfriends, remaining lifelong bachelors. Sniff if you must, you skeptics, but I do assure you that was Laurie's environment. She tried to bring me up in the same way, but I was a scholar not to be intimidated; with Carl she succeeded better, for he was naturally shy, a quiet person.

Silent, dour Nanna seems to have been no help. She even neglected to tell Laurie about menstruation;

why then would Nanna have broken the habits of a lifetime to tell Laurie what she was in for? Apparently she did not.

What happened on the honeymoon was rape. In those days it was quite a frequent occurrence. Exasperated by refusals to be let touch, have a feel—even look—the new husband finally resorted to forcible possession. He never equated what he did with rape, an act he continued to deplore. A wife was a legal belonging and had taken solemn vows to yield up her body. In 1932 whatever money a wife had passed automatically to him unless some other provision had been made; she couldn't borrow money in her own name, or, if unmarried, obtain a mortgage.

That was Laurie's world. The seeds of her hatred of Jim were sown; so was her horror of the sexual act.

To add to Laurie's woes, Jim was an inveterate miser. He put her to work as a house cleaner in North Queensland, collected her pay himself, and gave her a tiny allowance of the sort she had to itemize down to the price of anything she bought. Before he gave her the next instaliment, she had to produce proof that she had no money left—and God help her if she spent foolishly. Her cleaning job included her accommodation; Jim had begun to cut sugar cane and lived in barracks, so he pocketed almost every penny they earned.

With logic on her side for once, Laurie quit Queensland to go home to Nanna and the brothers.

Jim visited from time to time, apparently paying Laurie an allowance that didn't demand receipts; the brothers must have said something. She was down in mood and eating very little; when, nearly five years after her marriage, she learned that she was pregnant, she ate even less.

I was born on June 1st, 1937, a runt who weighed less than five pounds. For the first three months of my life I starved because the milkless Laurie insisted on breast-feeding me; she had read in some magazine that babies had to be breast-fed, and that was that. Nanna told her she didn't have any milk, but Laurie turned a deaf ear. Luckily the local midwife was more aggressive, and threatened to have Laurie declared an unfit mother unless she put me on a bottle. From then on, I thrived. Whether because of the milk fiasco or because I was a girl, Laurie conceived a dislike of me.

Nearly as thin as a concentration camp victim and still anorexic, Laurie went into a second pregnancy. Carl was born on September 23rd, 1938, almost sixteen months after me. He too weighed less than five pounds, but went straight on to a bottle, and thrived from the beginning.

Laurie didn't like pain, so I've wondered if she starved herself to have small babies, thus making childbirth easier. If she did, it didn't work. Carl and I were both very long labors with forceps deliveries. My theory is that Laurie made labor worse by fighting against it rather than going with it, but I don't know. With Laurie, that is my perpetual plaint: I don't *know*.

She was never loath to tell me that all she ever wanted was a baby boy with hair so blond it was white, the bluest of blue eyes, and tiny little ears set close to his head. In Carl she got it all, even the ears. By sheer willpower, I am utterly convinced; even God would not have dared gainsay her. Deeming me a failed attempt, she had vowed to do it once more, and get it right. After that, no more sex. Laurie had exactly what she wanted at last.

We received our names in the oddest way. Though both are ethnic, ethnicity didn't enter into it. It was war to the teeth as usual when I was born; Jim wanted to call me Margaretta, while Laurie wanted Patricia. Neither would bend. Finally Nanna produced a book of names and suggested that I be called by the first name that meant "female." That was Colleen, the Erse for girl. When Carl was born, the same duel flourished anew; Jim wanted Robert, Laurie wanted Dallas. So Nanna produced the book of names. Carl is Swedish for "male".

★ ★ ★

There were two critical illnesses that I know of.

The first took place when I was about four, a pneumonia (statistically the great killer before antibiotics) that saw Nanna spreading gooey, dark grey poultices on Laurie's chest and back. I was old enough to understand that she was dying, a strange, horrible notion all tangled up with whispers, threats about making noise, trying to find a corner to hide in. Jim wasn't there. But she recovered.

The second was mysterious, and occurred when I was about six. As best I can reconstruct events, Laurie was in Sydney at the time, though we weren't living there; something extremely unusual must have transpired to cause Laurie to journey to the big city without her children. After surgical removal of her reproductive organs in toto, she hovered on the brink of death for weeks. Nanna took Carl and me to Sydney and we stayed at the People's Palace, a hostelry for the impoverished not far from the main rail station. Jim was there; I have memories of him and Nanna conversing in hushed voices, and of an effigy in a bed in a dimly lit room, not a ward.

When Laurie told me about menstruation it was gruffly, her tone unemotional: once a month all women bled for several days, she said. Nanna hadn't breathed a word about it to her, so when her own menses appeared, she thought she was dying. A nun at her school had explained. Therefore, growled Laurie to me, she had sworn that if she had a daughter, that daughter would know in advance about the bleeding. I was eleven: two years were to go by before my turn came.

Then she tacked on a curious sequel. Her own periods, she said, had been such a torment that she had known something was wrong, and sought a gynaecologist. As our region didn't have one, she set off to Sydney, where she couldn't find one either. Eventually someone gave her the name of a gynaecologist in practice five miles from Liverpool rail station.

In 1943 Liverpool was the very outermost of all Sydney's suburbs, famous chiefly for its massive army camp: this latter function helped me fathom the mystery later on, as it happened. Liverpool's streets were not tar-sealed, nor was Liverpool yet sewered. And, said Laurie, she had no money, so she walked from the train station. The gynaecologist saw her and said she had fibroids, but made no arrangements. So she started to walk back to the train station down the dirt road, five miles in blistering heat for a second time. Halfway there she haemorrhaged.

Why she bothered telling me all this I have absolutely no idea; it was a classic Laurie lie. Even knowing that much, I had no answer until years after I left home. The incident had been long buried far below consciousness when something occurred to trigger recollection. Suddenly the lie made sense. Even in 1943 (the worst year of World War II for Australians) one didn't find a Sydney gynaecologist at the end of five miles of dirt road in Liverpool. What one found was a gigantic army camp—and an abortionist. Laurie was seeking an abortion.

Poor wretched woman! As if I were present, I could see a stunned Laurie realizing she was pregnant, and vowing to be rid of this unwanted child. Being Laurie, she shifted heaven and earth to find an abortionist, and did—exactly where one would have lurked. It was a shocking crime in 1943. In Laurie's world of puritanical hellfire, everything that ever happened to her afterward was retribution.

What Jim thought, I have no way of guessing beyond the little giveaways a mostly absent father betrayed. He was not Catholic and he was certainly a miser, but somehow I cannot see him as the *deus ex machina* of Laurie's abortion. That smacks of Laurie, of her mad dashes onto the rocks of her own follies. Poor husband material though he was, he would not have left her to take that walk alone and without a penny beyond the £5 an abortion would have cost. No, it was Laurie.

I wonder what that third child might have been like?

Thanks to Laurie's idiocies, Carl and I had terrible illnesses as children.

When I was three and Carl two, Laurie decided she was moving to Sydney and living on what Jim sent her from Queensland. The only house she could afford to rent was in a Sydney slum suburb; she justified it by declaring that it was on a tram line and very near a shopping centre. The place oozed filth. At night Carl and I were smothered in huge cockroaches. If a cockroach appears in my house to this day, I move out. That is not an exaggeration. I have a pathological dread of cockroaches. There were rats too, but they confined their perambulations to the floor, maybe why I have never minded rats.

The Sydney sojourn didn't last long. The Phoney War was becoming the real War with a vengeance, most of the brothers had enlisted and gone to fight Rommel in North Africa; Nanna needed company. Jim didn't enlist. None of the men was obliged to join up as they worked on the land, but the brothers were fiercely patriotic; Jim was a dedicated Communist—but that belongs to his story, also in this collection.

Laurie returned to Nanna with a mortally ill son. Carl had contracted several critical diseases at one and the same moment, including rheumatic fever and gastroenteritis. Though he shook them off, his health was never robust as a child, and his first growth spurt didn't happen until his eighteenth year. That awful house was to blame, with its rats and cockroaches; had he been exposed to that kind of environment earlier he might have developed the antibodies to cope, but he was a rural child from a dry and healthy place.

When we were respectively eight and seven years old, Laurie decided to end Jim's carefree bachelor existence in the sugar cane, and dragged us off to North Queensland, where we remained for about two years. Odd though it may sound, I have no idea where we lived, apart from the fact that Laurie eked out her stipend from Jim by working as a cleaner. A boarding house seems right, as one of my strongest impressions about childhood is that we were terrified of making a noise, getting underfoot, "making a nuisance" of ourselves.

Carl had an appalling bout of chicken pox; he even had the ulcers inside his throat. Another close shave for Laurie.

There had been something wrong with my skin since birth; it broke down into weeping vesicles called dermatitis, but in 1945 no one knew how to treat it. I kept telling Laurie that the dermatitis was due to soap; her response was to call me a dirty pig of a girl and make sure I scrubbed harder. And yes, of course it was soap! It wouldn't have been Laurie were it any other substance. Luckily when I entered my teens I had a little more privacy for my ablutions, and managed to avoid the soap for most of the time. That entailed wetting the cake; Laurie always checked. But this is about Laurie, not about me, so I do have a purpose in recounting the tale of my dermatitis.

The place in North Queensland where we lived was on the same latitude south of the Equator as Belize is north—17°. That's the real tropics, not some pallid imitation. It was permanently humid, and the rainfall was literally 300 inches a year—*7.7 metres*. No one carried an umbrella or wore a mackintosh; the clouds open like a waterfall, one is drenched, the rain stops, and ten minutes later the clothes are dry again. However, the rain was fairly seasonal monsoon: November to March, summer.

Though thanks to Auntie Mary and the priest the family had quit the Catholic Church decades before, Carl and I were sent to Catholic schools because Laurie believed they gave children a better education. Schools in the plural.

The particular Catholic School I had been attending in New South Wales owned a very fancy uniform, utterly unsuited for heat of any kind: I wore a black serge tunic with narrow box pleats, a long-sleeved shirt with collar and tie, long socks, a serge wool blazer, and a black velour hat with the school band. Carl's school saw him wearing a black serge suit, long-sleeved shirt with collar and tie, and a grey felt hat.

North Queensland disgusted Laurie. Not only was she in a menial job, but she had no way to show these tropical yokels how socially superior she was. I have vague memories of Jim's having a cousin of some kind where we were, and of staying with the cousin and his family when we first arrived. We were not there long, so it's pounds to peanuts that Laurie snooped and we were asked to leave, after which the boarding house. For certainly Laurie knew people in our town on a better basis than if her only contact was through cleaning. And she was determined to cock a snook at them, demonstrate how top-class she and her children actually were. Her solution was to send Carl and me to the little state school we attended—it was the only school in forty miles—wearing our school uniforms.

When we duly appeared clad in our uniforms we created a sensation—but not of the kind Laurie envisioned. The local yokels laughed themselves sick.

Not that Laurie saw or heard them. As usual, she was in her own world. Luckily it was a mixed school, so I could protect Carl—no one messed with him!

We walked two miles to school along a blood-red dirt road, the air filled with the stench of molasses from the sugar mill on the bend of a wide, treacherous river, its currents tugging at masses of dark green weed, its water teeming with gigantic salt-water crocodiles, the vast mountains dense with jungle as a backdrop. It was so humid! Never having known humidity, we western N.S.W. children were utterly miserable.

The backs of my legs from buttocks to knees had broken down into dermatitis. I couldn't bear the weight of that heavy tunic banging against them, so I walked holding the tunic out off my legs with both hands, kicking my suitcase of books ahead of me. Just recovering from the chicken pox and hardly owning the strength to carry his own case, Carl couldn't carry mine as well. A softer person than I, he wept.

The toilets at the school were vile. Boys were segregated from girls, but that was the only nicety. A board affair with holes in it had been constructed to fit standard sized drums beneath it, drums that caught the faecal matter and urine. The height meant children had to scramble up and sit; there was no way to avoid contact with those filthy boards if one were eight years old. Looking into a "honey can" (as it was known) was to look into a stinking, lumpy brown liquid seething with fat white worms. I will never forget it, especially the worms.

My dermatitis became badly infected, but Laurie, having no experience of the tropics, thought it would "clear up". While, it seems, I was cooking septicaemia. The headmaster caught me holding my heavy tunic off the back of my legs, looked at them, and took my temperature. A wild drive later and I was in the hospital, where I was to remain for six months, one of the first civilian patients in Australia to have injections of penicillin, the new wonder drug. Strangely, I don't remember being gravely ill. My memories are of wonderful peace and quiet, of hugely high ceilings clattering with revolving fans, of friendly faces. It was always bliss to escape from the turmoil of Laurie's world, disorganized almost to chaos.

I recount these incidents to illustrate Laurie's incredible obstinacy. Once she took an idea into her head, nothing could shift it, even when any fool could see that, for instance, she was endangering her children's lives. I shrink from calling that stupidity, but, looking back, it's hard to find a kinder word. Yet it wasn't a dumbly brutish stupidity; in many ways Laurie was as quick as the next one. As a neuroscientist, I wonder about unopened neural pathways in her brain, of a checkerboard cerebrum whose fundamental nuclei were as likely to retard her thought processes as to sharpen them. Her emotions were so strong that they impaired her ability to reason; in my own life I have known many others with this same handicap. A boots-and-all mentality that fills me with sorrow for the missed opportunities, the tragedies that a little thinking out would have averted.

She was not a merciful mother, for all she was capable of great mercy toward those she didn't know well. Family members dwelled in a different house from all other people.

A great many of the appalling mistakes she made as a mother have to be laid at the door of a genuine confusion; if she had no idea what to do, she did nothing, on the theory that whatever the problem was would eventually go away of its own accord.

At seven years of age I was hospitalized for some months in a Sydney isolation hospital; I went in an ordinarily sized little girl, and came out overweight. I was never again to be an ordinary size.

Laurie hated, hated, hated having a fat daughter. My life became a passing parade of diets. Until I left home for good at seventeen, I was always on a diet. The weight was yet one more reason to dislike me, particularly because I was muscular rather than jelly-obese, and had inherited Jim's height. Laurie was a physical shrimp who yearned for presence, and size endows anyone with a certain amount of presence.

All her love was lavished upon Carl, though the outcome contradicts Freud: I pitied him, and he envied me. Why on earth would any child hunger to be the centre of a parent's universe? The constriction! The suffocation! I used to see it every day. Poor Carl couldn't blink without Laurie's pouncing—why did he do that, what was the meaning of this? She tied him with every trick at her command, and she had thousands of tricks. How he envied me my emancipation from her!

We were not alike in temperament, which makes something of a puzzle out of our enormously close bond. Unless, as I tend to think, Carl and I had joined each other at the hip in an effort to survive Laurie. His character was gentle, sympathetic, understanding of human frailty, and a little puritanical; his patience was so etched into his spirit that, as he put it, he obtained more pleasure from spending two weeks teaching a mentally retarded child to tie their shoelaces than he did from teaching a class of geniuses. His ambition was always to be a teacher of mentally retarded children.

His prose style was far better than mine and his love of history equally great, but he had no scientific or mathematical streak. Like me, he drew and painted well, but unlike me, he was a born athlete. If I had to find one word to describe him, it would be "perfect".

So he became adept at escaping from Laurie's gyrations by using her own tools against her.

We moved to Sydney in 1949, into a big brick semi-detached house a five-minute walk from the beach; Laurie's brothers bought it, though it was put in Jim's name. A gift to Carl.

We had a phone now that sat in an alcove halfway down the very long front hall; the door between the hall and the living room was always closed. If the phone rang—always for Jim or Carl or me—there would be Laurie's shadow flickering under the door as she strained mightily to hear. Telling her not to listen was wasted breath. We couldn't keep our papers or notes or letters safe from her; she would find them and read them, and knew so little shame that if she found an uncomplimentary reference to herself, she would fly at the culprit like a virago, accusing whoever of lying about her. She poked and pried into everything.

But when Jim brought The Thing home, he defeated her. The Thing was a huge wooden box with many padlocks in which he kept his money and his documents; try though she did, Laurie could not open it. Once she took an axe to it, but it remained quite impervious; she was so angry that she left it sitting in the middle of Jim's bedroom floor with the axe still embedded in it.

To hear her talk, she hated her life, and was perpetually threatening to end it. A threat nobody believed for a second. We knew Laurie wouldn't be done with living until she'd battered and minced it into a blood-soaked lump comprising the people she loathed—a long, long list.

Now comes the one facet of Laurie's character that I find hardest to understand, given her volcanic nature and the sheer power of her emotions. In all our lives as children and as young man and young woman, Laurie never once kissed, hugged or cuddled either of us. The only hand she laid on us was an angry one. Why is that? How can that be? I walked and talked at nine months of age, Carl about the same—whole, properly constructed sentences that I mention only to indicate that memory for both Carl and me was an early business. Yet neither of us could find one single memory of our mother giving us overt physical affection. I was an adult before I thought to question the lack: children assume every other child lives in exactly the same way, so it never occurred to us that children might be kissed or cuddled. And Nanna? A pat on the shoulder.

Did Laurie's omission scar us? Damage us? I really don't know. The only conclusion I can arrive at is that judgement in this matter has to come from the people we have known intimately since "home" became something we made for ourselves. And in Carl's case, that might be no one at all. Despite our closeness, we didn't spend our adult time together raking up childhood.

Carl finally escaped by following me to England, giving as his reason the fact that he had exhausted the Australian avenues of instruction in teaching the mentally retarded. I should qualify that by explaining that until he left for England, Carl's teaching duties had been in underprivileged rather than special schools. Australia was very late into special schools.

Laurie had no choice other than to accept Carl's reasons for going; she let him go, not without retreating into one of her "saintly" phases—sighs, woebegone face, hastily mopped up tears, more sighs, her fire extinguished. Ten thousand miles were just too many, she would never have the money to visit him.

Whether it was his delicate health as a child, or whether Laurie had gotten to him in ways I hadn't plumbed, or whether some innate tendency naturally inclined him that way, Carl was deeply depressed. At the time I didn't put a name to it, just knew he was terribly down. Our consciousness of emotional mental disorders today is so highly developed that we forget how recently this has happened. In 1963, we were ignorant. So in that ignorance perhaps I went about a cure in the wrong way by deciding that what Carl really needed was time spent apart from all the members of his family. Including me. Thus in London we didn't do what we had once done in Sydney, rent a place and share it. What fun we had then!

My own work was very demanding, his was in a different London area; we lived separate lives. Twice a week we met for dinner, our only contact; he shared digs with his best friend, I shared a room with a girl I hardly knew. It was all wrong, though I didn't realize it then. Besides, there may have been no right way. I am not foolish enough needlessly to blame myself for what will always be a mystery.

I saw him off on a journey down the eastern Mediterranean Sea, hoping that the experience would cheer him up; he wasn't alone, his best friend was with him.

On the surface his death was an heroic rescue rather than a suicide, but why didn't he drown? The U.S. Air

Force found him forty hours later floating face up, fifteen miles out to sea. If the water was too cold and the effort was too huge, with his history of rheumatic fever he might have died of a heart attack; but we lost his body for eight years, and I will never know. He was a few days short of his twenty-seventh birthday, unmarried and uncommitted.

I had to telephone Laurie and tell her that Carl was dead. What I didn't tell her—or anyone else—was about the letter he had written to me. It turned up in London six weeks after he died, and it's that letter convinces me that somehow he managed to commit suicide. So alone. I couldn't tell her, ever.

Laurie took the news of his death nobly, didn't cry or refuse to talk about him. However, it marked the kind of shift in her that a major earthquake does the continental plates. She never forgave Carl for dying, or me for living. This most shattering crisis of her life left Laurie with the wrong child.

It genuinely doesn't hurt to say that. It is a *fait accompli* and it could only have hurt if I had existed in ignorance of how Laurie felt about her children. I saw it as inevitable.

Her way of mourning Carl was extraordinary. She burned all of him that she still had. His car she gave to his best friend, his clothes to the Salvation Army, and his books, his papers, his every flammable memento, she burned. Every photograph that contained him, even as background, she burned. Imperishable and useless mementos were sent to the garbage dump. So that by the time she was finished, it was as if her son had never been.

After Carl's death Laurie wasn't as much different, as *more*. The family kept dwindling. I was gone, never to come home again, and the brothers died one by one until only Tom, the youngest, was left. Then Jim died. The spice went out of life for Laurie. The story of his bizarre death is told elsewhere, but once the fuss quietened down and everyday living resumed, it became clear that, in losing Jim, Laurie had no grand target left at whom to loose her barbs. I would have done nicely, but I wasn't there.

Did she cry for Jim? Did she mourn him? I don't know, and I never will know. Out of a forty-one-year married life, they had spent relatively little time living together. I rarely saw them interact in any other way than shouting matches. All I do know is that the war between them was a vital necessity. Divorce was freely available to the working classes, so either one could have sought a legal sundering. Carl and I used to beg Laurie to divorce Jim; after we were working, we offered to pay the court costs. She wouldn't hear of it.

They were welded together as firmly as steel plates: war to the bitter end, war to the death.

I had a telephone in my Connecticut apartment, through the medium of which Laurie and I talked every month. Once I had used a telephone to give her the news of Carl's death, but when Jim died she didn't phone me. She sent me a telegram. It said: DADDY PASSED AWAY PEACEFULLY THIS MORNING. ALL MY LOVE.

Was it a way of informing me that she would have preferred to have had the news about Carl in a telegram? A tangible thing she could display rather than repeat vanished conversation? The wording was sheer hypocrisy, but for whose benefit? How long did it take her to draft it?

Carl died in 1965, Jim in 1973.

Save for one visit to sort out Jim's death, I hadn't been back in Australia since 1963. After Jim's death Laurie's company went down to Tom, a happy-go-lucky sort of man fully ten years her junior. Of all her brothers, Tom was the most emancipated, but after severe injuries in a car crash in 1975 he returned home to live; Laurie sank her claws in, and Tom never managed again to get away. They were to live together for twenty-three years. There was a certain amount of tension between them because Tom adamantly refused to stop visiting his club—an ex-soldiers' football association—or seeing his friends. As he owned a very comfortable car (Laurie couldn't drive), he was essential; constantly complaining about his friends, Laurie put up with Tom for the sake of riding in a nice car and having a man in the house at night. Her dread of an intruder was so profound that every window and every door belonging to her house was kept locked top, bottom, and middle. Not unsurprisingly, no intruder ever did break in, though from time to time she would be full of tales of the prowler (her favorite word for a potential intruder) who had gone along every window and door trying to get in. This was never something I discussed with her, so I have no idea whether she was afraid of murder or rape: just that it was one of the two. Or both.

Few things Laurie did ever had the power to hurt me, but her reception of my first novel, *Tim*, was one of them. There I was, a neuroscientist, writing a first novel good enough to be accepted by Harper & Row, a most prestigious New York firm—*and* it received wonderful reviews in all the important literary channels, including the *New York Times*. I was chuffed, I admit it.

But Laurie? Laurie was utterly disgusted. Now the whole world knew that her thirty-plus spinster daughter was a loose woman—*Tim* contained love scenes! She could find nothing good to say about the book, and apparently burned the copy I sent her. Jim died scant weeks later, and Laurie found out that he had a copy on order from a bookstore (her copy was an advance); she cancelled it. I wonder what Jim might have thought had he lived to read it?

But maybe there was a little bit of payback in *The Thorn Birds*, with its large wodges of family history in the opening chapters, and a thinly disguised rape-style honeymoon for the heroine. Maybe the world would assume that Laurie had had an affair with a priest? Not bloody likely, but still …

In attempting payback, I hit paydirt. *The Thorn Birds* was a gargantuan bestseller the whole world over, crossing racial as well as ethnic barriers; at one stage I was mobbed by Hindu teenaged girls, to name one result. Naturally it was viciously panned by the same critics who had hailed *Tim* as brilliant—it earned far too much money to have any literary merit, and nowhere was this enmity more pronounced and long-lasting than in my own country, Australia, where the literati still put me down.

Laurie *loved* it! A dissipated daughter? Never! At last she had fame and money, and she was greedy for both.

At first I found her behavior inexplicable. Our house was in ghastly condition, but she absolutely refused to let me get the builders in. I bought her masses of gorgeous clothes, shoes, bags, even commissioned her a sable car coat with a snappy sable hat. Yet she never wore any of the clothes, shoes, bags, furs. I'd ask her to go to a reception in my honor, and she'd decline. Then I'd see her at the reception, huddled into a corner, wearing her oldest rags, carrying a tatty plastic bag, looking pathetic.

It was only when a journalist came to the house and gaped around at the cracked and peeling, badly furnished interior that the penny dropped. I caught the look on Laurie's face: smugly satisfied, gleeful. You awful old cow! I thought. You want the world to think that your rich and famous daughter neglects you, even abuses you.

The builders went in the next day against her protests and I threw out all her old clothes. Though, alas, I couldn't stop her shopping at Kmart for replacements, and she never did wear any of the lovely things I bought her.

I took her on a holiday to New Zealand, since she hadn't been back after leaving at ten years of age. It was hell. Laurie whined, complained, criticized, roared with rage, demanded, was annoyed by trifles, and whined all over again. I tried so hard to please her! The trouble was that she'd made up her mind before she left that she wasn't going to have a good time.

A holiday to England proved even worse. Because I had many unavoidable commitments, I gave her into the charge of two sweet elderly ladies who took her to the most wonderful places, but she wouldn't even be nice to this pair of relative strangers. If I drove out of London to find her, I just aimed for the blackest cloud in the sky; there she'd be, standing under it. You think I joke, or exaggerate? Well, I don't. I had known by then for many years that Laurie could control the weather. I tried to join her and her two companions as often as I could—a nightmare. It seems that Laurie had decided her companions were confidence tricksters out to separate me from my money—manifestly ridiculous. I was so grateful for their kindness and patience in the face of Laurie's rudeness and incivility that I gave them a bonus, and that was far from extortion.

During this six-month holiday Laurie spent in the British Isles an underlying, lifelong paranoia began to show in more overt ways; when she started calling me Joyce, I should have realized that she was beginning a dementia, but I didn't. Joyce, if you remember, was the name of brother Jack's slattern bride, and Laurie's snooping had failed to detach Jack from her. In the years to come, I became Joyce more and more.

★ ★ ★

When I married, she was furious. I hadn't expected her to like Ric, and she didn't. For one thing, he deeply offended the snob in her, as he worked with his hands for a living, thus detracting from her (and my) social status. So she summoned up the kind of hatred for him that she had cherished for Jim, but it didn't work one place removed. Ric's detestation of her was cold, and she was smart enough to recognize it as partisan. In Ric, I had a champion, whereas she had none. Though she had never owned a single particle of common sense, she divined that Ric was exactly the sort of man Carl would have liked immensely, and that capped her hatred. Ric was a *man*, which made him so alien that she couldn't even begin to find his weaknesses.

Suddenly living in Sydney didn't suit her. She demanded to sell the house and move up to the Blue Mountains, yet one more good turn Ric did me. The easier driving in less traffic enabled Tom to survive; had they remained in Sydney, the driving would have killed an old man with a wobbly heart.

One day when Ric and I were visiting them in Laurie's new home, we both noticed that Laurie was (as Ric elegantly phrased it) "slipping a cog". Once we did notice, her dementia became obvious; my being Joyce made sense of a kind.

We sat Tom down and made him tell us what was happening. Tom confessed that she was terrorizing him. The poor man got no sleep; Laurie would wake him several times during one night yelling at him to evict his drunken friends from her house this very moment. Then she would drag him around pointing out pools of urine and heaps of faeces that weren't there. She screamed abuse at him in the middle of supermarkets. Nothing he did had the power to please her.

By this time she was into her eighties, and had lost all central vision in both eyes. Her hearing went too. But she refused to help herself, just withdrew more and more into some world of her own. All the tricks that now I myself am using, she rejected—talking books, page magnifiers, developing better peripheral vision, having first-class hearing aids, using headphones. Whatever the device or the trick, Laurie rejected it. But she wouldn't reject the visceral act of living. That she clung to grimly. If there be an art to negativism, Laurie not only found it, she refined it.

All that was left was the tyrant. The personality, when it broke, fractured along the lines the pattern of a lifetime had drawn. Laurie demented was sweet as syrup to those not of her family, and filthy-mean to Tom, Ric, and me.

She went into a kind of Hilton Hotel for the aged, there to continue her downhill slide. At first she had her own apartment, then a full-time carer moved into the apartment with her, and finally she was hospitalized, unable to care for herself in any way. Being free of her gave my uncle Tom a new lease on life; he moved to Norfolk Island and lived with his dog in a little house a stone's throw from ours. Known to everyone as Uncle Tom, he was much loved, and lived another nine years, dying at ninety-two.

While Laurie still spoke to me, I became Joyce more frequently. Her choice of this name is fascinating; it must have been etched in letters of fire far deeper in her brain than her speech areas, even the emotional ones for curse words, yes and no. Perhaps her clash with Joyce had been the first of Laurie's life that didn't go the way she wanted, and she never got over the huge insult to her ego? Setting that aside, I became the hated Joyce, a woman she had discussed with Nanna over thousands and thousands of cups of tea as the years passed. I could have no illusions about Joyce and what she meant to Laurie.

The brain may have been dissolving to a pulp infested by tiny haemorrhages, but Laurie's body was immensely strong. While she lived in her apartment, she took marathon walks. One saw her cross most of the vast city of Sydney from its far northern beaches to the corner of the street in which her old Sydney home was situated—a distance of fifty kilometres. The police discovered her with not a penny in her battered old plastic handbag, and brought her back. After that she wore a SAT-NAV receptor on an eighteen-carat gold bracelet studded with diamonds—she wouldn't wear "rubbish" at any inducement. The walks continued, never with any money in her purse, and $30,000 around her wrist. No one molested her; the word would go out to the police, and back to her apartment went Laurie. No matter how vigilant the watch put on her, she evaded her keepers as if she were a ghost.

When she was first admitted to the hospital segment of her aged complex, Laurie bit, scratched, kicked and punched all who came near her. Then a new Laurie appeared: sweetly pleasant, unfailingly co-operative. Somewhere among the frightful jumble of her thought processes an instinct for self-preservation must have surfaced and told her that she must strive mightily to make these new carers as devoted to her as the apartment ones had been. Having switched personalities, she became liked again, even loved.

After she went into the hospital segment, the moment I hove in her vicinity to visit her, Laurie's mouth would set into a straight, hard line as her eyes took me in; she wasn't totally blind by any means. She would emit a noise of angry exasperation, and turn her head away. No matter how long I stayed, she would sit with head turned away, ignoring me. Never once did she acknowledge me, even as Joyce.

One does weird things after being resolutely ignored by one's mother. Following a whole series of visits with the head turned obdurately away, I chanced to see a television documentary about the racket in funerals. Dismissing the racket slant, I obtained a great deal of new knowledge about funerals. So the next day I went out and bought Laurie the poshest funeral I could find. I chose a beautifully carved mahogany casket that would have held six Lauries (she loathed being crowded), with white satin and lace padded interior, and gold-plated knobs and handles. Every detail was perused more thoroughly than NASA does a moon mission: the pallbearers, the sleekest hearse—the full catastrophe, as Zorba might have said. Buying Laurie that funeral did me the world of good. I was able to face another round of visits, though I never stayed long. It wasn't a scrap of use, beseech and beg though I did to see her face, have her say something to me. She wouldn't.

★★★

She didn't seem to know how to die—but then, she hadn't known the secret of living either. And when she didn't know what else to do, when she didn't know the answer, she did nothing.

Those last few years were an agony for her, I believe: of lying in a bed, of being bathed, of being put into a padded reclining chair, of being fed, of being bed-panned, of being medicated, of being put back to bed again.

And what did the observer see? A tiny, emaciated, incredibly old woman who dozed away the hours and the days, rousing only to do battle with that terrible monster, Joyce, by turning her head away. Exquisitely clean, yet giving off the subtle aroma of dying cells.

She had an ineffable nose for sensing the right moment to do the wrong thing, and that even included her dying, for after nearly a hundred years of living, I think all of us who were left had forgotten that she might actually *die*.

Bruni, my friend and musical collaborator from Hamburg, had managed to find two precious weeks to come to Norfolk Island to work with me on an opera about Cleopatra. Her commitments in Europe were extremely heavy, but there were reasons why I could not travel any farther than Sydney, so it had to be Bruni who climbed on a plane. I met her in Sydney, and took the time to see Laurie, who was bed-bound by now and hardly ever awake. I sat down on the side of her bed, leaned over and spoke to her; but the eyelids remained shut, the mouth slightly gaping, toothless and cavelike. I continued to sit, I continued to speak to her. No response. Then a little vulturine claw groped across the covers to find my hand, took it, and gently pressed it. Slowly it slipped away, her sleep became a soft snore. I left.

Bruni and I flew from Sydney to Norfolk Island immediately after that visit, and I confess that a part of my mind couldn't get away from Laurie's taking my hand, squeezing it.

Ric woke me in the middle of that first night home. Laurie had died. My reaction wasn't filial; all I could think was how Laurie had managed to do it again. I would have to fly to Sydney and spend at least half of Bruni's precious time seeing to the obsequies of my mother. Planes to and from Norfolk Island don't fly every day, or even every second day.

Then Ric had a brilliant idea.

In the morning I called the undertaker in Sydney. "I don't suppose you could pop my mother in the fridge for a couple of weeks?" I asked.

He gave a whoop of joy. "Oh, could I?" he asked. "I am swamped with burials at the moment. If you're absolutely sure you want this, I'd be delighted to oblige."

"Pop her in the fridge," I said.

So Bruni and I had a full two weeks of work, then flew with Ric to Sydney. Laurie came out of the fridge.

Her wish was to be cremated, so the service was held in a huge non-denominational chapel at a Sydney crematorium. There were six pallbearers and four mourners. Ric, our friend Michael and I were downstairs, while Bruni was in the choir loft with an organist. Bruni is an operatic diva as well as a composer. She sang Schubert's "Ave Maria" and her own "Kyrie". Never was a corpse so gloriously serenaded, though I am sure Laurie would have preferred Gounod's "Ave Maria" and "Climb Every Mountain". For once, the choice was mine.

I had the ashes interred in the crematorium rose garden. Laurie had asked that they be scattered over the Jamison Valley from the pinnacle of Echo Point, but that is a thousand-foot cliff, and I could see the newspaper headlines: HUNK OF TROCHANTER KILLS HIKER ON VALLEY FLOOR! COLLEEN McCULLOUGH'S MUM THE ALLEGED BLUNT INSTRUMENT! It would be just like her. Smell the roses instead, Joyce.